MW01069062

ROBOCOP™

//THE HUMAN ELEMENT//

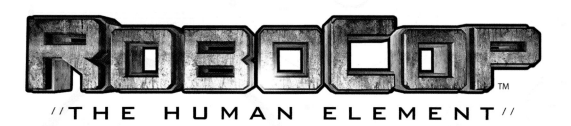

BOOM!™ STUDIOS

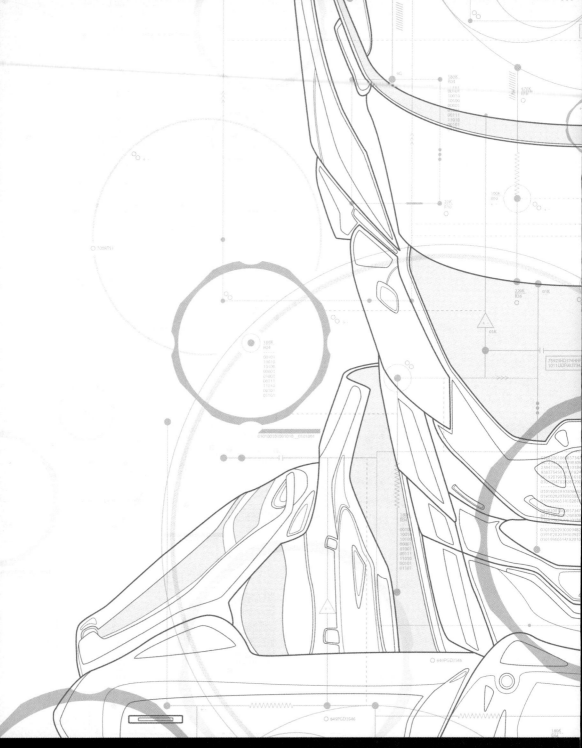

ROSS RICHIE CEO & Founder • **JACK CUMMINS** President • **MARK SMYLIE** Founder of Archaia • **MATT GAGNON** Editor-in-Chief • **FILIP SABLIK** VP of Publishing & Marketing • **STEPHEN CHRISTY** VP of Development
LANCE KREITER VP of Licensing & Merchandising • **PHIL BARBARO** VP of Finance • **BRYCE CARLSON** Managing Editor • **MEL CAYLO** Marketing Manager • **SCOTT NEWMAN** Production Design Manager • **IRENE BRADISH** Operations Manager
DAFNA PLEBAN Editor • **SHANNON WATTERS** Editor • **ERIC HARBURN** Editor • **REBECCA TAYLOR** Editor • **IAN BRILL** Editor • **CHRIS ROSA** Assistant Editor • **ALEX GALER** Assistant Editor • **WHITNEY LEOPARD** Assistant Editor
JASMINE AMIRI Assistant Editor • **CAMERON CHITTOCK** Assistant Editor • **HANNAH NANCE PARTLOW** Production Designer • **KELSEY DIETERICH** Production Designer • **EMI YONEMURA BROWN** Production Designer
DEVIN FUNCHES E-Commerce & Inventory Coordinator • **ANDY LIEGL** Event Coordinator • **BRIANNA HART** Executive Assistant • **AARON FERRARA** Operations Assistant • **JOSÉ MEZA** Sales Assistant • **ELIZABETH LOUGHRIDGE** Accounting Assistant

ROBOCOP: THE HUMAN ELEMENT, June 2014. Published by BOOM! Studios, a division of Boom Entertainment, Inc. ROBOCOP (2014) © 2014 Metro-Goldwyn-Mayer Pictures Inc. and Columbia Pictures Industries, Inc. ROBOCOP is a trademark of Orion Pictures Corporation. © 2014 Metro-Goldwyn-Mayer Studios Inc. All Rights Reserved. METRO-GOLDWYN-MAYER is a trademark of Metro-Goldwyn-Mayer Lion Corp. © 2014 Metro-Goldwyn-Mayer Studios Inc. All Rights Reserved. Originally published in single magazine form as ROBOCOP: BETA No. 1, ROBOCOP: MEMENTO MORI No. 1, ROBOCOP: TO LIVE AND DIE IN DETROIT No. 1, ROBOCOP: HOMINEM EX MACHINA No. 1. © 2014 Metro-Goldwyn-Mayer Pictures Inc. and Columbia Pictures Industries, Inc. All Rights Reserved. BOOM! Studios™ and the BOOM! Studios logo are trademarks of Boom Entertainment, Inc., registered in various countries and categories. All characters, events, and institutions depicted herein are fictional. Any similarity between any of the names, characters, persons, events, and/or institutions in this publication to actual names, characters, and persons, whether living or dead, events, and/or institutions is unintended and purely coincidental. BOOM! Studios does not read or accept unsolicited submissions of ideas, stories, or artwork.

A catalog record of this book is available from OCLC and from the BOOM! Studios website, www.boom-studios.com, on the Librarians Page.

BOOM! Studios, 5670 Wilshire Boulevard, Suite 450, Los Angeles, CA 90036-5679. Printed in Canada. First Printing. ISBN: 978-1-60886-389-1, eISBN: 978-1-61398-243-3

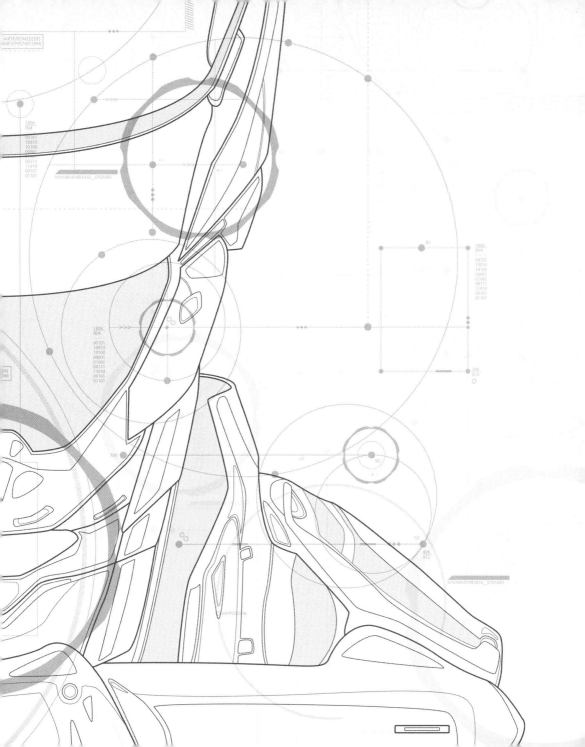

ROBOCOP™
"THE HUMAN ELEMENT"

"BETA"

WRITTEN BY
ED BRISSON

ART BY
EMILIO LAISO

COLORS BY
MICHAEL GARLAND

"MEMENTO MORI"

WRITTEN BY
FRANK J. BARBIERE

ART BY
JOÃO "AZEITONA" VIEIRA

COLORS BY
RUTH REDMOND

LETTERS BY
ED DUKESHIRE

COVER BY
GREG SMALLWOOD

DESIGN BY
SCOTT NEWMAN
AND EMI YONEMURA BROWN

"TO LIVE AND DIE IN DETROIT"
WRITTEN BY
JOE HARRIS

ART BY
PIOTR KOWALSKI

COLORS BY
VLADIMIR POPOV

"HOMINEM EX MACHINA"
WRITTEN BY
MICHAEL MORECI

ART BY
JASON COPLAND

COLORS BY
JUAN MANUEL TUMBURÚS

ASSISTANT EDITOR
ALEX GALER

EDITORS
IAN BRILL
ERIC HARBURN

SPECIAL THANKS
KAROL MORA

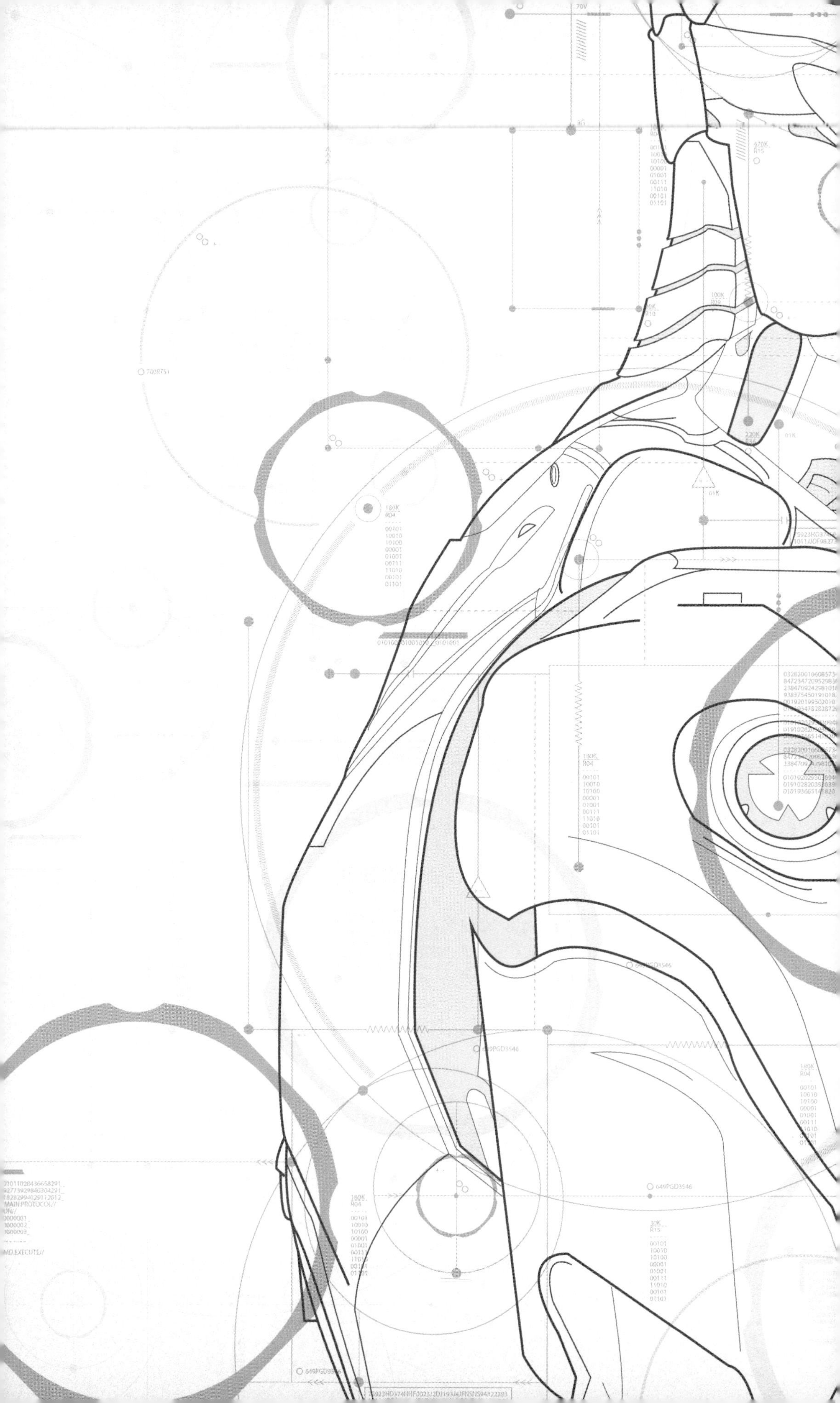

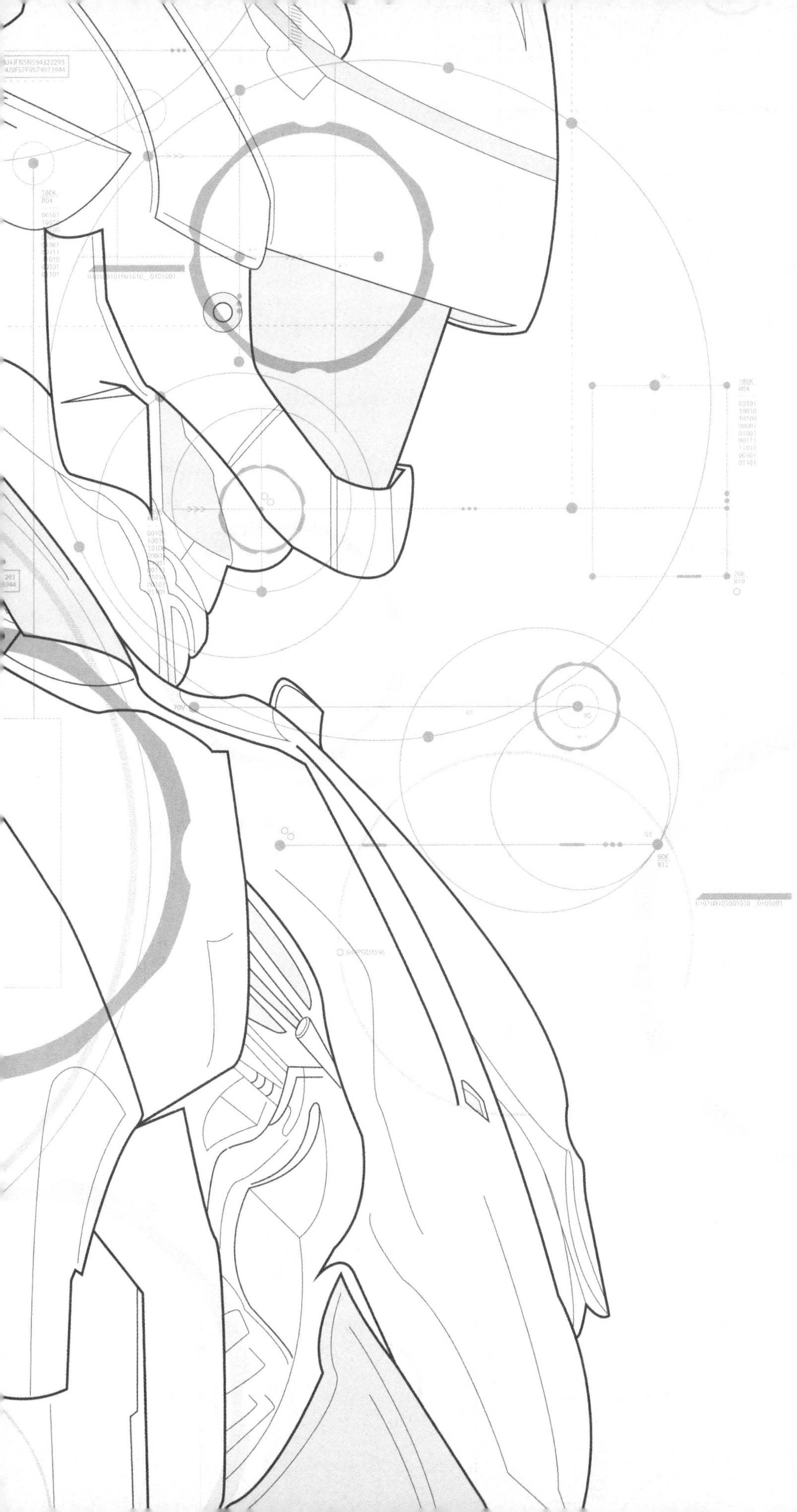

//BETA//

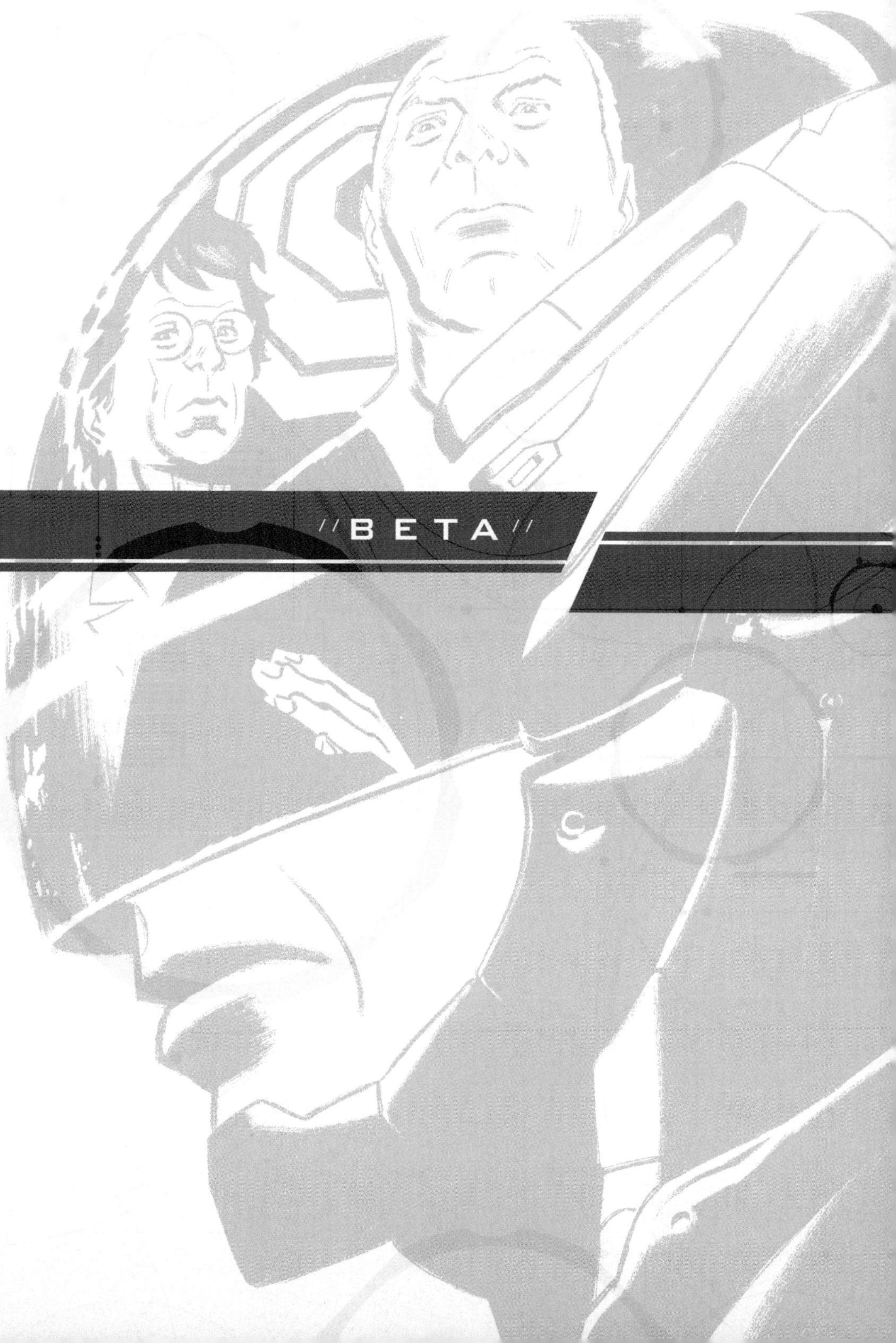

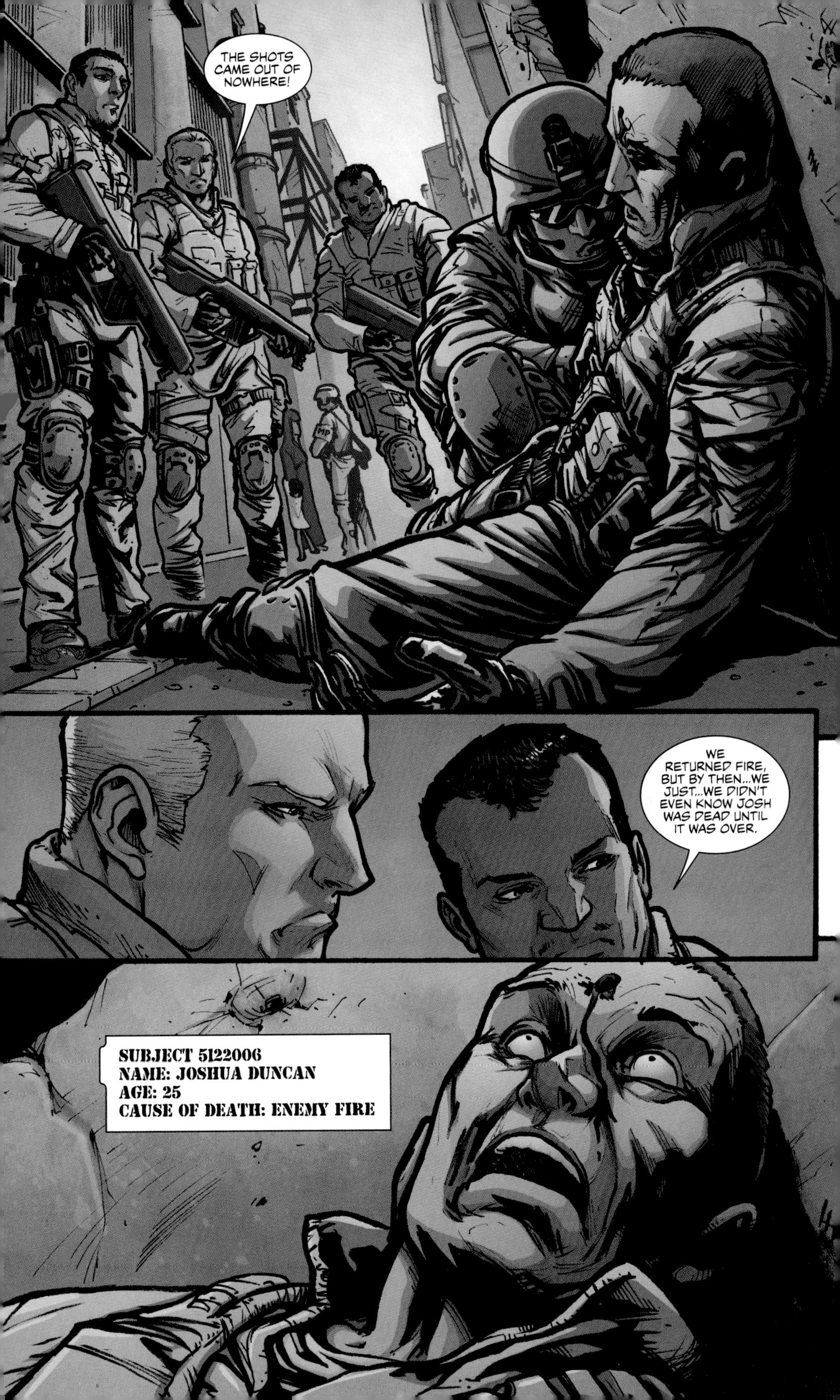
THE SHOTS CAME OUT OF NOWHERE!
WE RETURNED FIRE, BUT BY THEN...WE JUST...WE DIDN'T EVEN KNOW JOSH WAS DEAD UNTIL IT WAS OVER.
SUBJECT 5122006
NAME: JOSHUA DUNCAN
AGE: 25
CAUSE OF DEATH: ENEMY FIRE

[redacted]

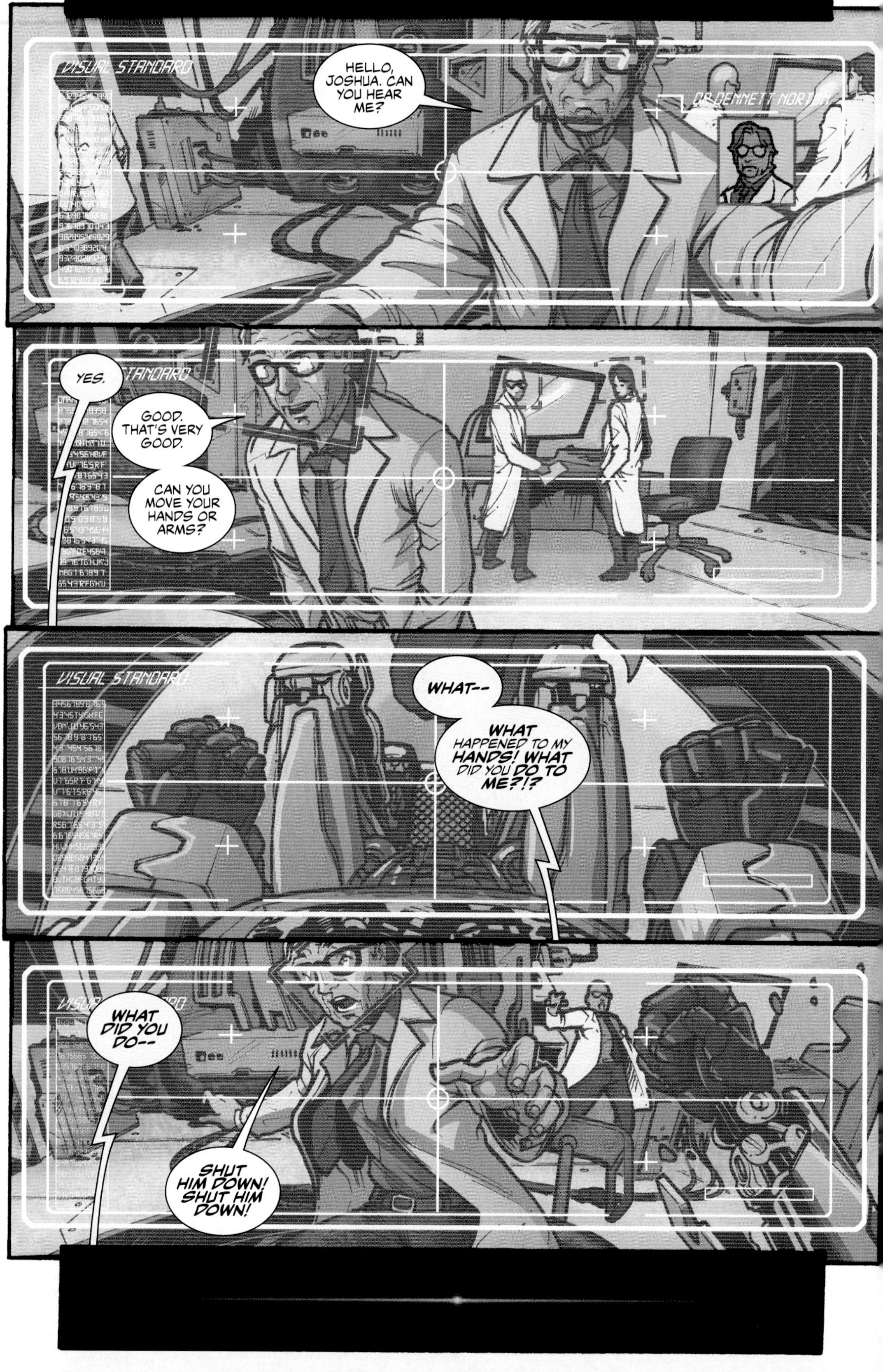
VISUAL STANDARD
HELLO, JOSHUA. CAN YOU HEAR ME?
DR DENNETT NORTON
YES.
GOOD. THAT'S VERY GOOD.
CAN YOU MOVE YOUR HANDS OR ARMS?
VISUAL STANDARD
WHAT--
WHAT HAPPENED TO MY HANDS! WHAT DID YOU DO TO ME?!?
WHAT DID YOU DO--
SHUT HIM DOWN! SHUT HIM DOWN!

[redacted]

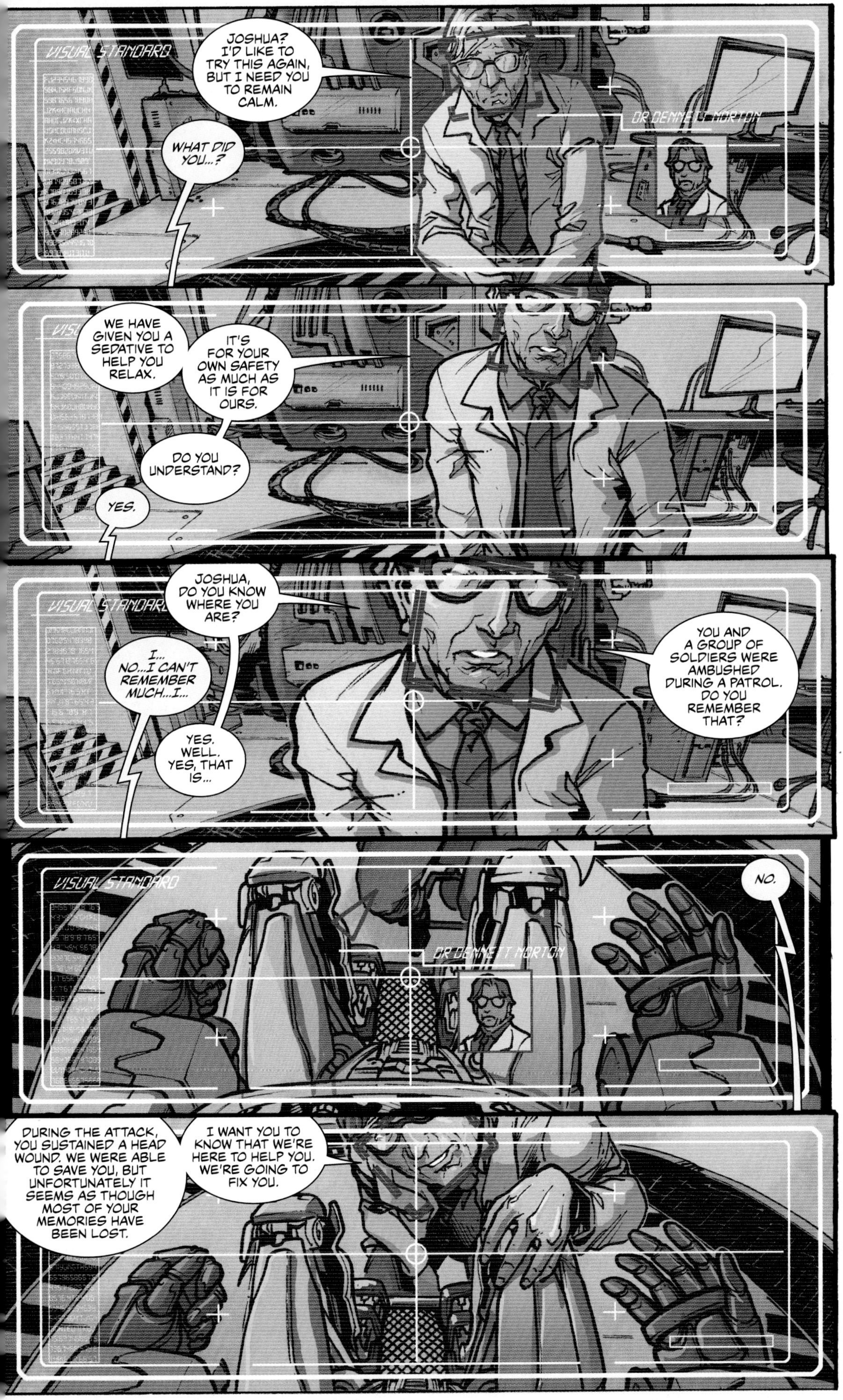
VISUAL STANDARD
JOSHUA? I'D LIKE TO TRY THIS AGAIN, BUT I NEED YOU TO REMAIN CALM.
DR DENNETT NORTON
WHAT DID YOU...?
WE HAVE GIVEN YOU A SEDATIVE TO HELP YOU RELAX.
IT'S FOR YOUR OWN SAFETY AS MUCH AS IT IS FOR OURS.
DO YOU UNDERSTAND?
YES.
VISUAL STANDARD
JOSHUA, DO YOU KNOW WHERE YOU ARE?
I... NO...I CAN'T REMEMBER MUCH...I...
YES. WELL. YES, THAT IS...
YOU AND A GROUP OF SOLDIERS WERE AMBUSHED DURING A PATROL. DO YOU REMEMBER THAT?
VISUAL STANDARD
NO.
DR DENNETT NORTON
DURING THE ATTACK, YOU SUSTAINED A HEAD WOUND. WE WERE ABLE TO SAVE YOU, BUT UNFORTUNATELY IT SEEMS AS THOUGH MOST OF YOUR MEMORIES HAVE BEEN LOST.
I WANT YOU TO KNOW THAT WE'RE HERE TO HELP YOU. WE'RE GOING TO FIX YOU.

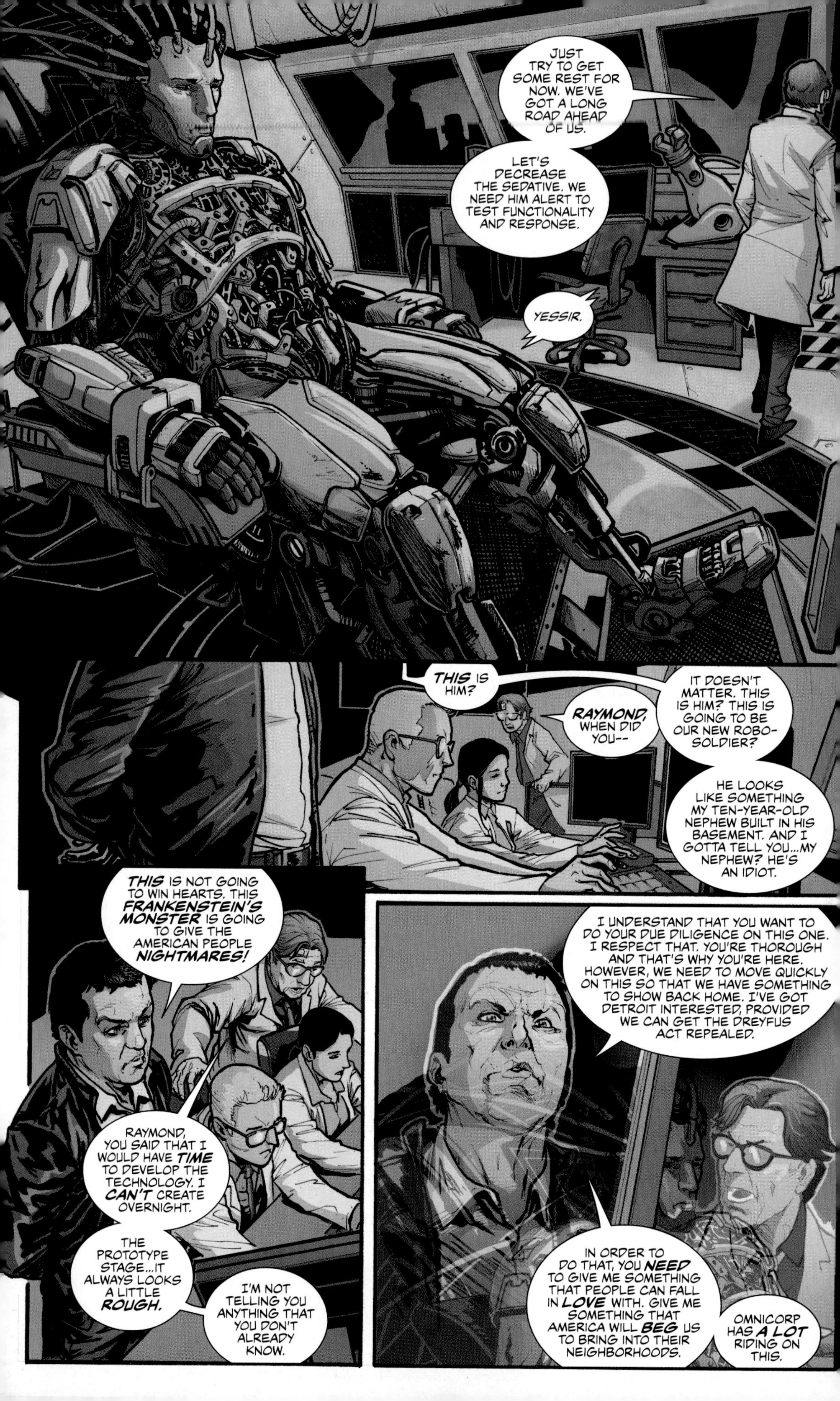
JUST TRY TO GET SOME REST FOR NOW. WE'VE GOT A LONG ROAD AHEAD OF US.
LET'S DECREASE THE SEDATIVE. WE NEED HIM ALERT TO TEST FUNCTIONALITY AND RESPONSE.
YESSIR.
THIS IS HIM?
RAYMOND, WHEN DID YOU--
IT DOESN'T MATTER. THIS IS HIM? THIS IS GOING TO BE OUR NEW ROBO-SOLDIER?
HE LOOKS LIKE SOMETHING MY TEN-YEAR-OLD NEPHEW BUILT IN HIS BASEMENT. AND I GOTTA TELL YOU...MY NEPHEW? HE'S AN IDIOT.
THIS IS NOT GOING TO WIN HEARTS. THIS FRANKENSTEIN'S MONSTER IS GOING TO GIVE THE AMERICAN PEOPLE NIGHTMARES!
RAYMOND, YOU SAID THAT I WOULD HAVE TIME TO DEVELOP THE TECHNOLOGY. I CAN'T CREATE OVERNIGHT.
THE PROTOTYPE STAGE...IT ALWAYS LOOKS A LITTLE ROUGH.
I'M NOT TELLING YOU ANYTHING THAT YOU DON'T ALREADY KNOW.
I UNDERSTAND THAT YOU WANT TO DO YOUR DUE DILIGENCE ON THIS ONE. I RESPECT THAT. YOU'RE THOROUGH AND THAT'S WHY YOU'RE HERE. HOWEVER, WE NEED TO MOVE QUICKLY ON THIS SO THAT WE HAVE SOMETHING TO SHOW BACK HOME. I'VE GOT DETROIT INTERESTED, PROVIDED WE CAN GET THE DREYFUS ACT REPEALED.
IN ORDER TO DO THAT, YOU NEED TO GIVE ME SOMETHING THAT PEOPLE CAN FALL IN LOVE WITH. GIVE ME SOMETHING THAT AMERICA WILL BEG US TO BRING INTO THEIR NEIGHBORHOODS.
OMNICORP HAS A LOT RIDING ON THIS.

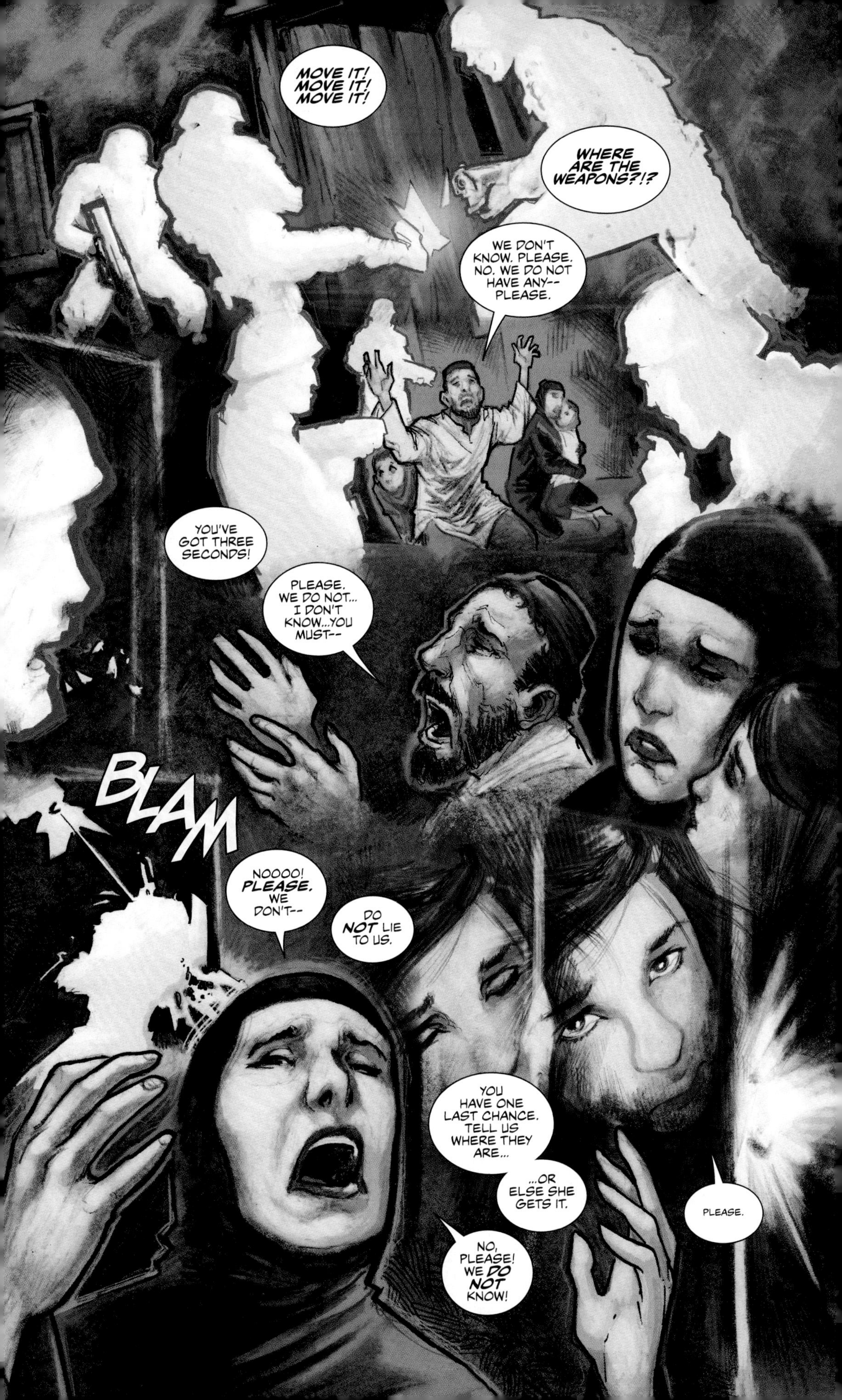

MOVE IT! MOVE IT! MOVE IT!
WHERE ARE THE WEAPONS?!?
WE DON'T KNOW. PLEASE. NO. WE DO NOT HAVE ANY-- PLEASE.
YOU'VE GOT THREE SECONDS!
PLEASE. WE DO NOT... I DON'T KNOW...YOU MUST--
BLAM
NOOOO! PLEASE. WE DON'T--
DO NOT LIE TO US.
YOU HAVE ONE LAST CHANCE. TELL US WHERE THEY ARE...
...OR ELSE SHE GETS IT.
PLEASE.
NO, PLEASE! WE DO NOT KNOW!

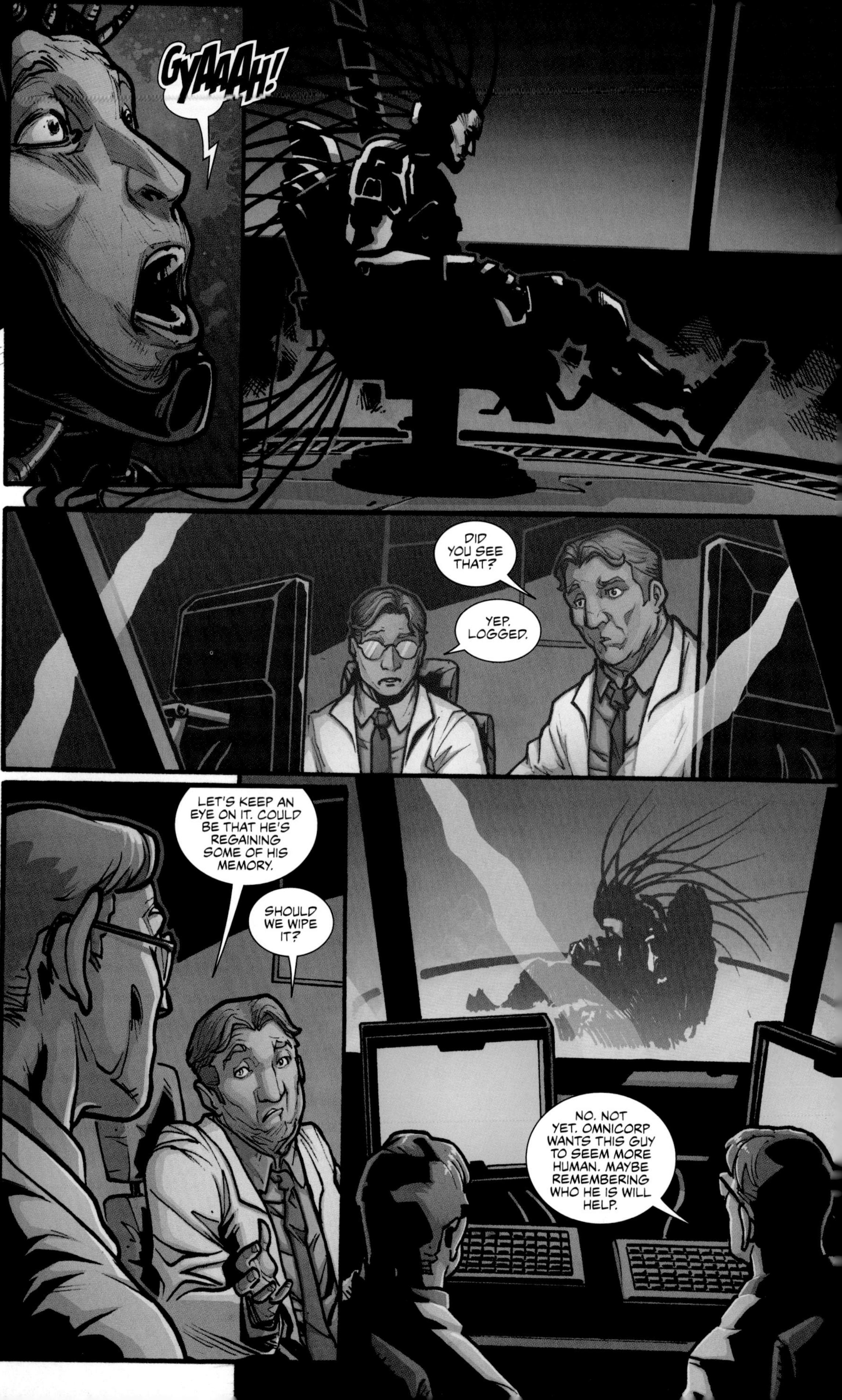
GYAAAH!
DID YOU SEE THAT?
YEP. LOGGED.
LET'S KEEP AN EYE ON IT. COULD BE THAT HE'S REGAINING SOME OF HIS MEMORY.
SHOULD WE WIPE IT?
NO. NOT YET. OMNICORP WANTS THIS GUY TO SEEM MORE HUMAN. MAYBE REMEMBERING WHO HE IS WILL HELP.

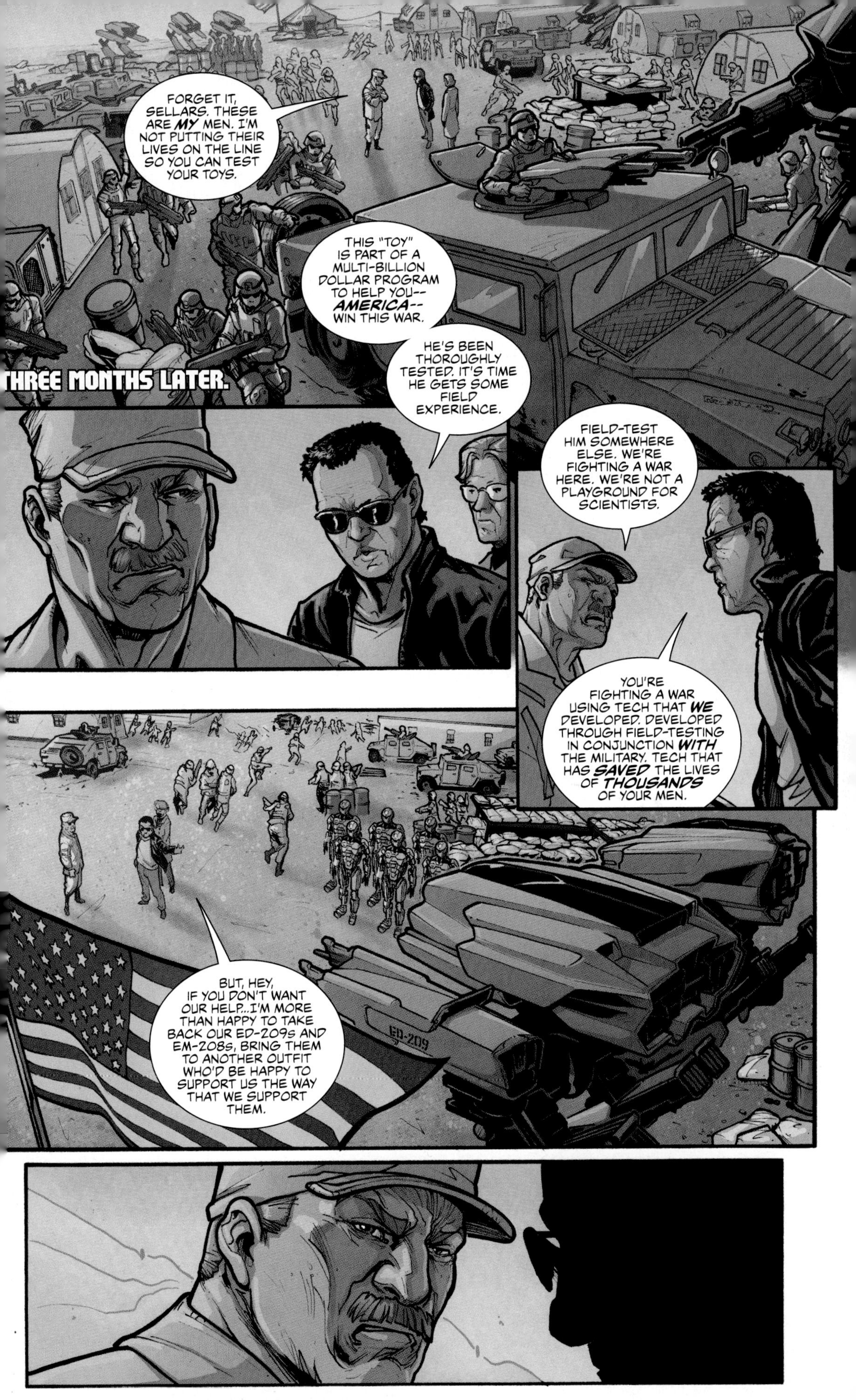
FORGET IT, SELLARS. THESE ARE MY MEN. I'M NOT PUTTING THEIR LIVES ON THE LINE SO YOU CAN TEST YOUR TOYS.
THIS "TOY" IS PART OF A MULTI-BILLION DOLLAR PROGRAM TO HELP YOU-- AMERICA-- WIN THIS WAR.
THREE MONTHS LATER.
HE'S BEEN THOROUGHLY TESTED. IT'S TIME HE GETS SOME FIELD EXPERIENCE.
FIELD-TEST HIM SOMEWHERE ELSE. WE'RE FIGHTING A WAR HERE. WE'RE NOT A PLAYGROUND FOR SCIENTISTS.
YOU'RE FIGHTING A WAR USING TECH THAT WE DEVELOPED. DEVELOPED THROUGH FIELD-TESTING IN CONJUNCTION WITH THE MILITARY. TECH THAT HAS SAVED THE LIVES OF THOUSANDS OF YOUR MEN.
BUT, HEY, IF YOU DON'T WANT OUR HELP...I'M MORE THAN HAPPY TO TAKE BACK OUR ED-209s AND EM-208s, BRING THEM TO ANOTHER OUTFIT WHO'D BE HAPPY TO SUPPORT US THE WAY THAT WE SUPPORT THEM.
ED-209

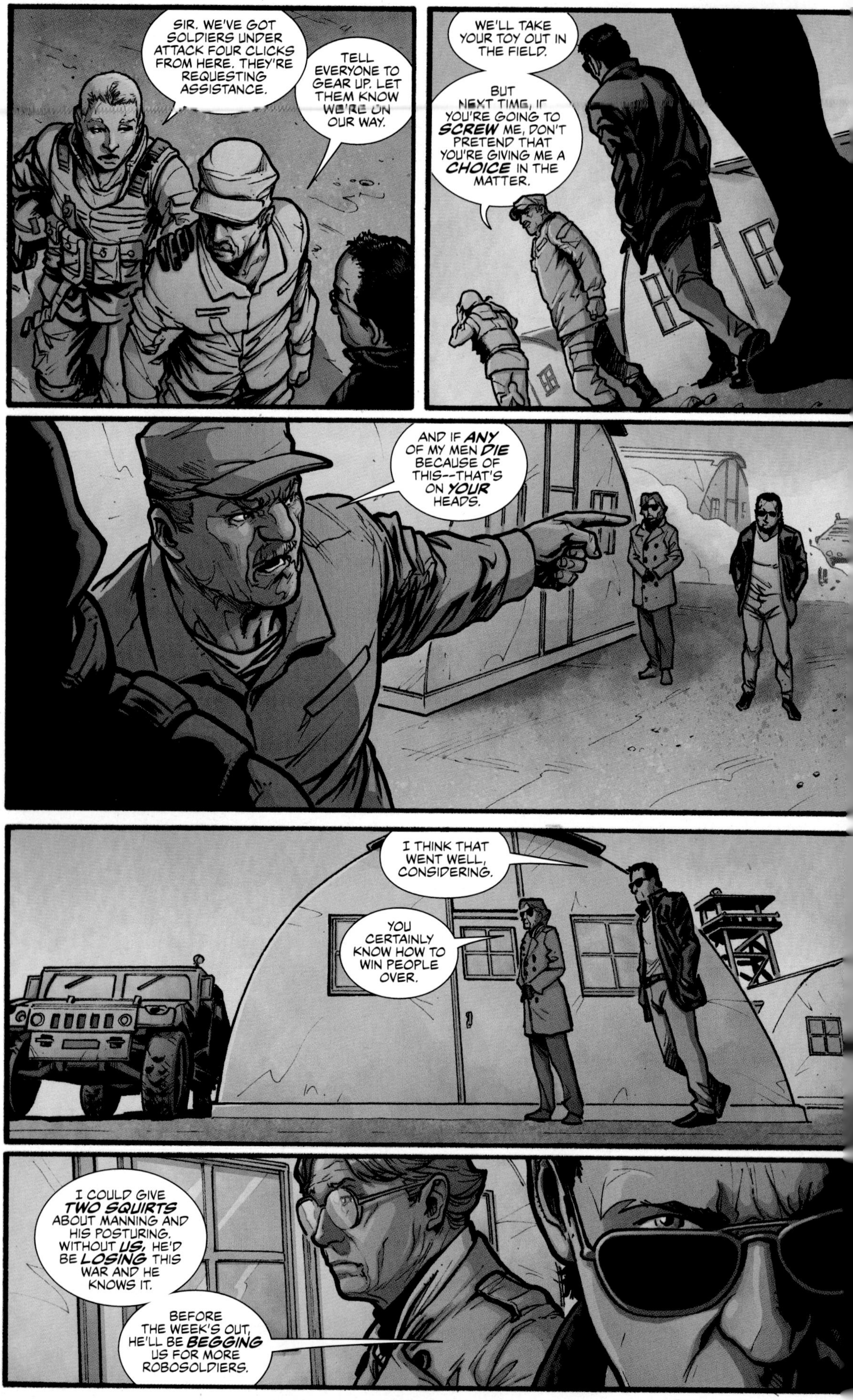
SIR. WE'VE GOT SOLDIERS UNDER ATTACK FOUR CLICKS FROM HERE. THEY'RE REQUESTING ASSISTANCE.
TELL EVERYONE TO GEAR UP. LET THEM KNOW WE'RE ON OUR WAY.
WE'LL TAKE YOUR TOY OUT IN THE FIELD.
BUT NEXT TIME, IF YOU'RE GOING TO SCREW ME, DON'T PRETEND THAT YOU'RE GIVING ME A CHOICE IN THE MATTER.
AND IF ANY OF MY MEN DIE BECAUSE OF THIS--THAT'S ON YOUR HEADS.
I THINK THAT WENT WELL, CONSIDERING.
YOU CERTAINLY KNOW HOW TO WIN PEOPLE OVER.
I COULD GIVE TWO SQUIRTS ABOUT MANNING AND HIS POSTURING. WITHOUT US, HE'D BE LOSING THIS WAR AND HE KNOWS IT.
BEFORE THE WEEK'S OUT, HE'LL BE BEGGING US FOR MORE ROBOSOLDIERS.

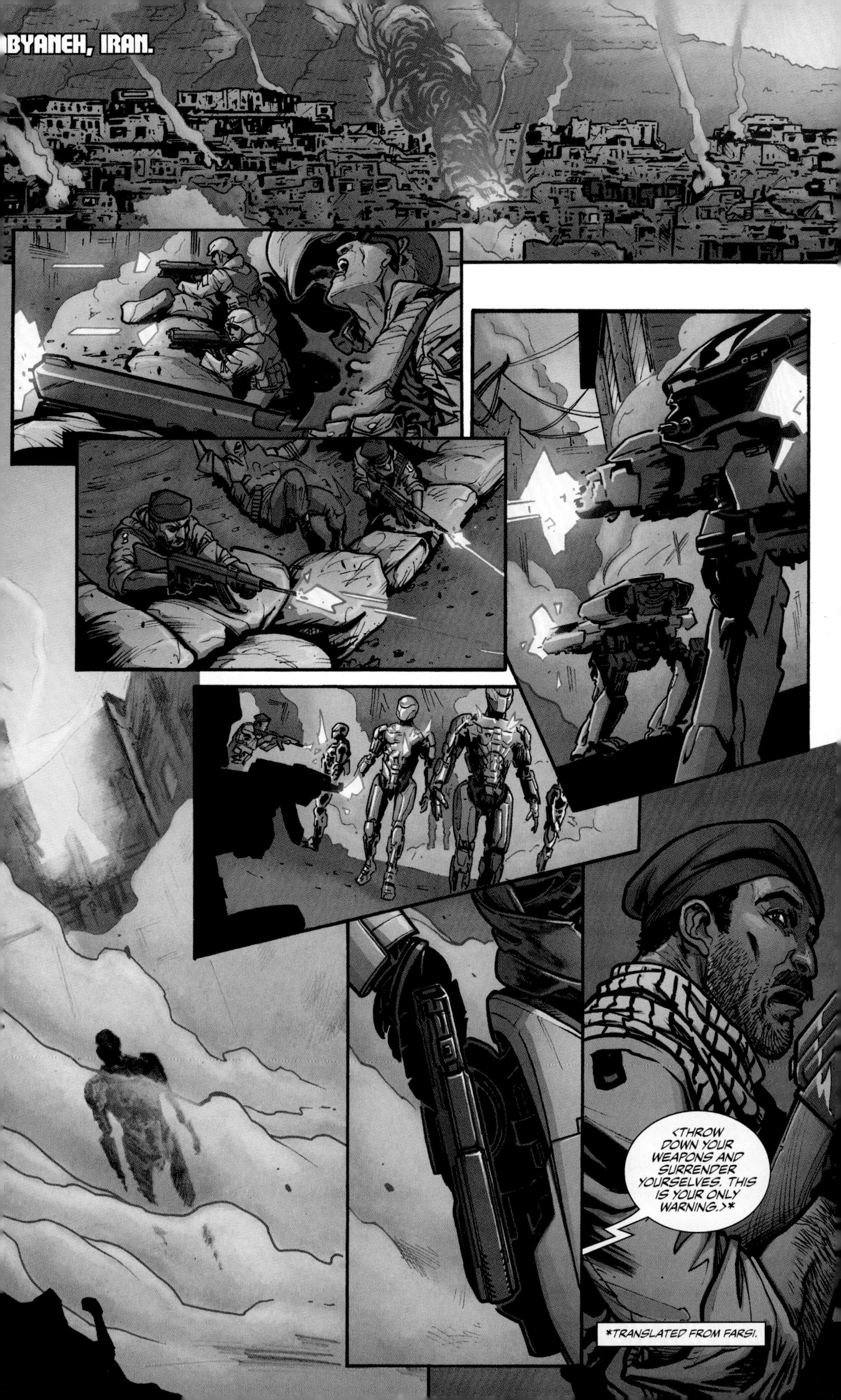
BYANEH, IRAN.
<THROW DOWN YOUR WEAPONS AND SURRENDER YOURSELVES. THIS IS YOUR ONLY WARNING.>*
*TRANSLATED FROM FARSI.

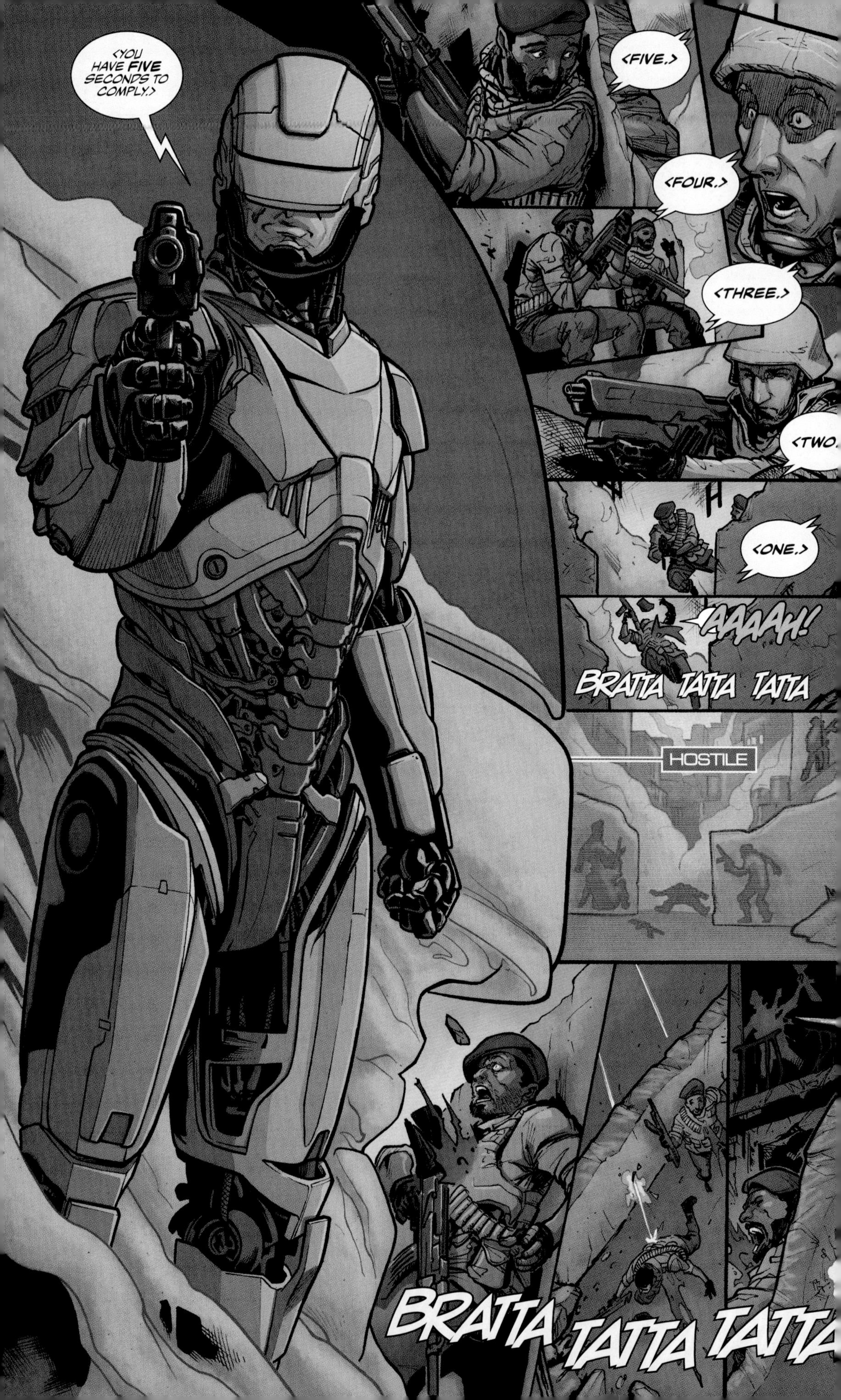

<YOU HAVE FIVE SECONDS TO COMPLY.>
<FIVE.>
<FOUR.>
<THREE.>
<TWO.
<ONE.>
AAAAH!
BRATTA TATTA TATTA
HOSTILE
BRATTA TATTA TATTA

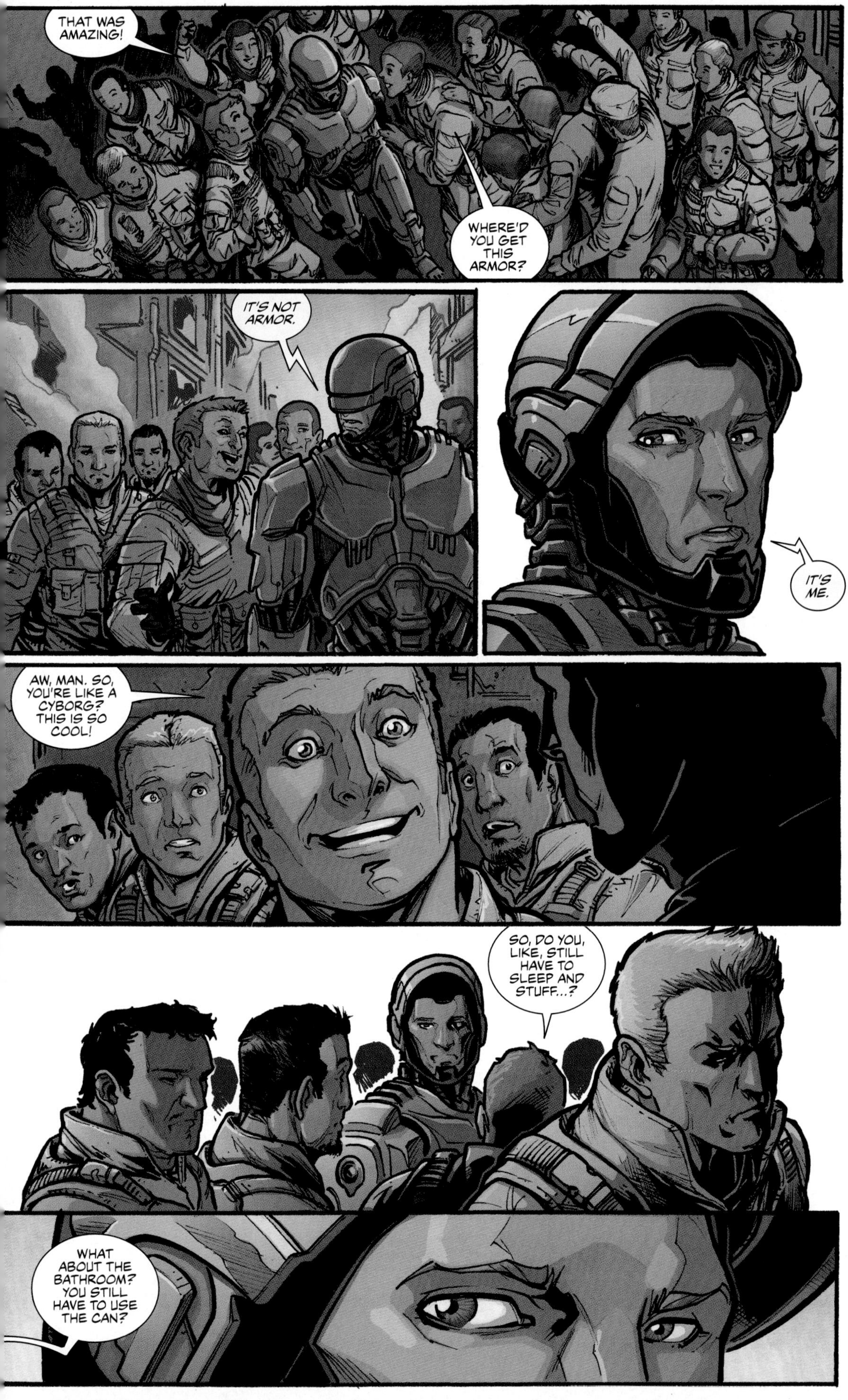
THAT WAS AMAZING!
WHERE'D YOU GET THIS ARMOR?
IT'S NOT ARMOR.
IT'S ME.
AW, MAN. SO, YOU'RE LIKE A CYBORG? THIS IS SO COOL!
SO, DO YOU, LIKE, STILL HAVE TO SLEEP AND STUFF...?
WHAT ABOUT THE BATHROOM? YOU STILL HAVE TO USE THE CAN?

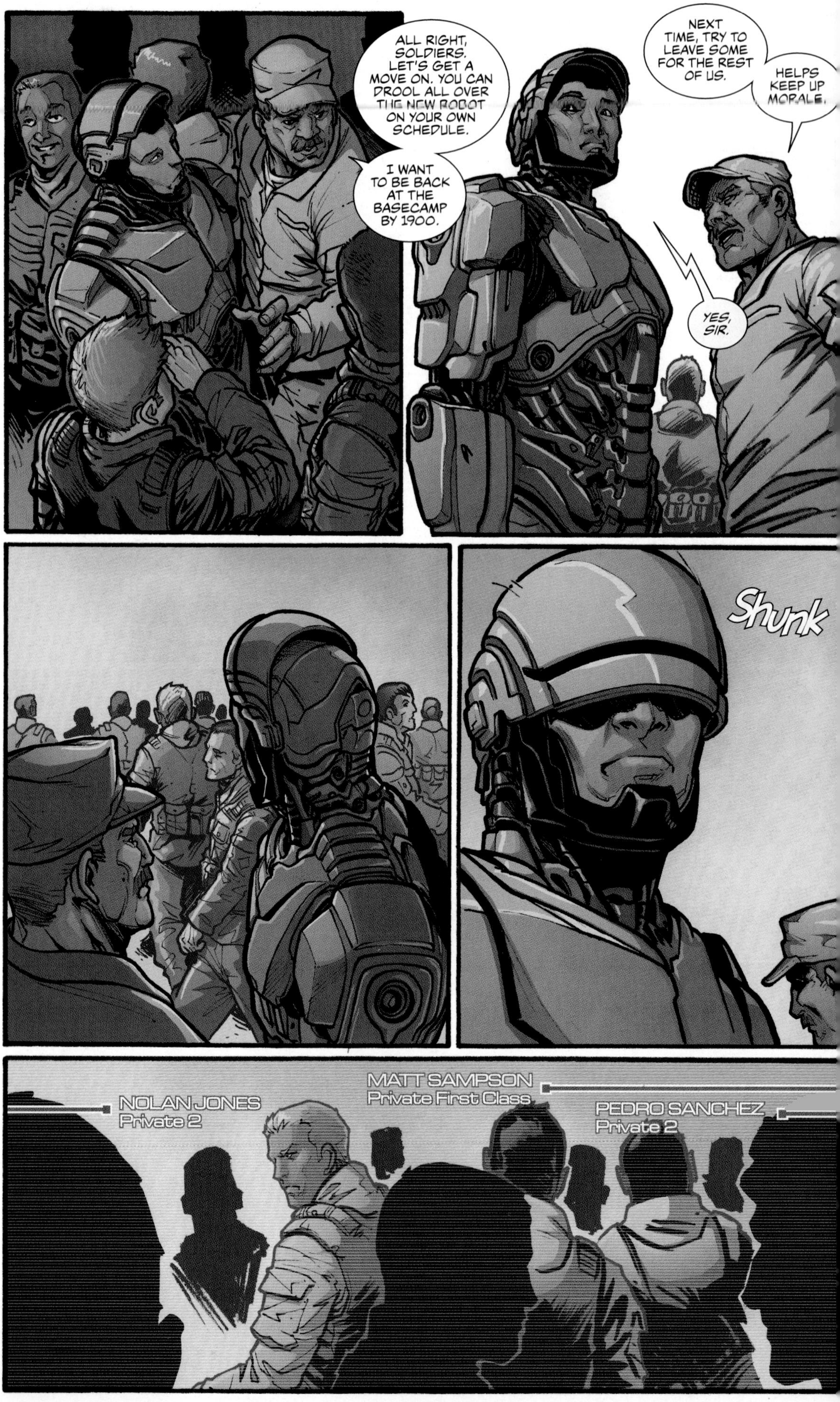
ALL RIGHT, SOLDIERS. LET'S GET A MOVE ON. YOU CAN DROOL ALL OVER THE NEW ROBOT ON YOUR OWN SCHEDULE.
I WANT TO BE BACK AT THE BASECAMP BY 1900.
NEXT TIME, TRY TO LEAVE SOME FOR THE REST OF US.
HELPS KEEP UP MORALE.
YES, SIR.
Shunk
NOLAN JONES
Private 2
MATT SAMPSON
Private First Class
PEDRO SANCHEZ
Private 2

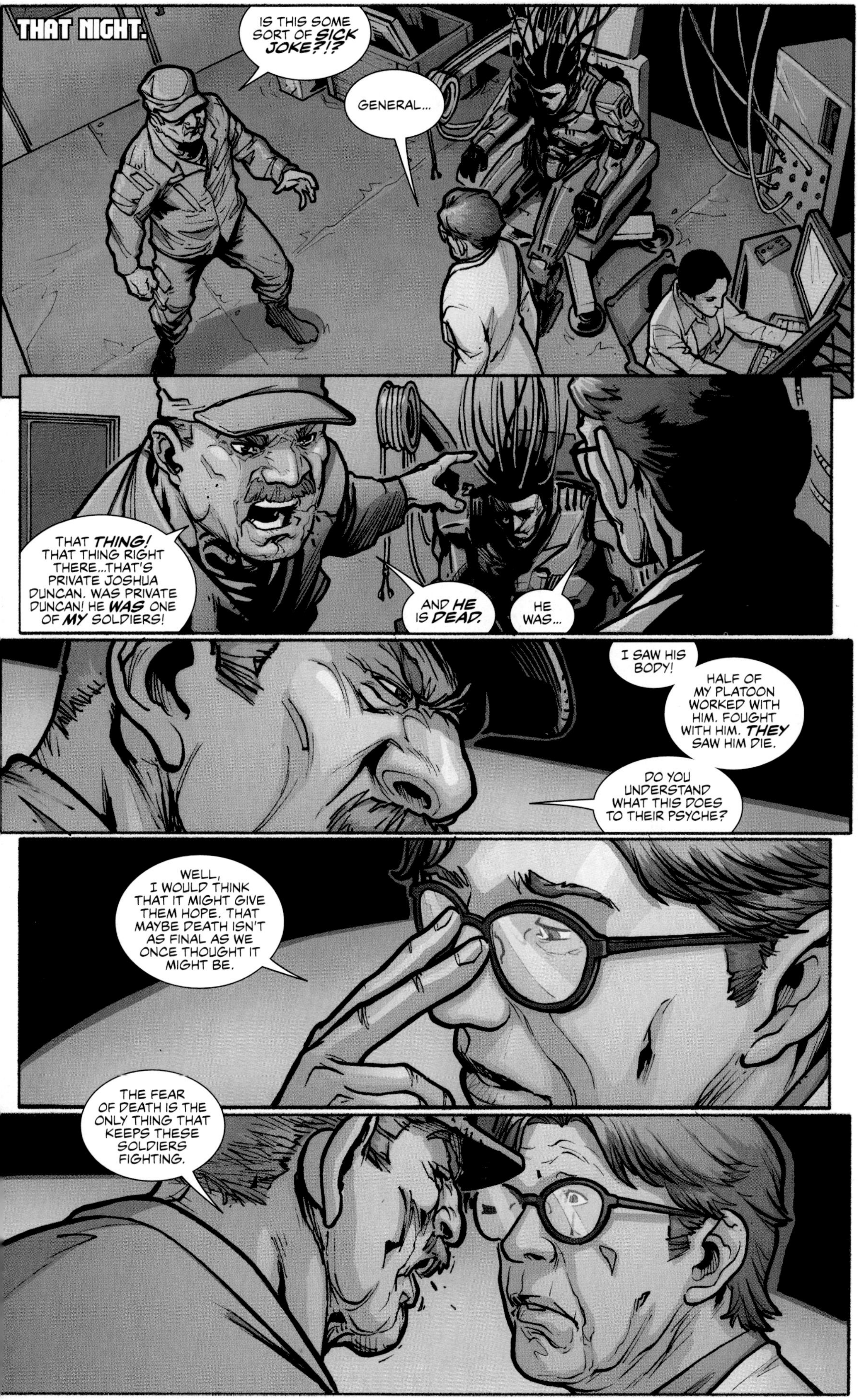
THAT NIGHT.
IS THIS SOME SORT OF SICK JOKE?!?
GENERAL...
THAT THING! THAT THING RIGHT THERE...THAT'S PRIVATE JOSHUA DUNCAN. WAS PRIVATE DUNCAN! HE WAS ONE OF MY SOLDIERS!
AND HE IS DEAD.
HE WAS...
I SAW HIS BODY!
HALF OF MY PLATOON WORKED WITH HIM. FOUGHT WITH HIM. THEY SAW HIM DIE.
DO YOU UNDERSTAND WHAT THIS DOES TO THEIR PSYCHE?
WELL, I WOULD THINK THAT IT MIGHT GIVE THEM HOPE. THAT MAYBE DEATH ISN'T AS FINAL AS WE ONCE THOUGHT IT MIGHT BE.
THE FEAR OF DEATH IS THE ONLY THING THAT KEEPS THESE SOLDIERS FIGHTING.

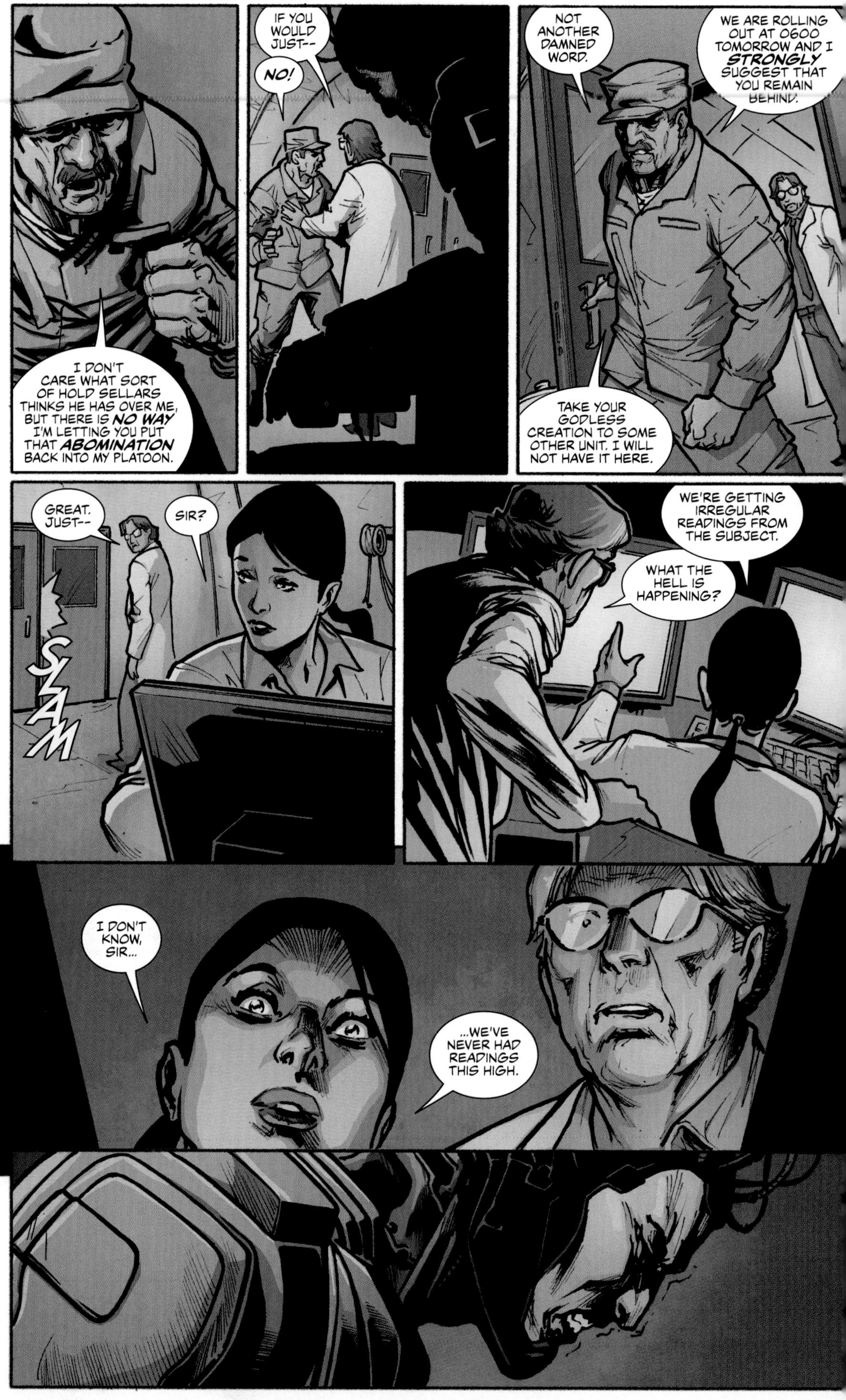

I DON'T CARE WHAT SORT OF HOLD SELLARS THINKS HE HAS OVER ME, BUT THERE IS NO WAY I'M LETTING YOU PUT THAT ABOMINATION BACK INTO MY PLATOON.
IF YOU WOULD JUST--
NO!
NOT ANOTHER DAMNED WORD.
WE ARE ROLLING OUT AT 0600 TOMORROW AND I STRONGLY SUGGEST THAT YOU REMAIN BEHIND.
TAKE YOUR GODLESS CREATION TO SOME OTHER UNIT. I WILL NOT HAVE IT HERE.
SLAM
GREAT. JUST--
SIR?
WE'RE GETTING IRREGULAR READINGS FROM THE SUBJECT.
WHAT THE HELL IS HAPPENING?
I DON'T KNOW, SIR...
...WE'VE NEVER HAD READINGS THIS HIGH.

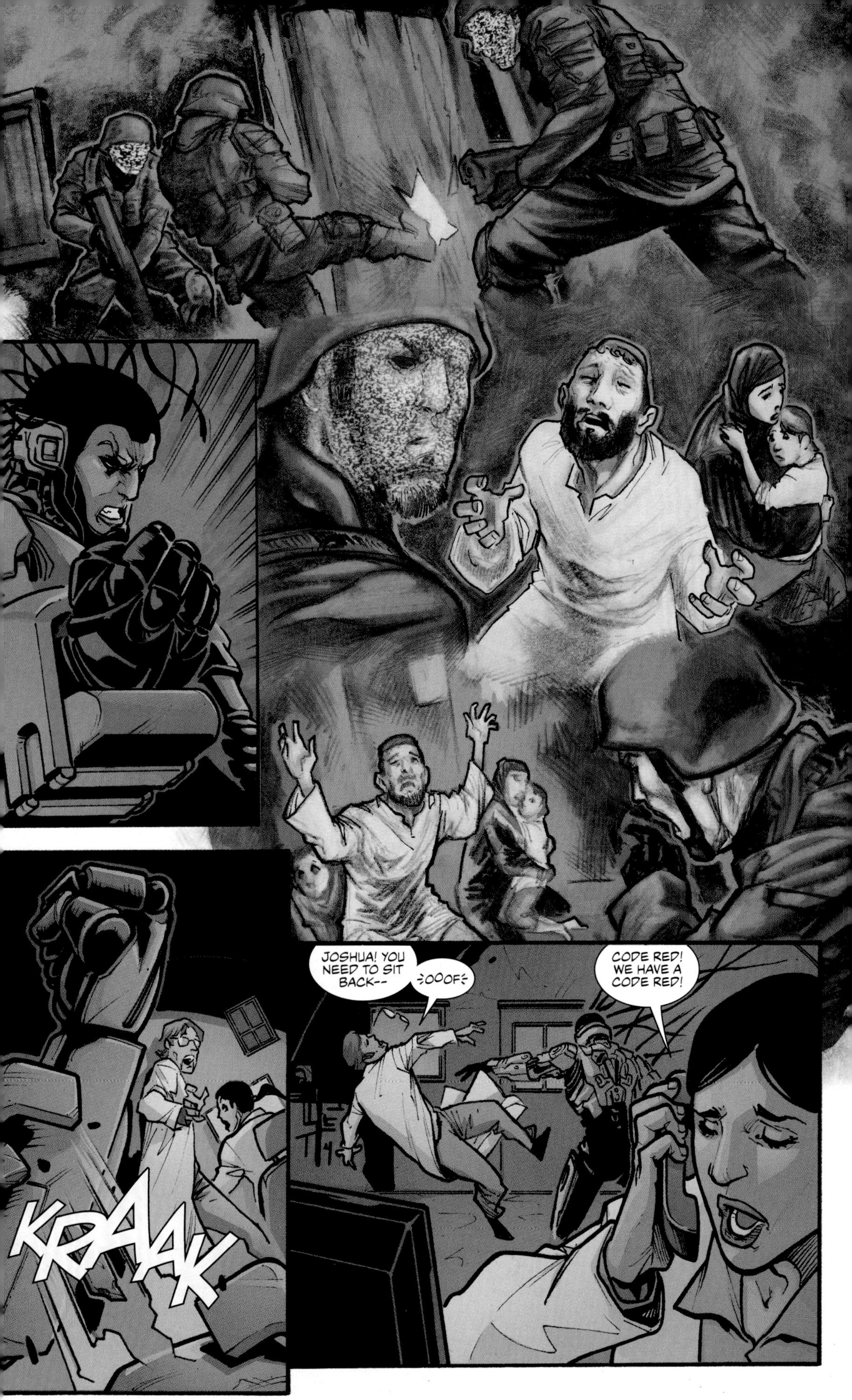
KRAAAK
JOSHUA! YOU NEED TO SIT BACK--
OOOF
CODE RED! WE HAVE A CODE RED!

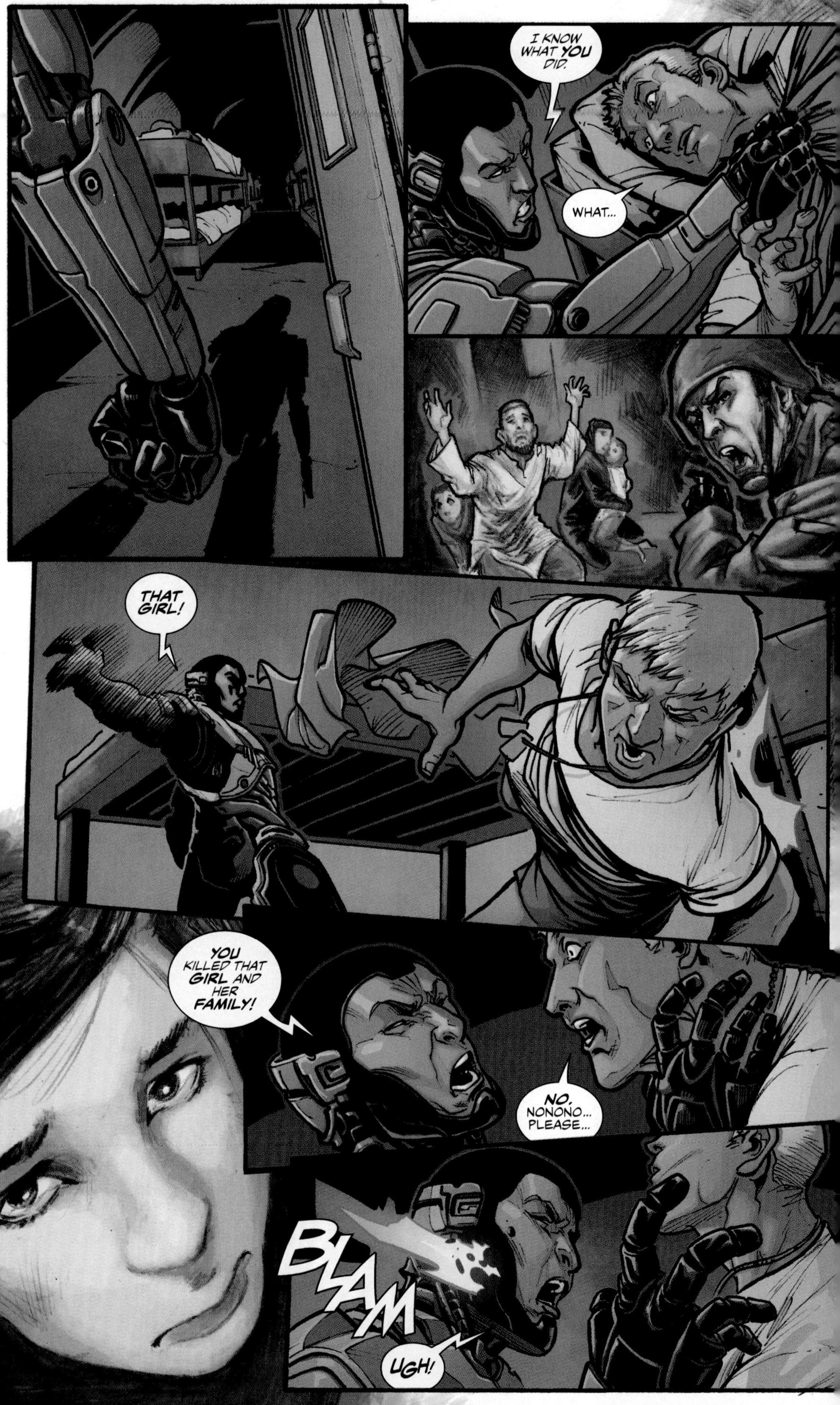
I KNOW WHAT YOU DID.
WHAT...
THAT GIRL!
YOU KILLED THAT GIRL AND HER FAMILY!
NO. NONONO... PLEASE...
BLAM
UGH!

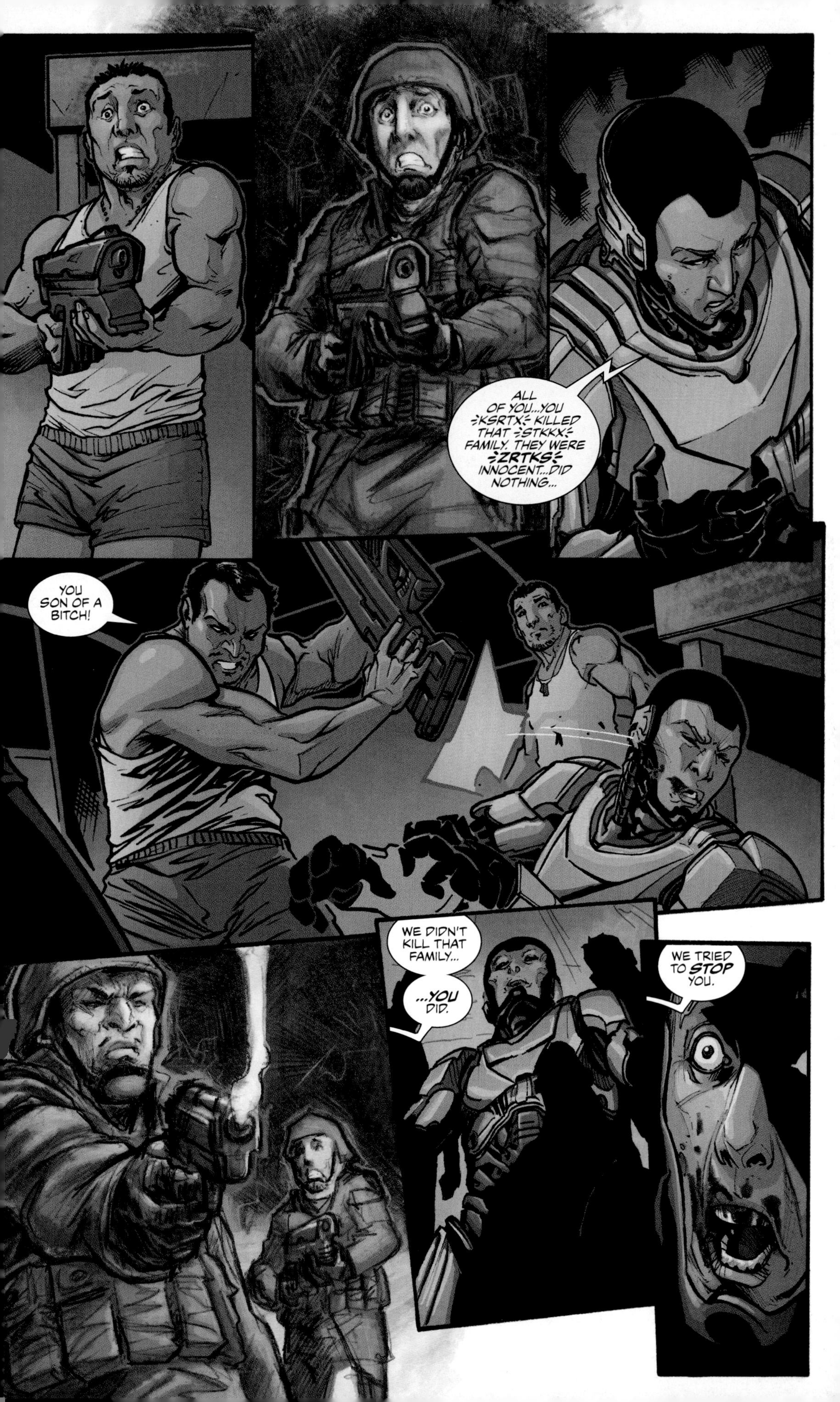
ALL OF YOU...YOU ⚡KSRTX⚡ KILLED THAT ⚡STKKX⚡ FAMILY. THEY WERE ⚡ZRTKS⚡ INNOCENT...DID NOTHING...
YOU SON OF A BITCH!
WE DIDN'T KILL THAT FAMILY...
...YOU DID.
WE TRIED TO STOP YOU.

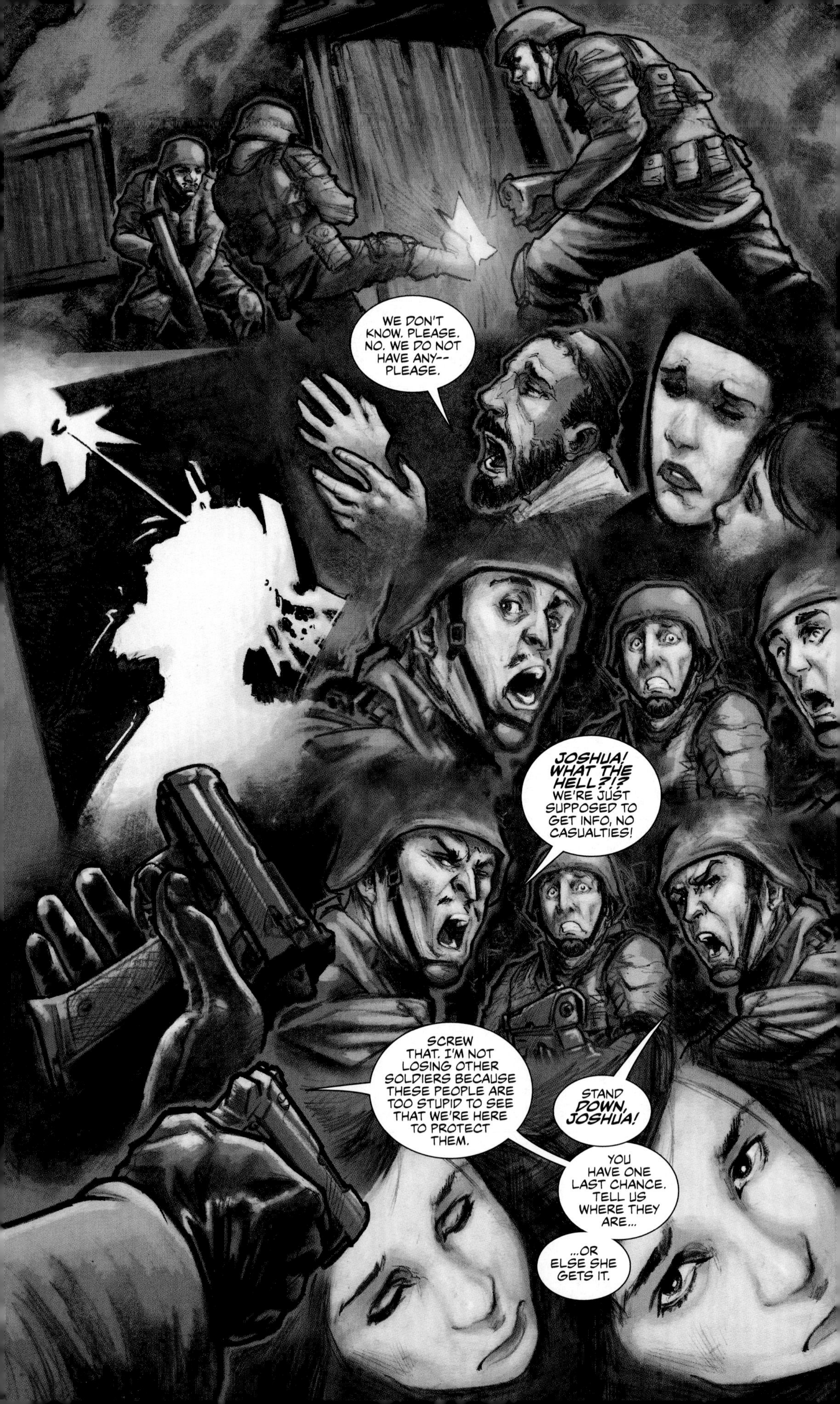
WE DON'T KNOW. PLEASE. NO. WE DO NOT HAVE ANY-- PLEASE.
JOSHUA! WHAT THE HELL?!? WE'RE JUST SUPPOSED TO GET INFO, NO CASUALTIES!
SCREW THAT. I'M NOT LOSING OTHER SOLDIERS BECAUSE THESE PEOPLE ARE TOO STUPID TO SEE THAT WE'RE HERE TO PROTECT THEM.
STAND DOWN, JOSHUA!
YOU HAVE ONE LAST CHANCE. TELL US WHERE THEY ARE...
...OR ELSE SHE GETS IT.

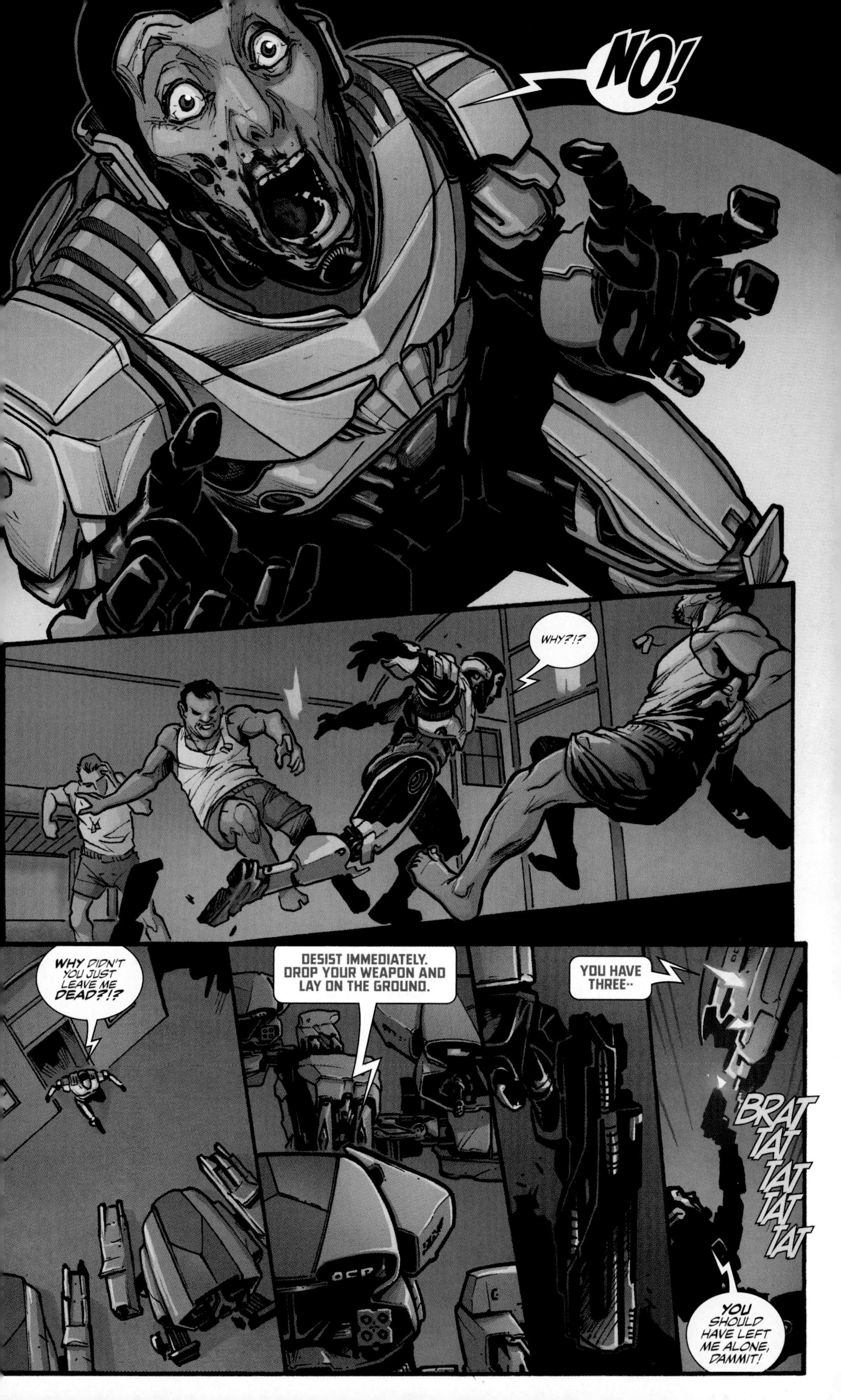
NO!
WHY?!?
WHY DIDN'T YOU JUST LEAVE ME DEAD?!?
DESIST IMMEDIATELY. DROP YOUR WEAPON AND LAY ON THE GROUND.
YOU HAVE THREE--
BRAT TAT TAT TAT TAT
YOU SHOULD HAVE LEFT ME ALONE, DAMMIT!

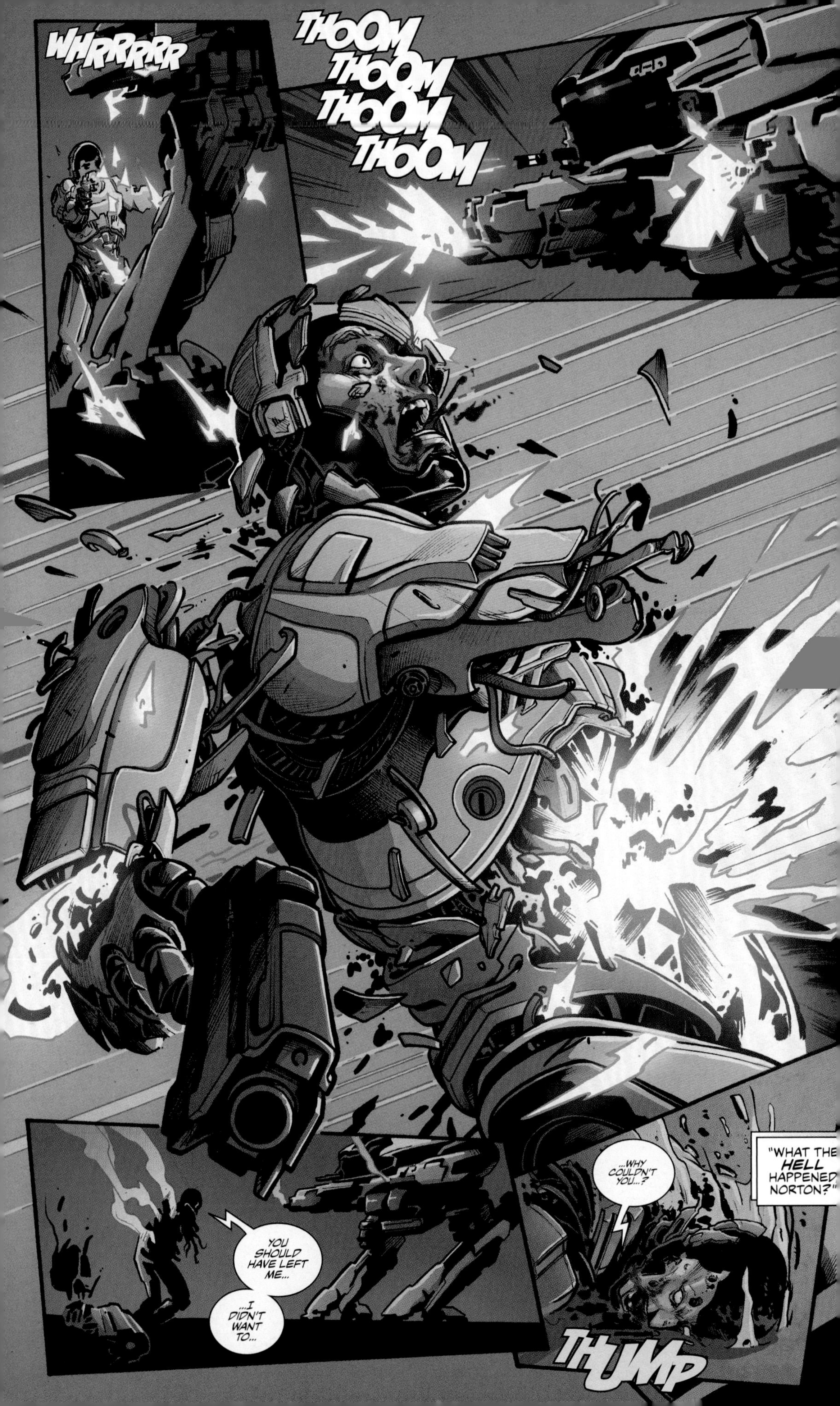
WHRRRRR
THOOM THOOM THOOM THOOM
YOU SHOULD HAVE LEFT ME...
...I DIDN'T WANT TO...
...WHY COULDN'T YOU...?
"WHAT THE HELL HAPPENED NORTON?"
THUMP

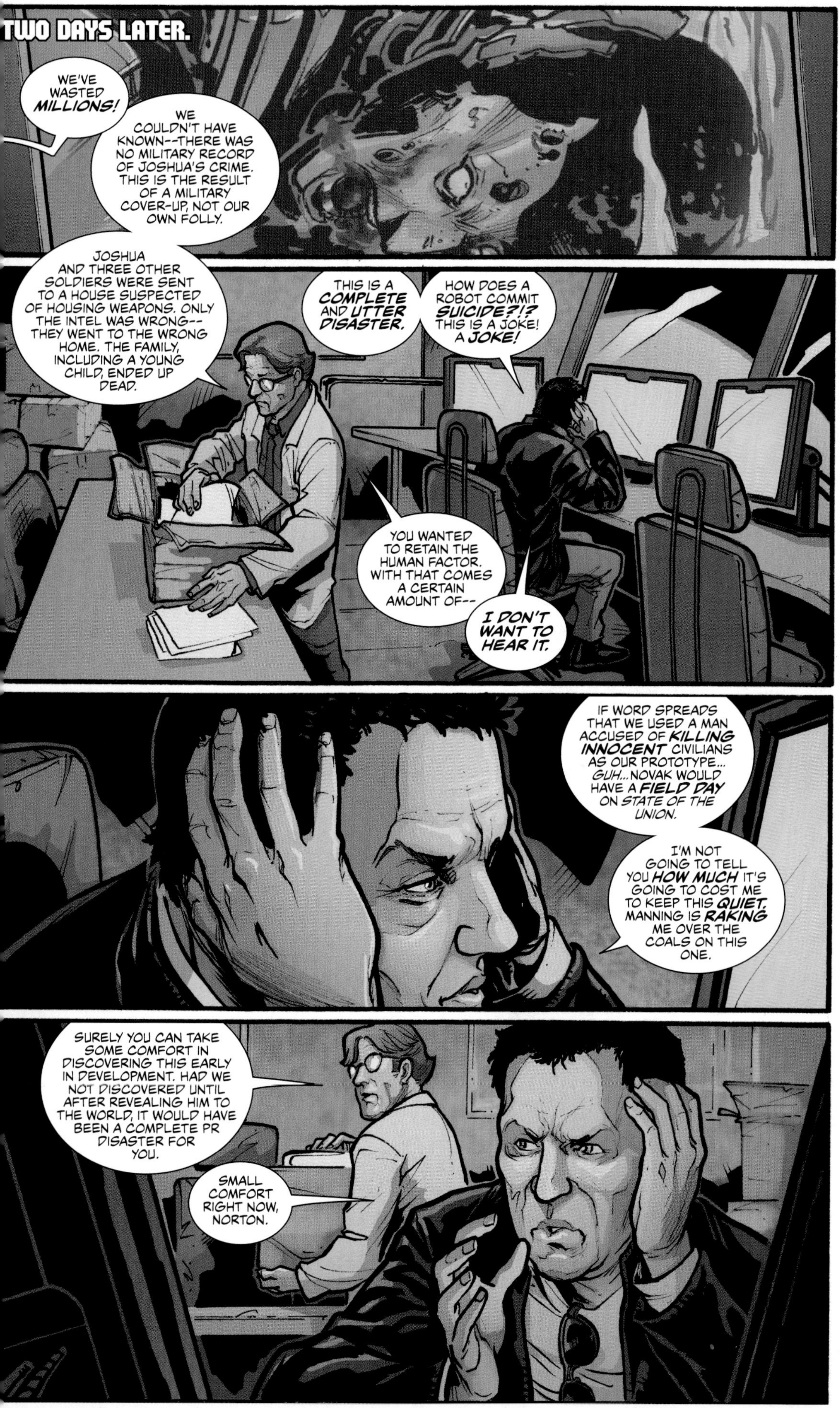
TWO DAYS LATER.
WE'VE WASTED MILLIONS!
WE COULDN'T HAVE KNOWN--THERE WAS NO MILITARY RECORD OF JOSHUA'S CRIME. THIS IS THE RESULT OF A MILITARY COVER-UP, NOT OUR OWN FOLLY.
JOSHUA AND THREE OTHER SOLDIERS WERE SENT TO A HOUSE SUSPECTED OF HOUSING WEAPONS. ONLY THE INTEL WAS WRONG--THEY WENT TO THE WRONG HOME. THE FAMILY, INCLUDING A YOUNG CHILD, ENDED UP DEAD.
THIS IS A COMPLETE AND UTTER DISASTER.
HOW DOES A ROBOT COMMIT SUICIDE?!? THIS IS A JOKE! A JOKE!
YOU WANTED TO RETAIN THE HUMAN FACTOR. WITH THAT COMES A CERTAIN AMOUNT OF--
I DON'T WANT TO HEAR IT.
IF WORD SPREADS THAT WE USED A MAN ACCUSED OF KILLING INNOCENT CIVILIANS AS OUR PROTOTYPE... GUH... NOVAK WOULD HAVE A FIELD DAY ON STATE OF THE UNION.
I'M NOT GOING TO TELL YOU HOW MUCH IT'S GOING TO COST ME TO KEEP THIS QUIET. MANNING IS RAKING ME OVER THE COALS ON THIS ONE.
SURELY YOU CAN TAKE SOME COMFORT IN DISCOVERING THIS EARLY IN DEVELOPMENT. HAD WE NOT DISCOVERED UNTIL AFTER REVEALING HIM TO THE WORLD, IT WOULD HAVE BEEN A COMPLETE PR DISASTER FOR YOU.
SMALL COMFORT RIGHT NOW, NORTON.

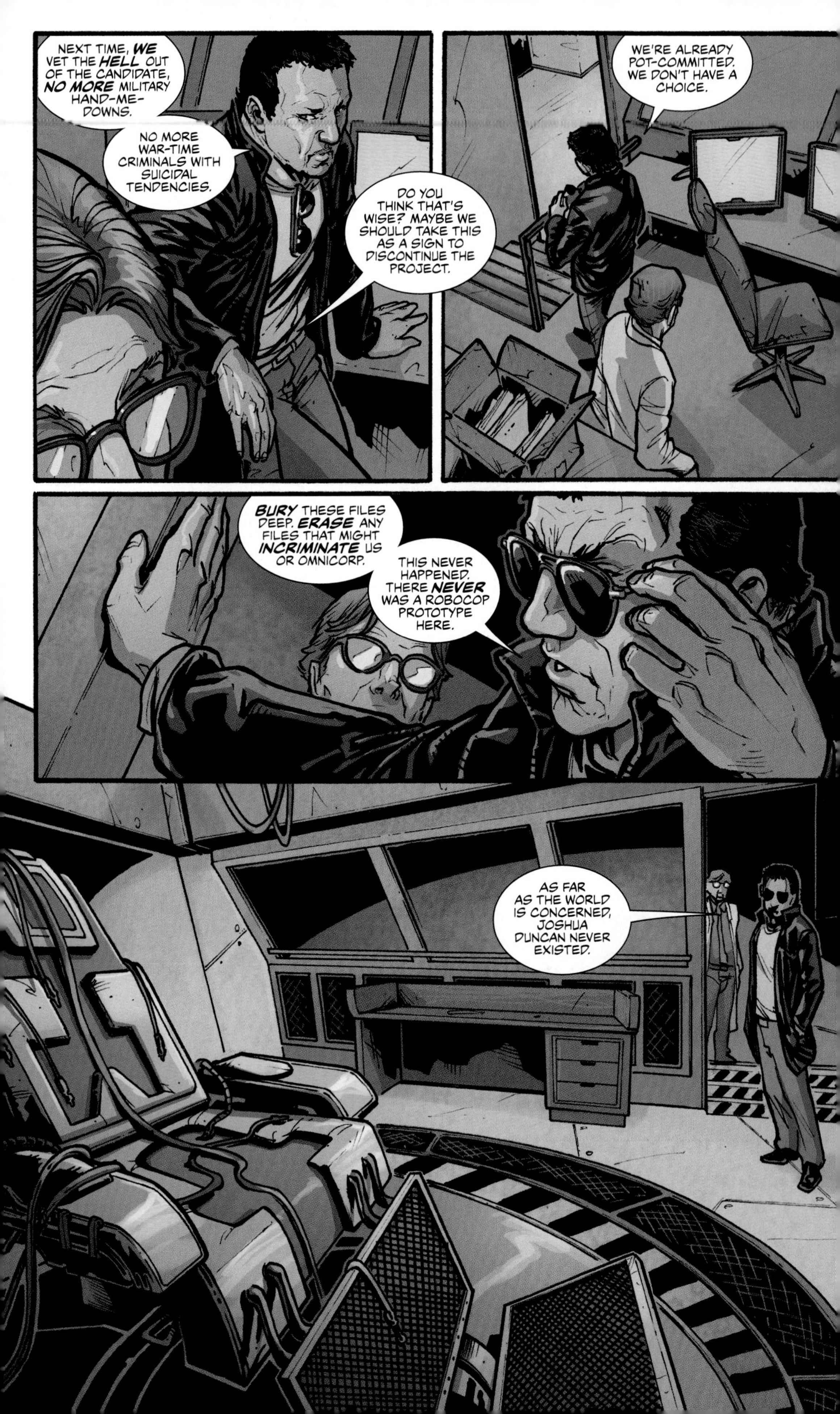
NEXT TIME, WE VET THE HELL OUT OF THE CANDIDATE, NO MORE MILITARY HAND-ME-DOWNS.
NO MORE WAR-TIME CRIMINALS WITH SUICIDAL TENDENCIES.
DO YOU THINK THAT'S WISE? MAYBE WE SHOULD TAKE THIS AS A SIGN TO DISCONTINUE THE PROJECT.
WE'RE ALREADY POT-COMMITTED. WE DON'T HAVE A CHOICE.
BURY THESE FILES DEEP. ERASE ANY FILES THAT MIGHT INCRIMINATE US OR OMNICORP.
THIS NEVER HAPPENED. THERE NEVER WAS A ROBOCOP PROTOTYPE HERE.
AS FAR AS THE WORLD IS CONCERNED, JOSHUA DUNCAN NEVER EXISTED.

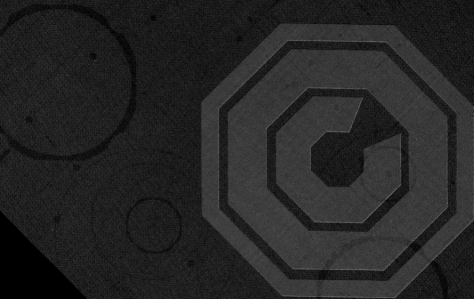

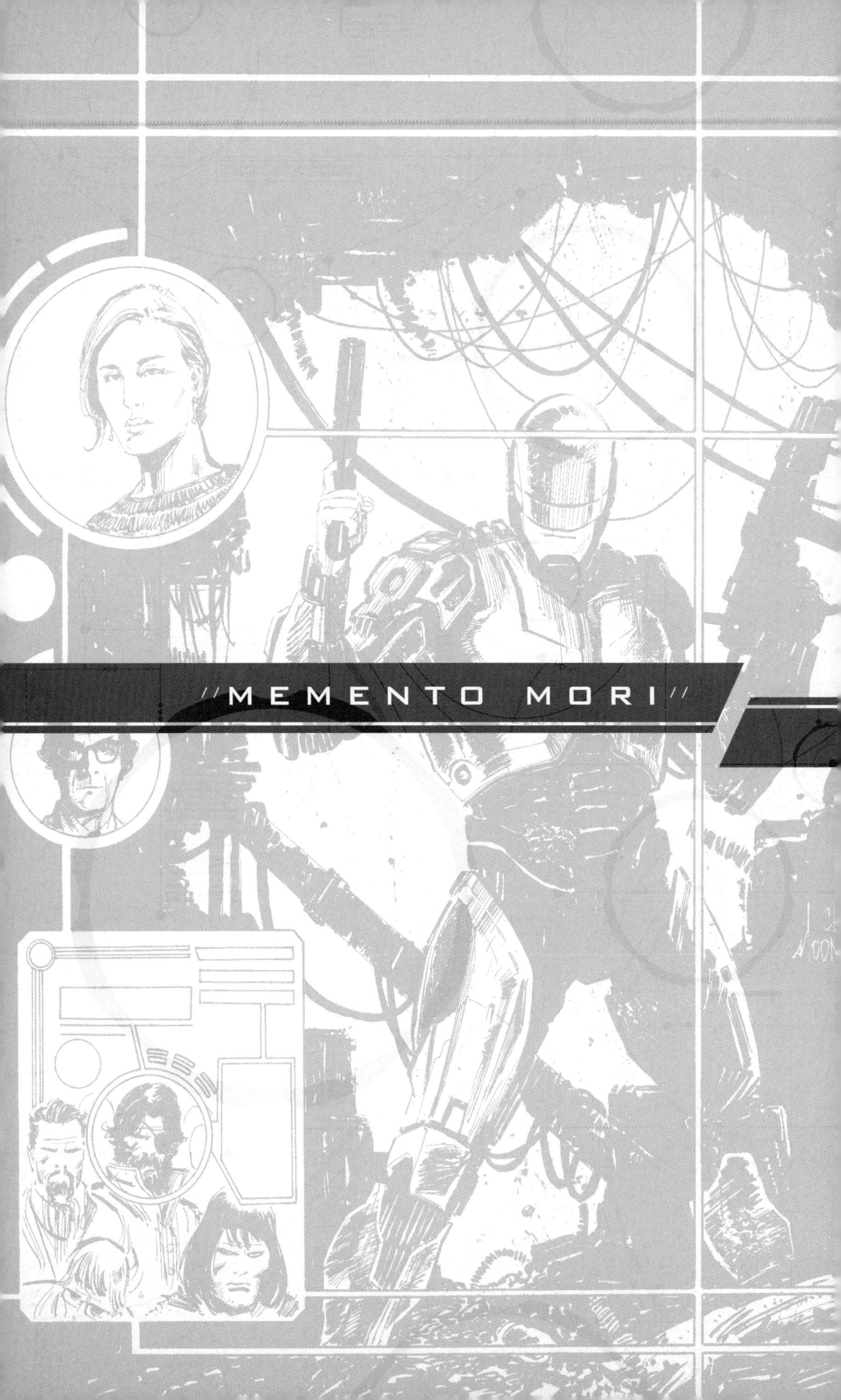
//MEMENTO MORI//

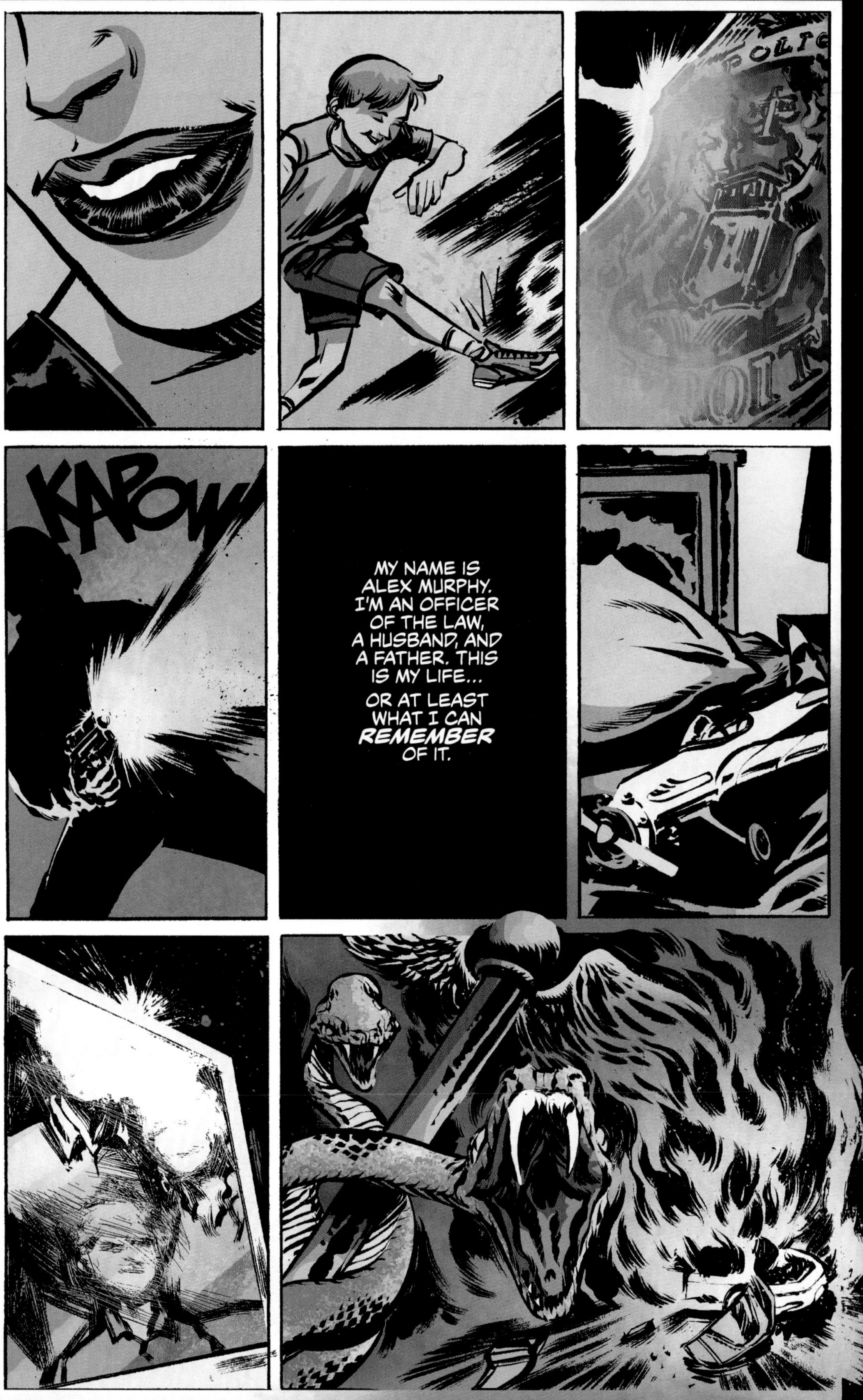
KAPOW
MY NAME IS ALEX MURPHY. I'M AN OFFICER OF THE LAW, A HUSBAND, AND A FATHER. THIS IS MY LIFE...
OR AT LEAST WHAT I CAN *REMEMBER* OF IT.

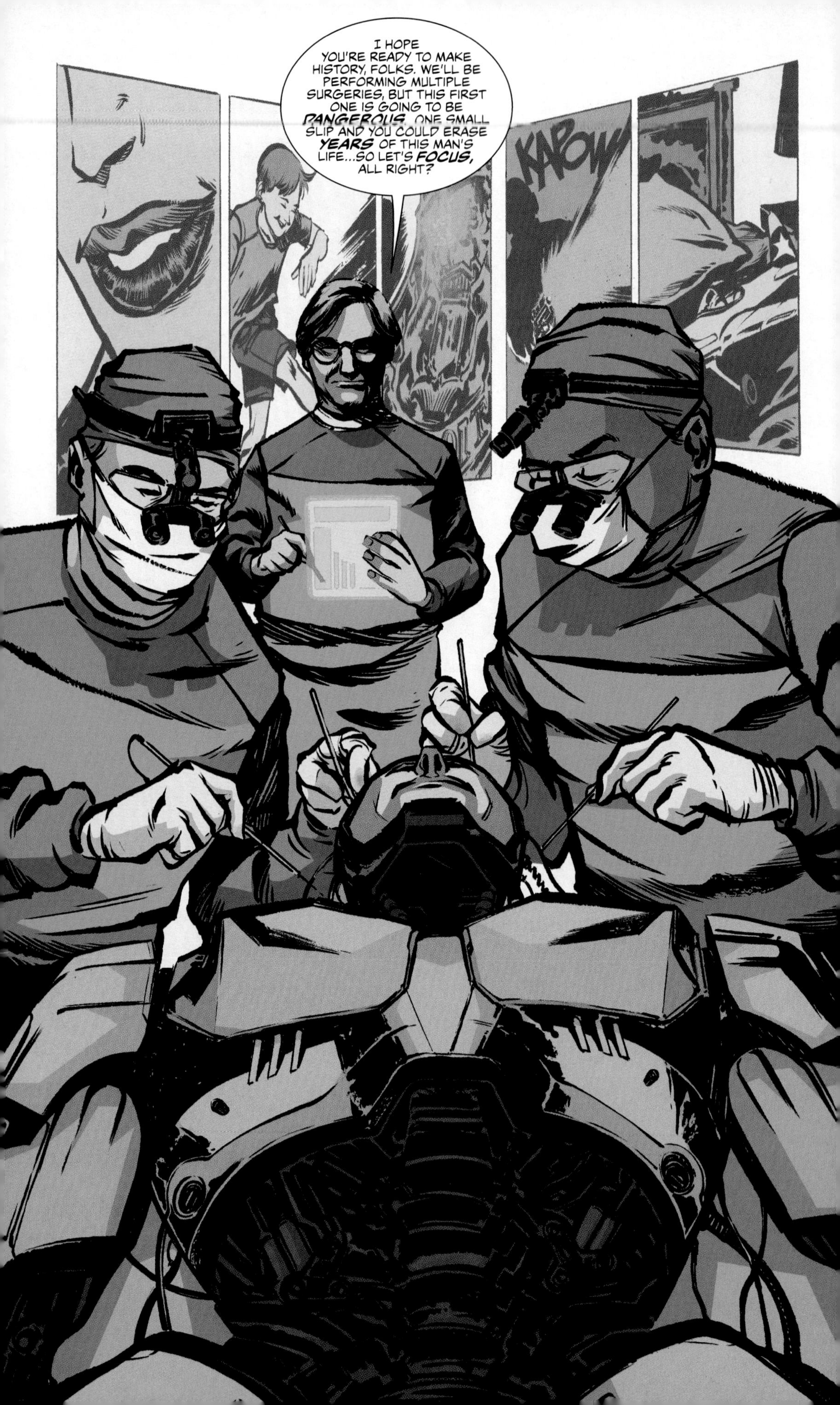
I HOPE YOU'RE READY TO MAKE HISTORY, FOLKS. WE'LL BE PERFORMING MULTIPLE SURGERIES, BUT THIS FIRST ONE IS GOING TO BE DANGEROUS. ONE SMALL SLIP AND YOU COULD ERASE YEARS OF THIS MAN'S LIFE...SO LET'S FOCUS, ALL RIGHT?
KAPOW

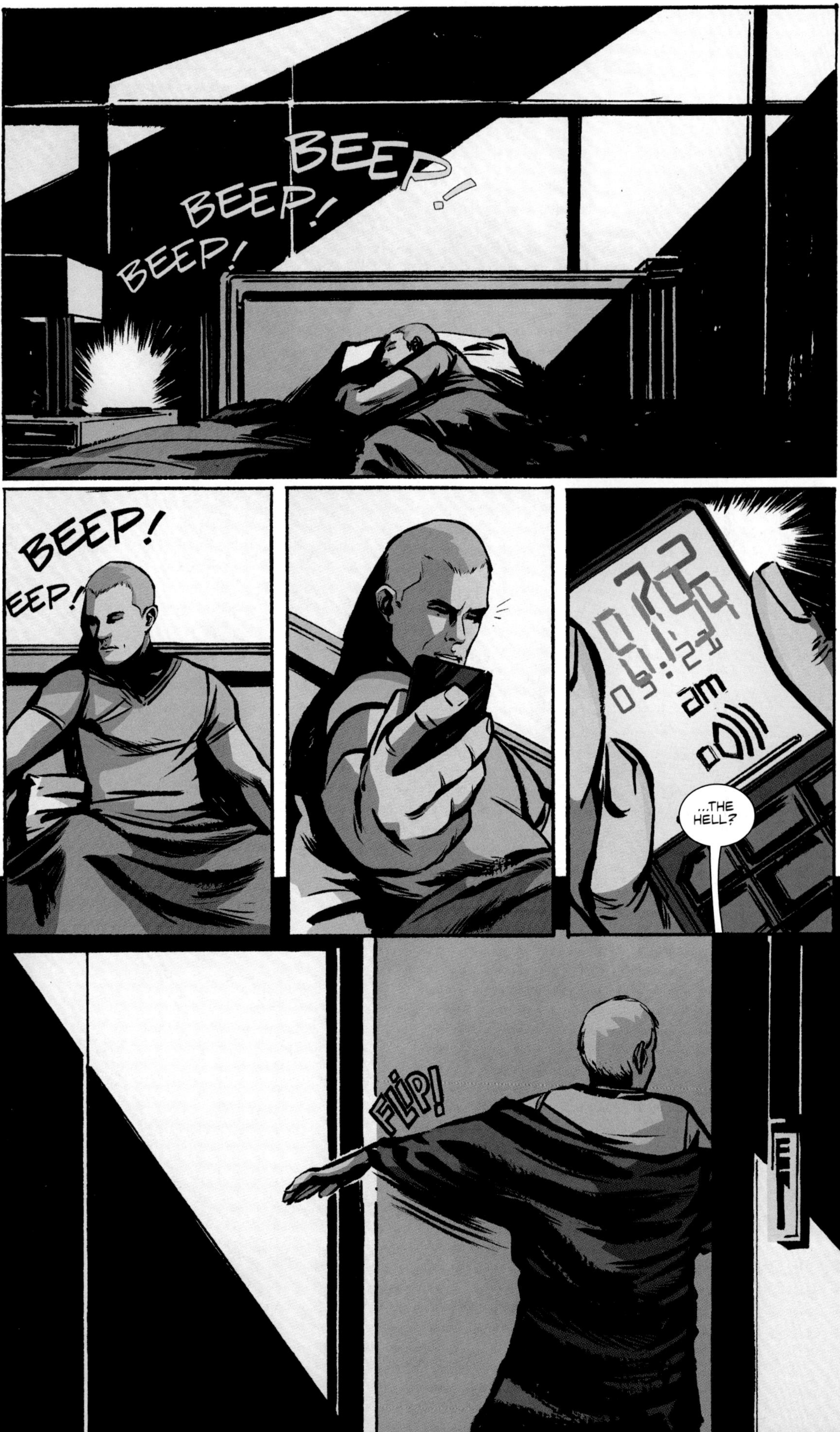
BEEP!
BEEP!
BEEP!
BEEP!
EEP!
...THE HELL?
FLIP!

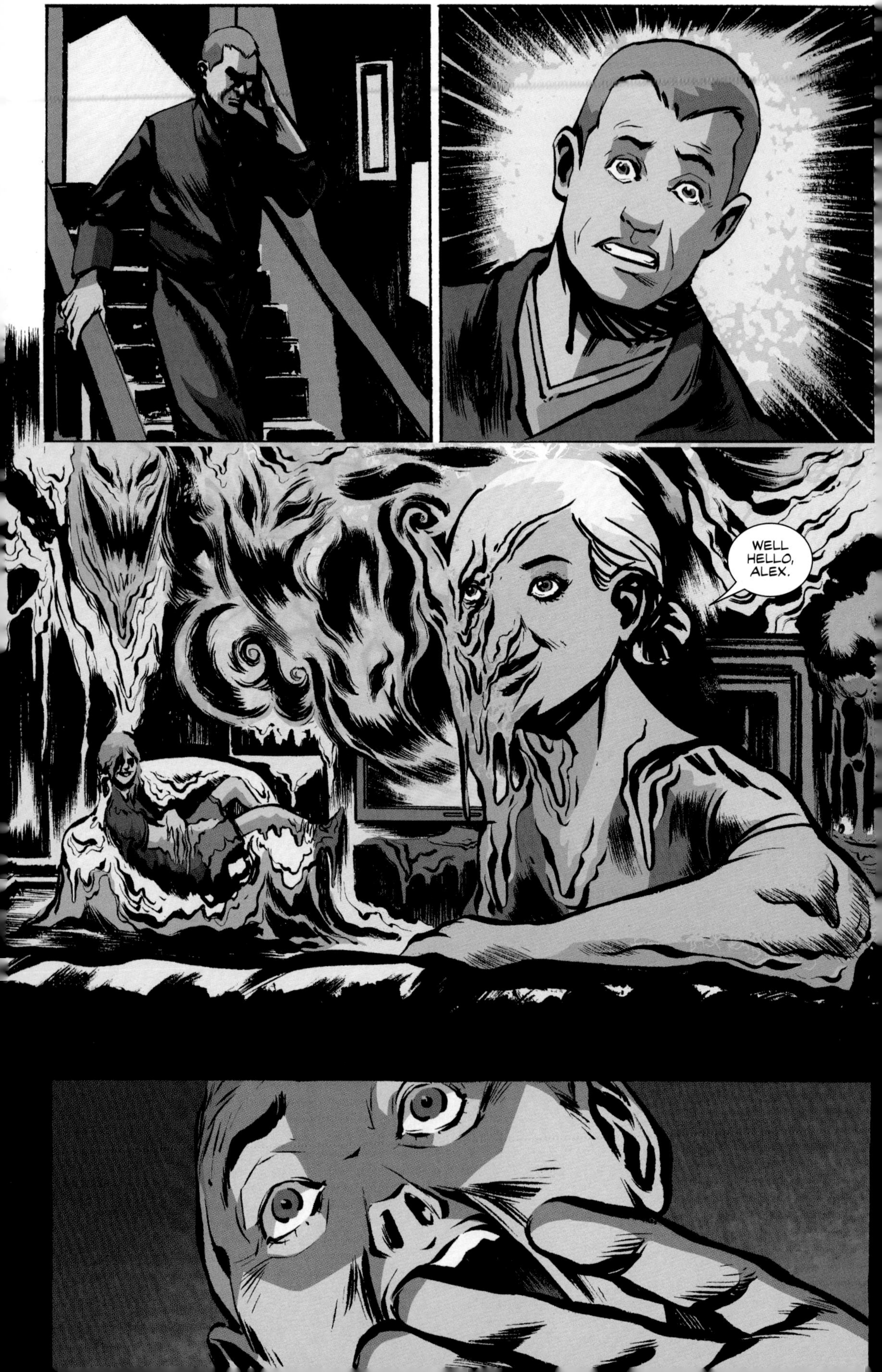
WELL HELLO, ALEX.

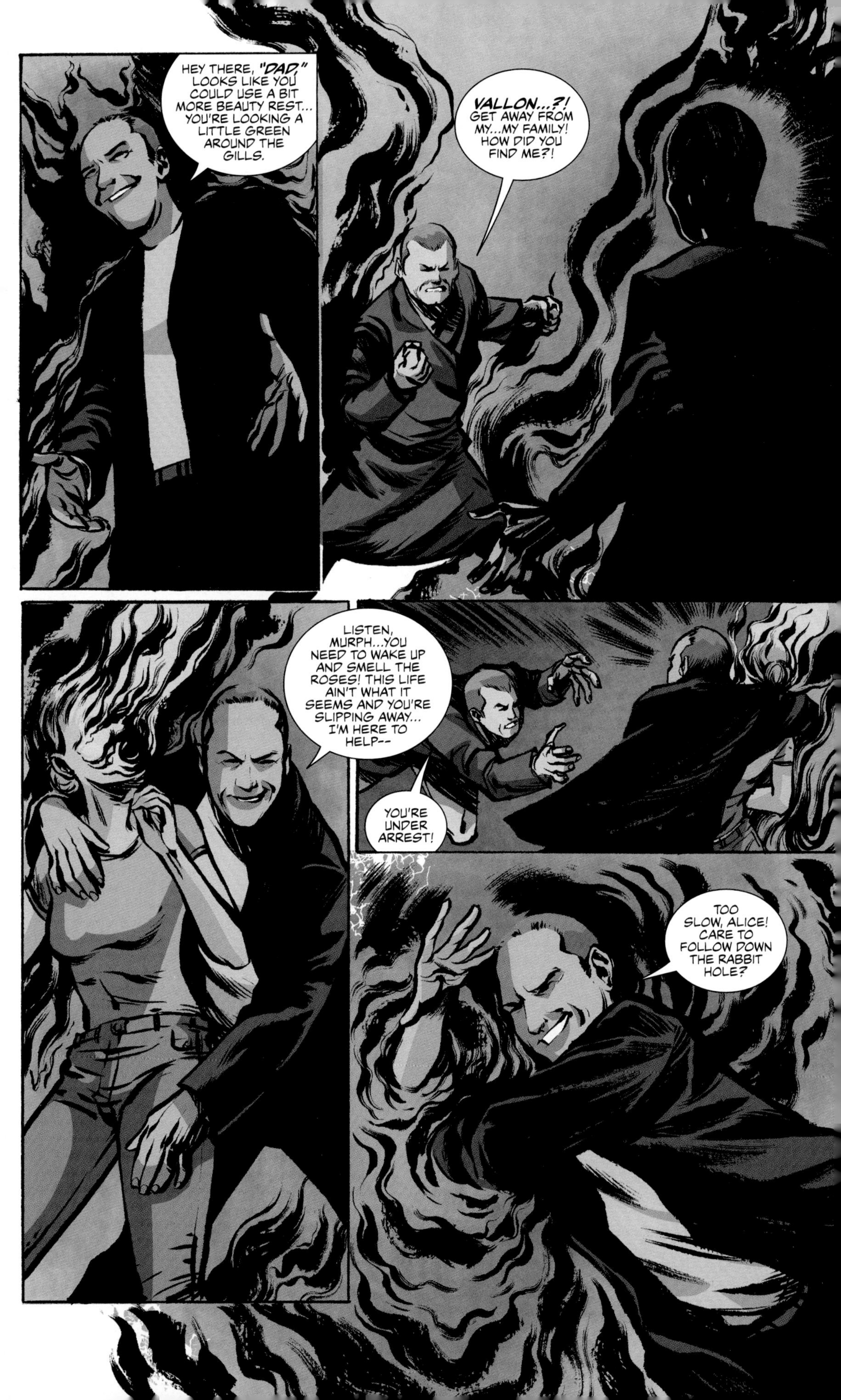
HEY THERE, "DAD." LOOKS LIKE YOU COULD USE A BIT MORE BEAUTY REST... YOU'RE LOOKING A LITTLE GREEN AROUND THE GILLS.
VALLON...?! GET AWAY FROM MY...MY FAMILY! HOW DID YOU FIND ME?!
LISTEN, MURPH...YOU NEED TO WAKE UP AND SMELL THE ROSES! THIS LIFE AIN'T WHAT IT SEEMS AND YOU'RE SLIPPING AWAY... I'M HERE TO HELP--
YOU'RE UNDER ARREST!
TOO SLOW, ALICE! CARE TO FOLLOW DOWN THE RABBIT HOLE?

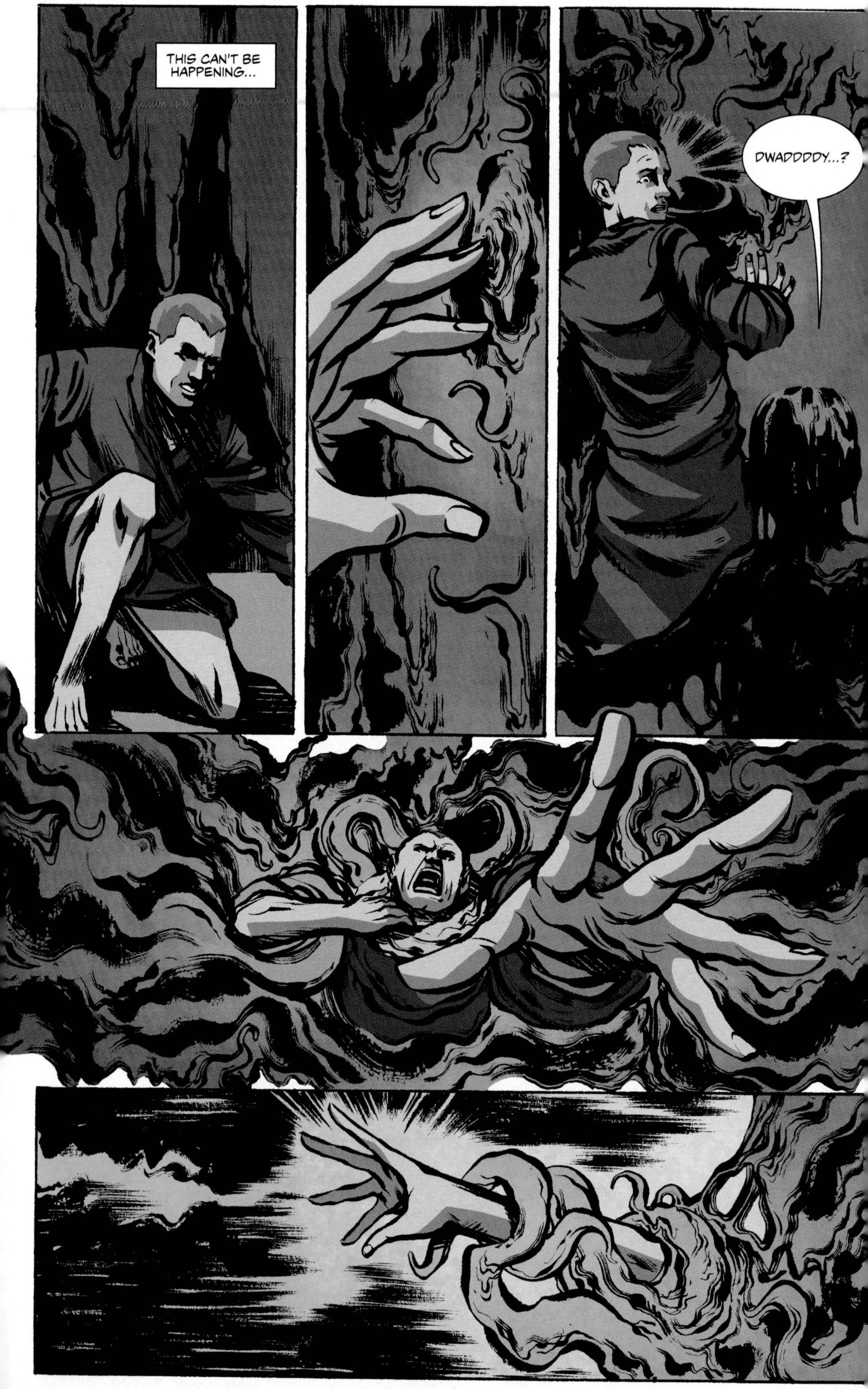
THIS CAN'T BE HAPPENING...
DWADDDDY...?

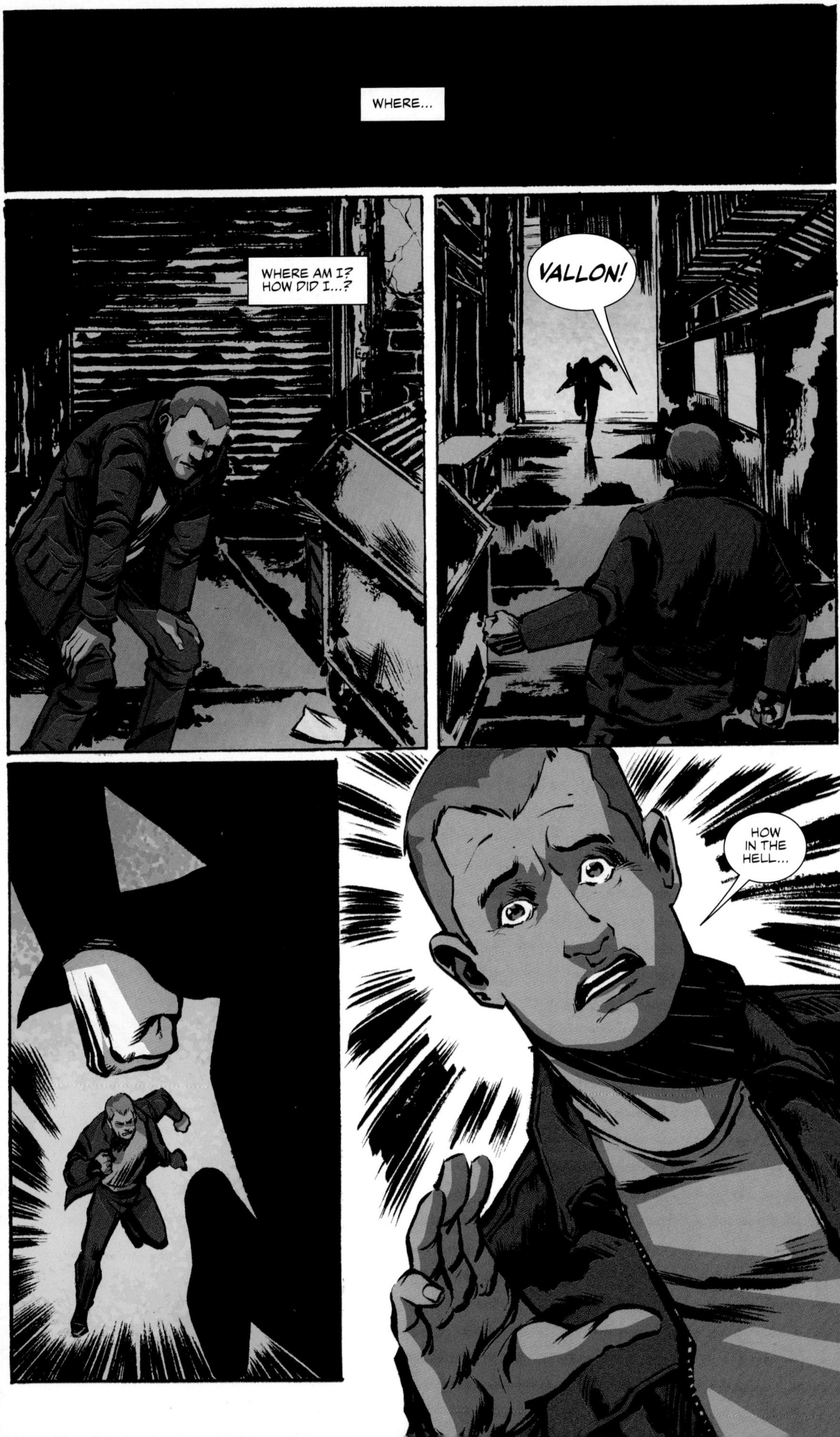

WHERE...
WHERE AM I? HOW DID I...?
VALLON!
HOW IN THE HELL...

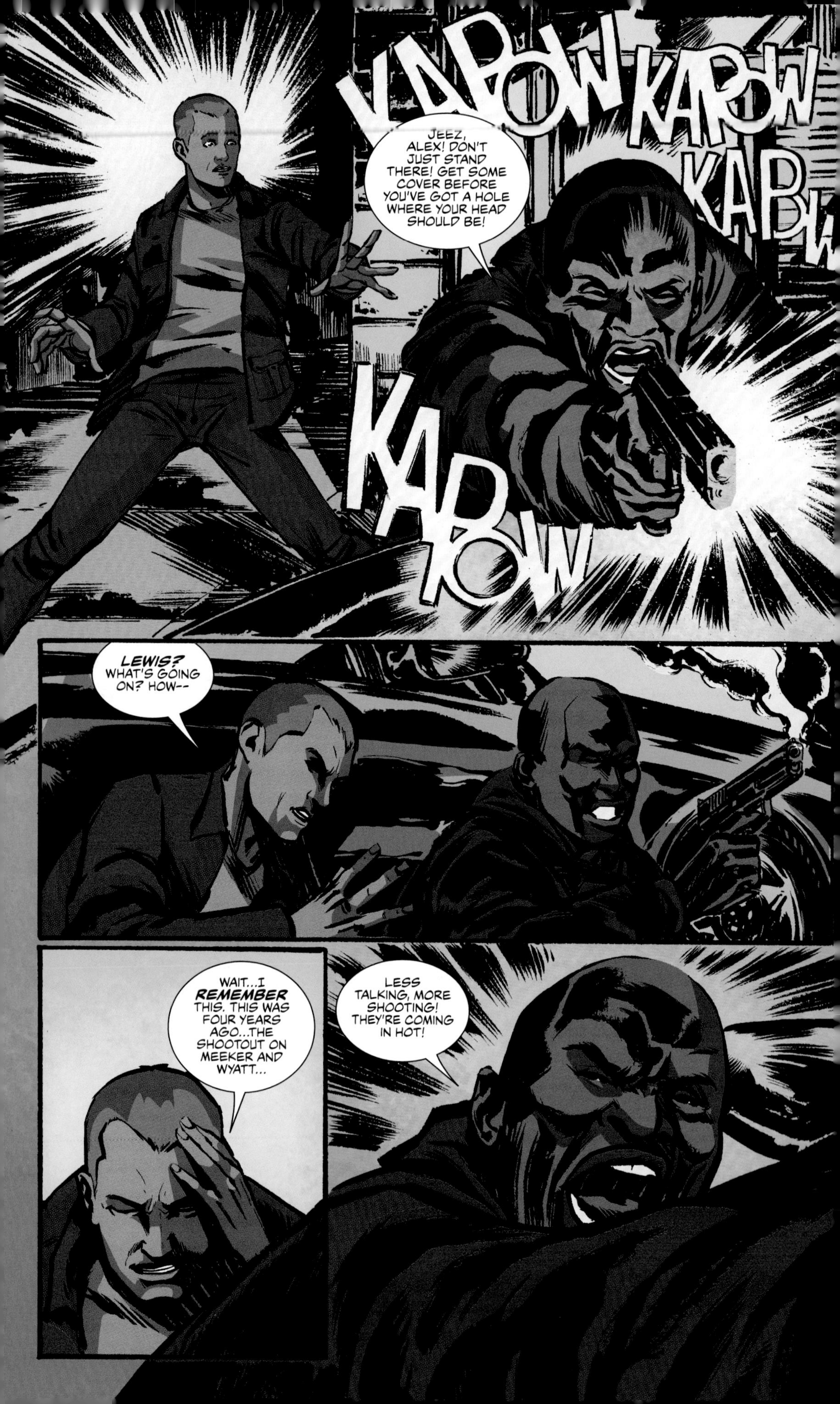
KAPOW KAPOW
KAPOW
JEEZ, ALEX! DON'T JUST STAND THERE! GET SOME COVER BEFORE YOU'VE GOT A HOLE WHERE YOUR HEAD SHOULD BE!
KAPOW
LEWIS? WHAT'S GOING ON? HOW--
WAIT...I REMEMBER THIS. THIS WAS FOUR YEARS AGO...THE SHOOTOUT ON MEEKER AND WYATT...
LESS TALKING, MORE SHOOTING! THEY'RE COMING IN HOT!

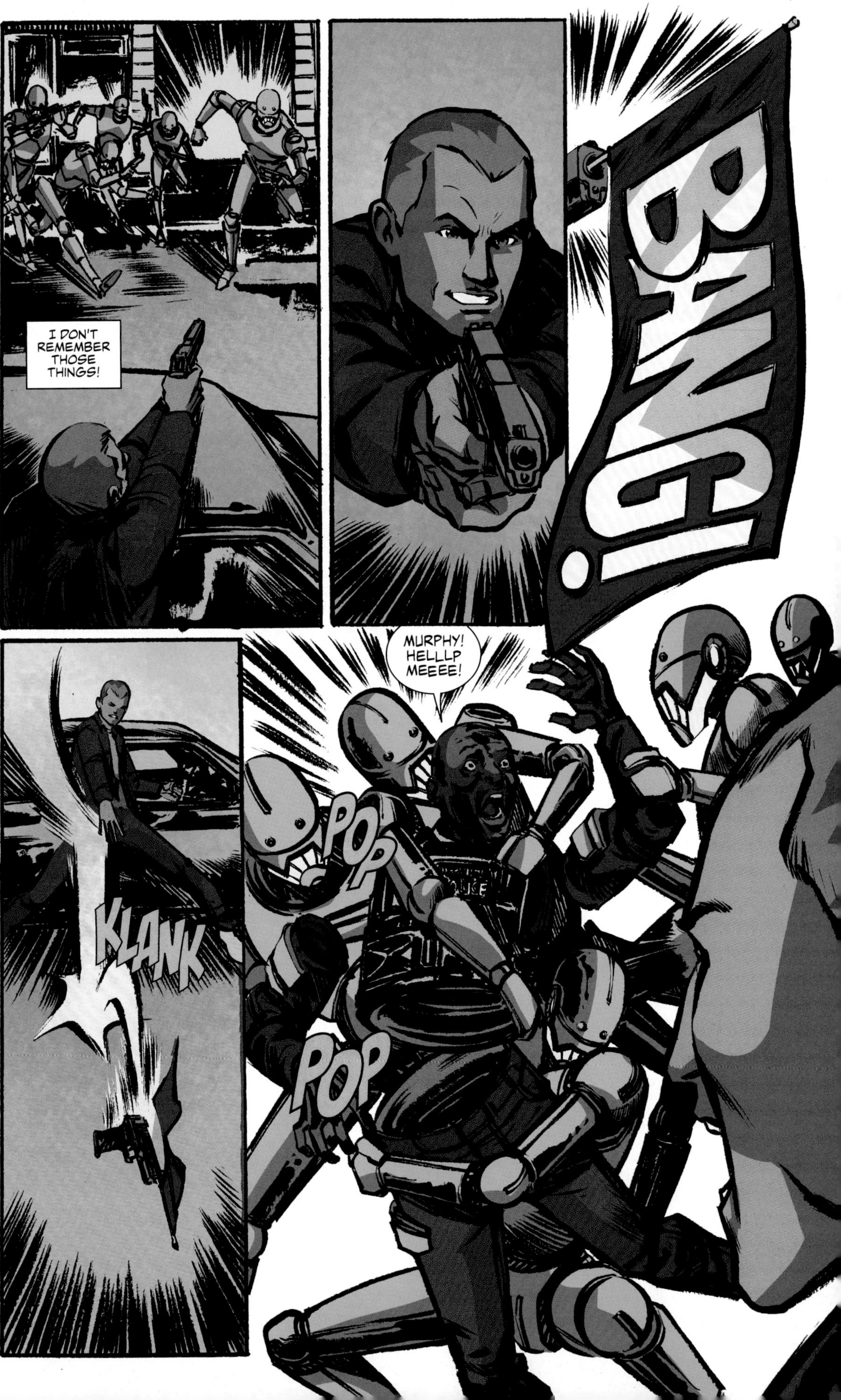
I DON'T REMEMBER THOSE THINGS!
BANG!
MURPHY! HELLLP MEEEE!
POP
POP
KLANK

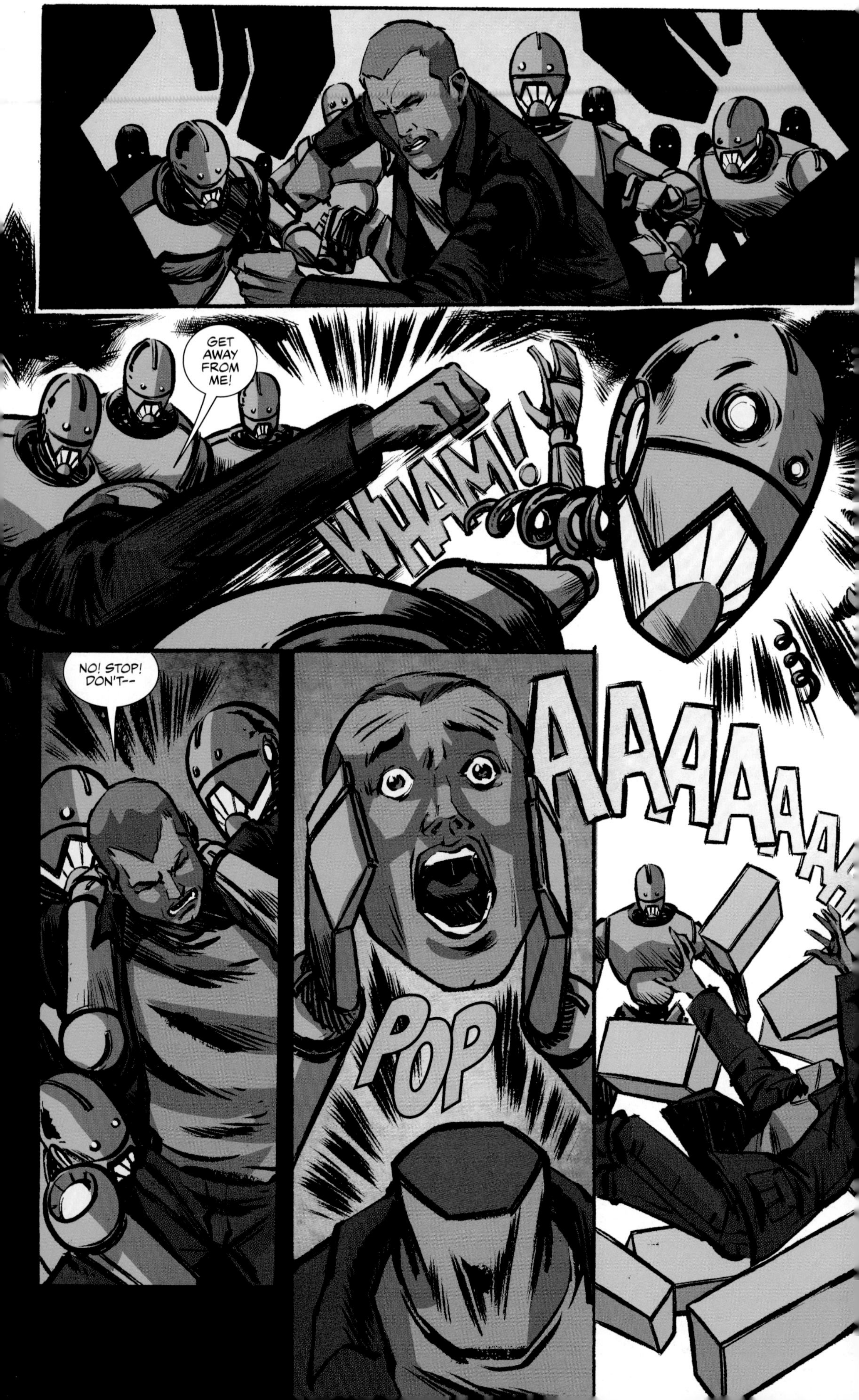
GET AWAY FROM ME!
WHAM!
NO! STOP! DON'T--
POP
AAAAAAAA

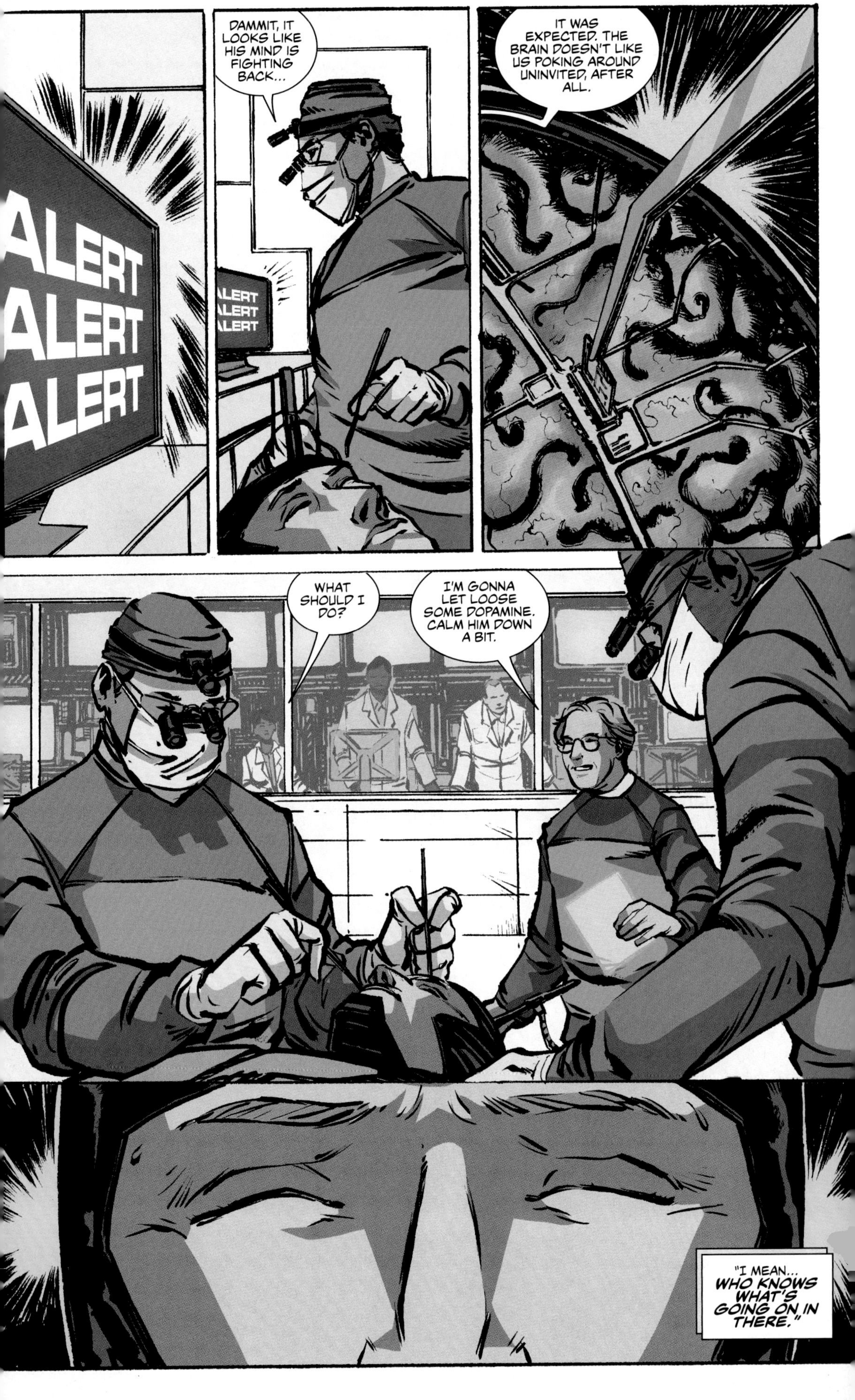
ALERT
ALERT
ALERT
DAMMIT, IT LOOKS LIKE HIS MIND IS FIGHTING BACK...
ALERT
ALERT
ALERT
IT WAS EXPECTED. THE BRAIN DOESN'T LIKE US POKING AROUND UNINVITED, AFTER ALL.
WHAT SHOULD I DO?
I'M GONNA LET LOOSE SOME DOPAMINE. CALM HIM DOWN A BIT.
"I MEAN... WHO KNOWS WHAT'S GOING ON IN THERE."

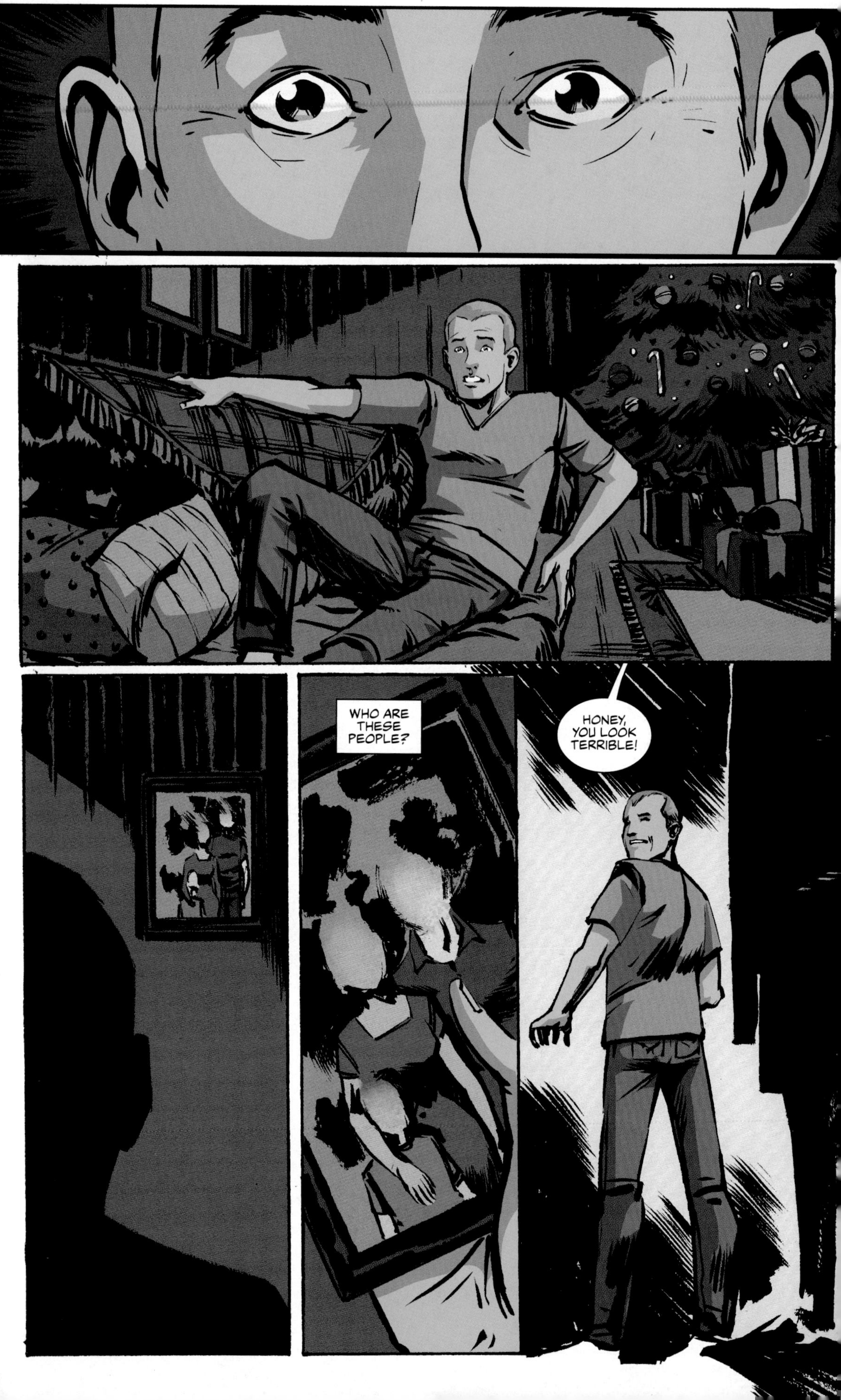
WHO ARE THESE PEOPLE?
HONEY, YOU LOOK TERRIBLE!

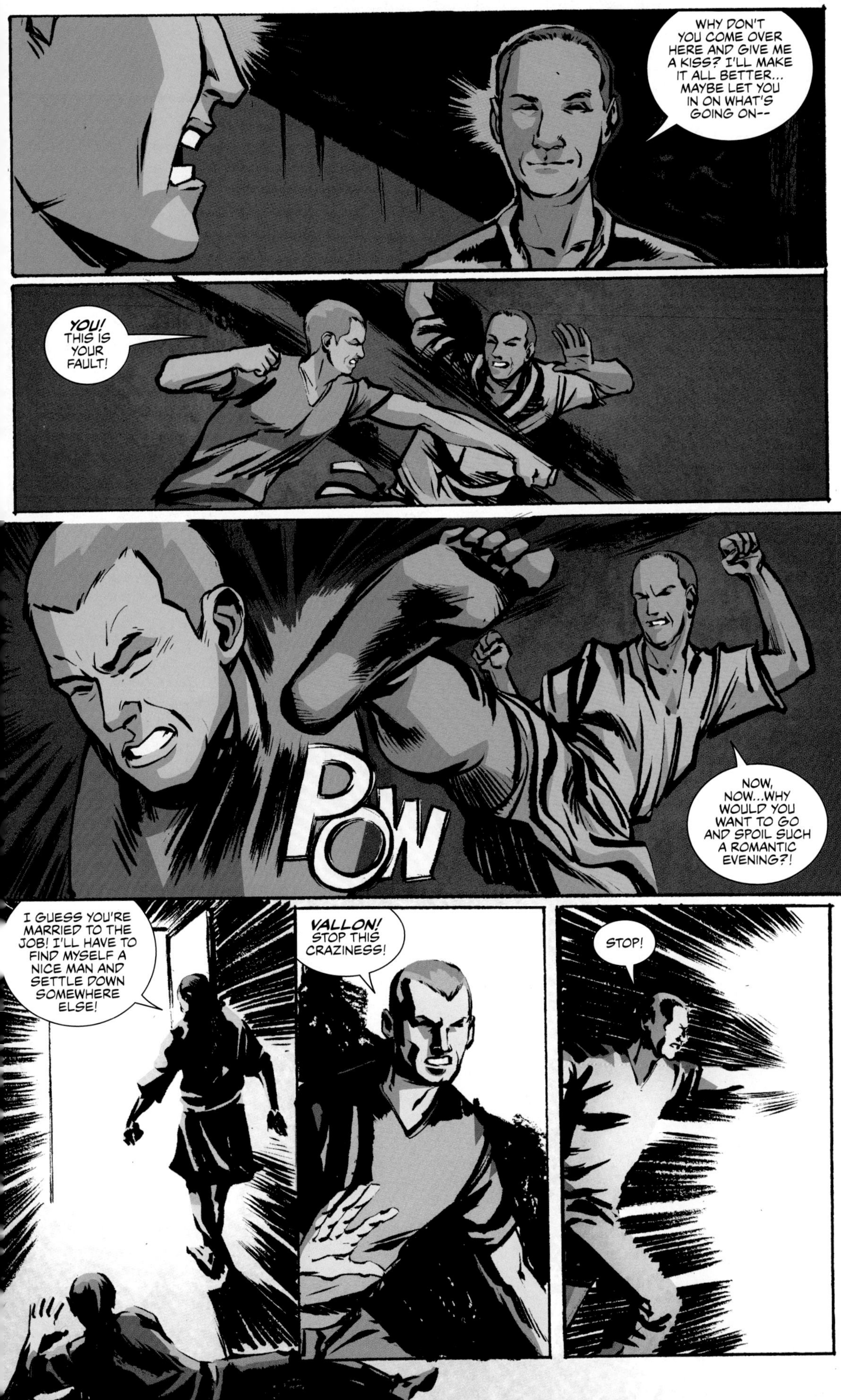
WHY DON'T YOU COME OVER HERE AND GIVE ME A KISS? I'LL MAKE IT ALL BETTER... MAYBE LET YOU IN ON WHAT'S GOING ON--
YOU! THIS IS YOUR FAULT!
POW
NOW, NOW...WHY WOULD YOU WANT TO GO AND SPOIL SUCH A ROMANTIC EVENING?!
I GUESS YOU'RE MARRIED TO THE JOB! I'LL HAVE TO FIND MYSELF A NICE MAN AND SETTLE DOWN SOMEWHERE ELSE!
VALLON! STOP THIS CRAZINESS!
STOP!

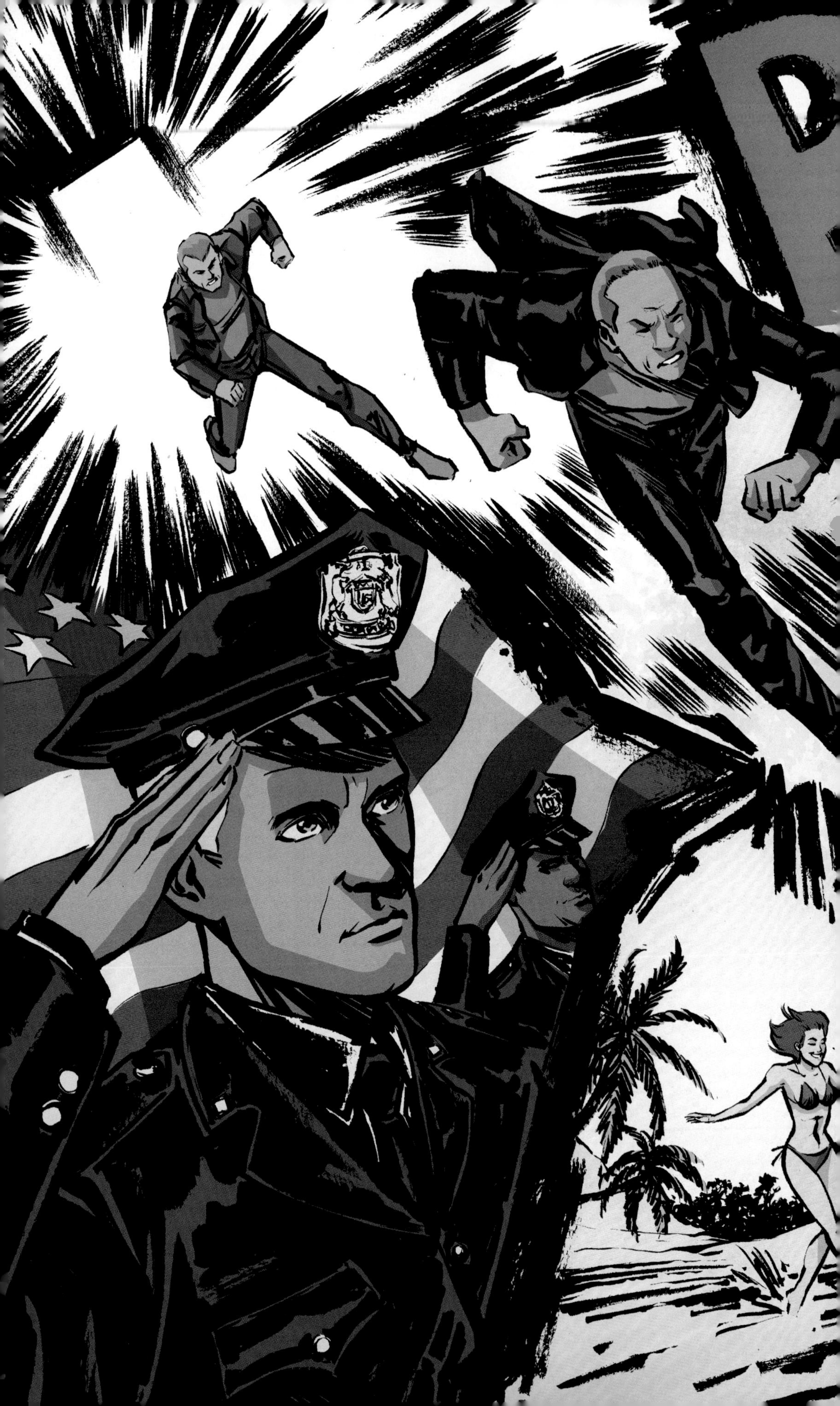

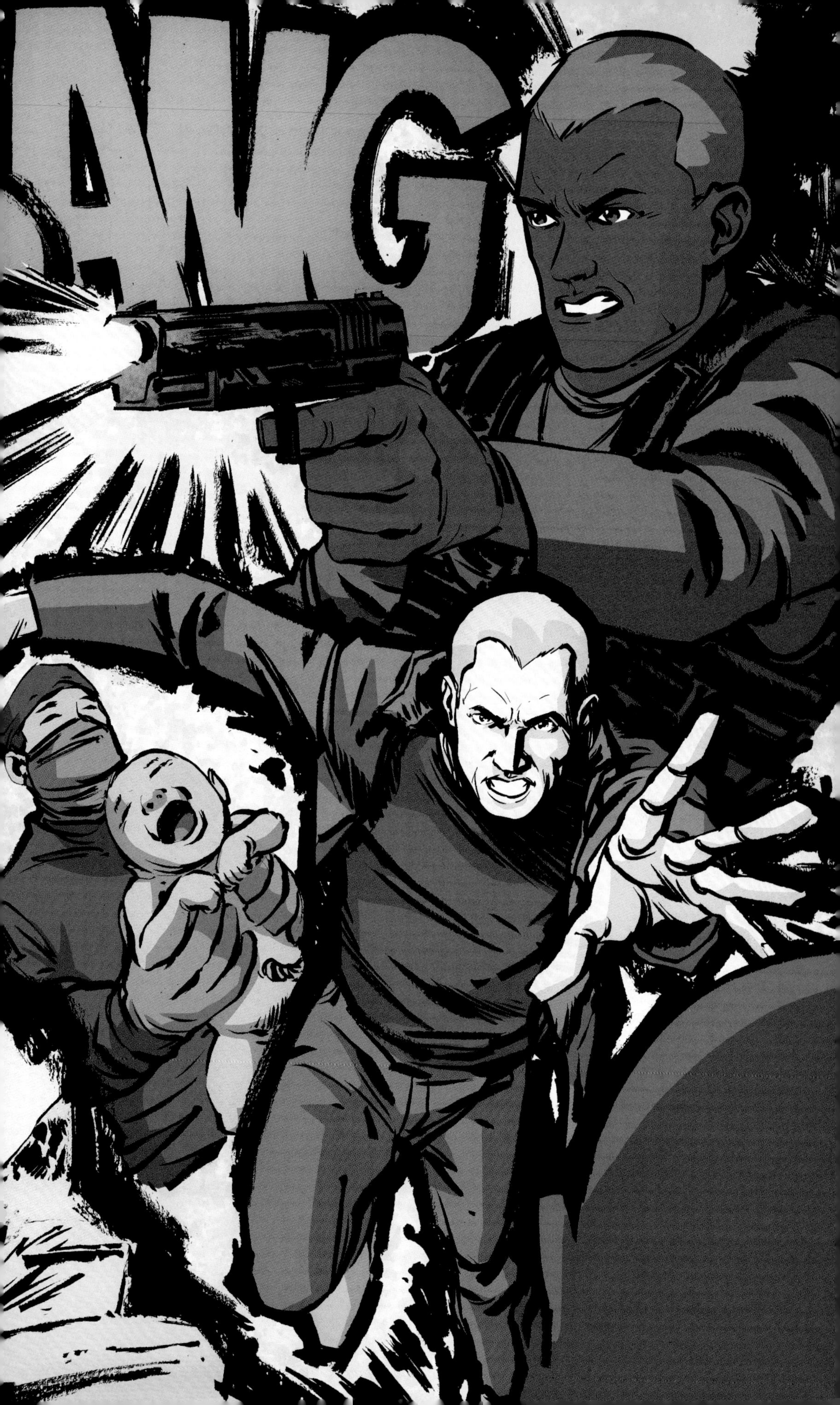
AWG

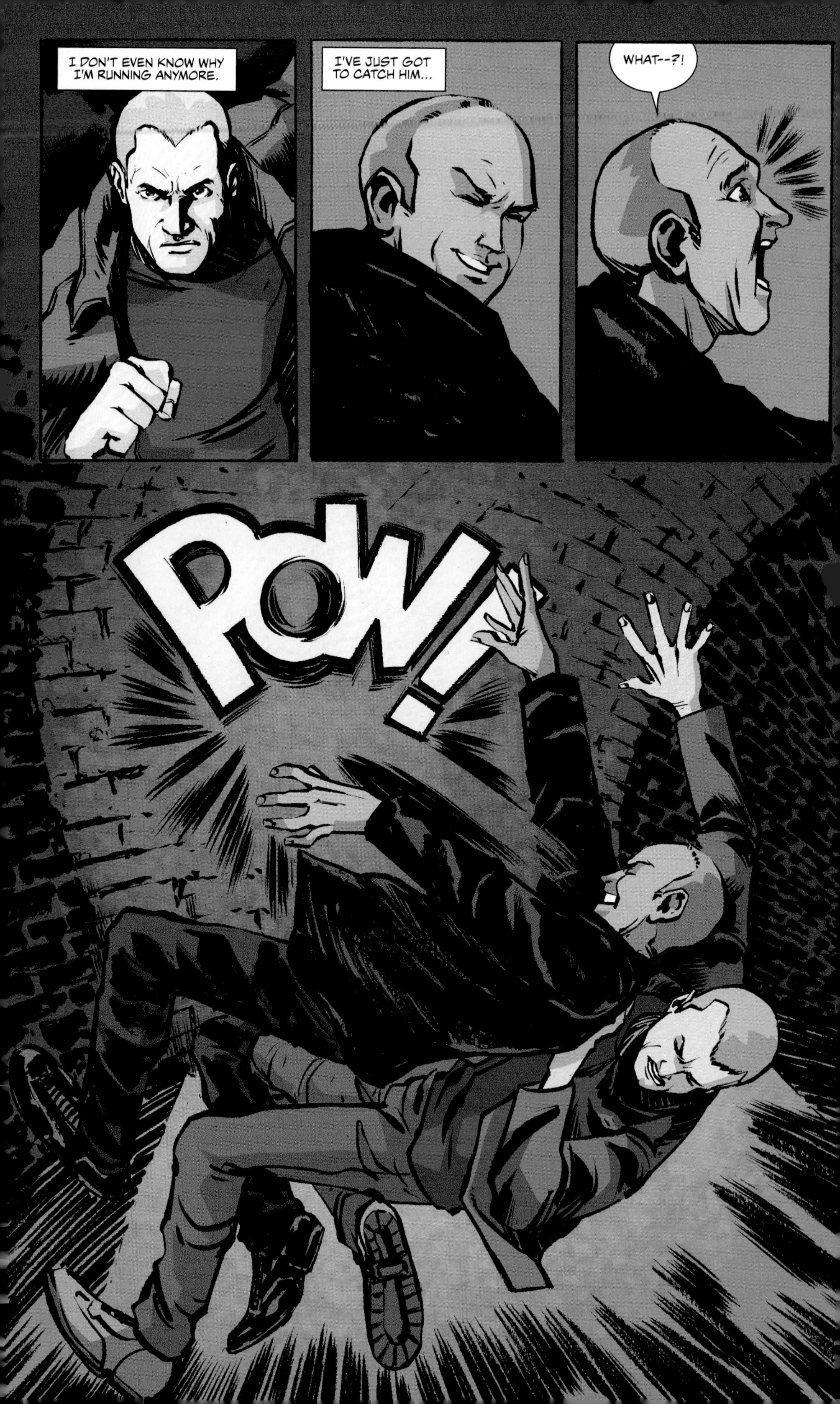
I DON'T EVEN KNOW WHY I'M RUNNING ANYMORE.
I'VE JUST GOT TO CATCH HIM...
WHAT--?!
POW!

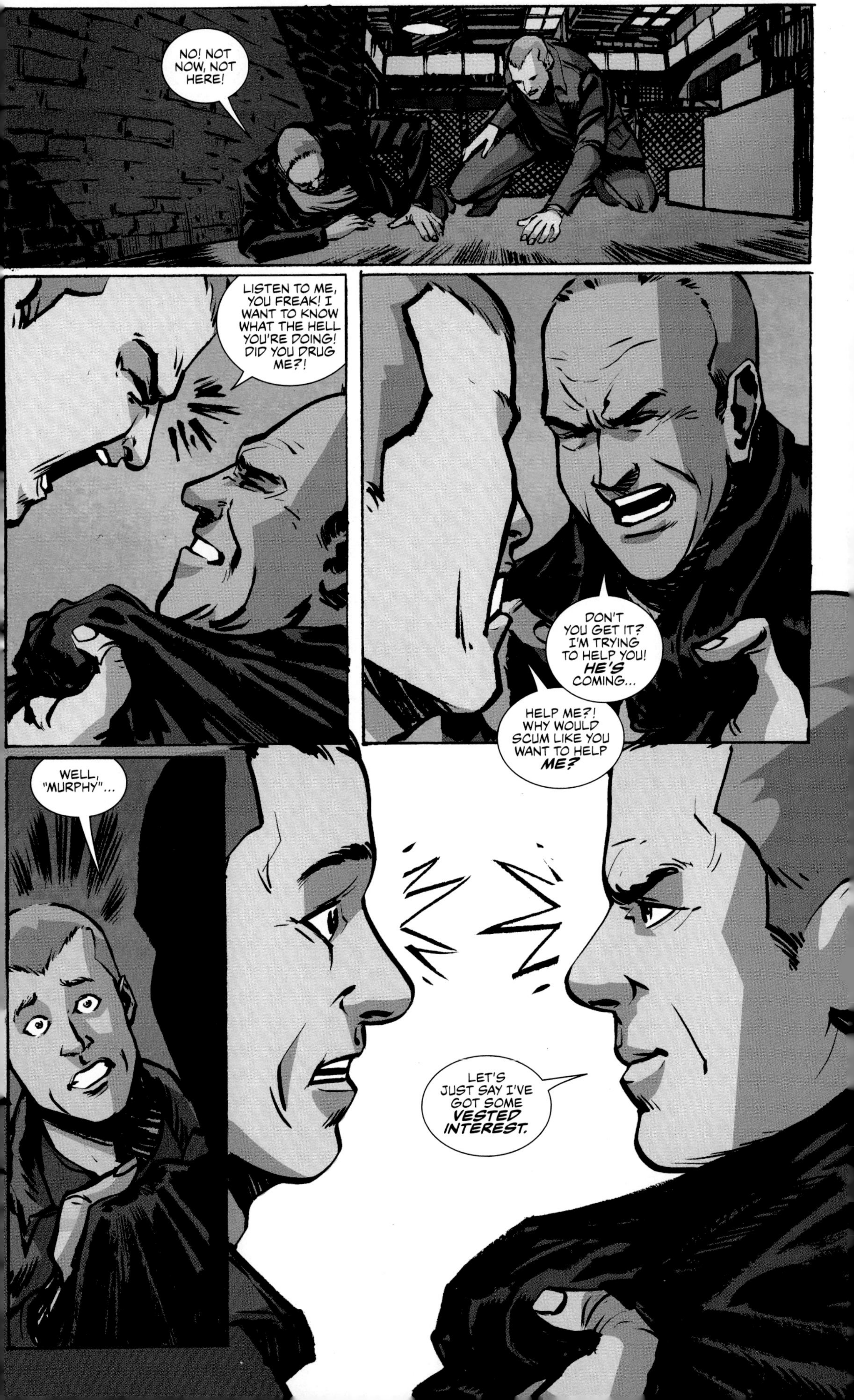
NO! NOT NOW, NOT HERE!
LISTEN TO ME, YOU FREAK! I WANT TO KNOW WHAT THE HELL YOU'RE DOING! DID YOU DRUG ME?!
DON'T YOU GET IT? I'M TRYING TO HELP YOU! HE'S COMING...
HELP ME?! WHY WOULD SCUM LIKE YOU WANT TO HELP ME?
WELL, "MURPHY"...
LET'S JUST SAY I'VE GOT SOME VESTED INTEREST.

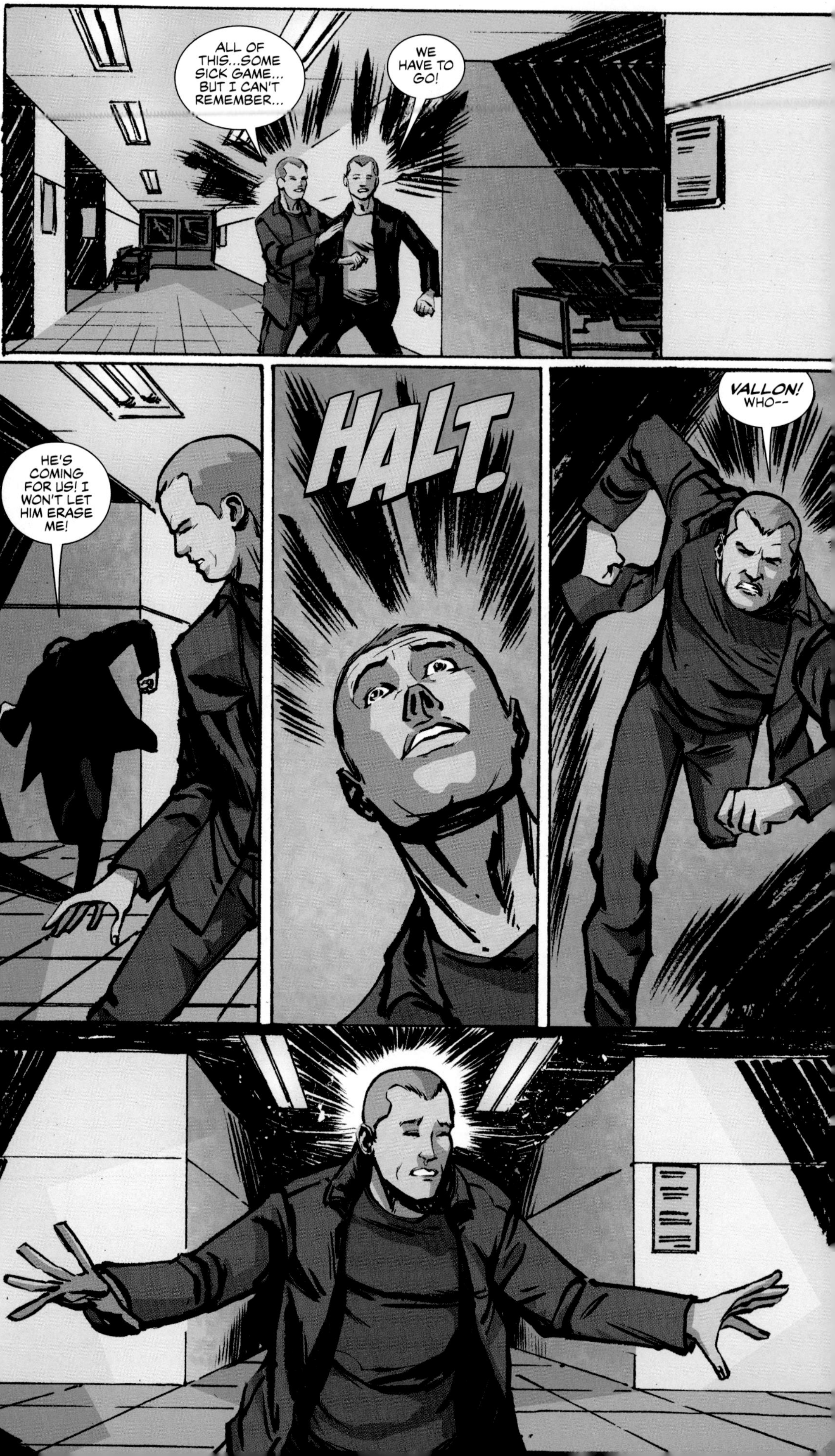

ALL OF THIS...SOME SICK GAME... BUT I CAN'T REMEMBER...
WE HAVE TO GO!
HE'S COMING FOR US! I WON'T LET HIM ERASE ME!
HALT.
VALLON! WHO--

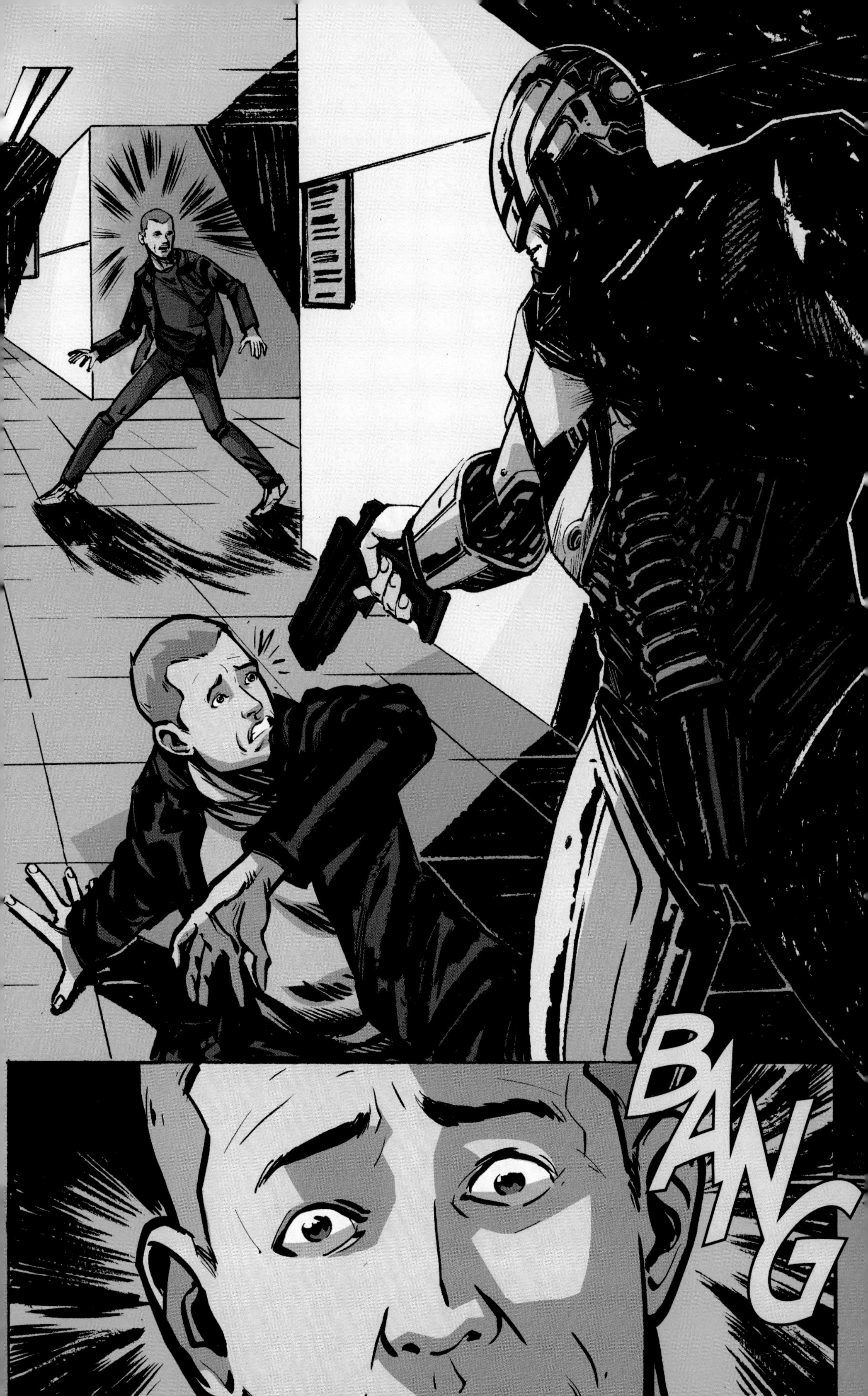
BANG

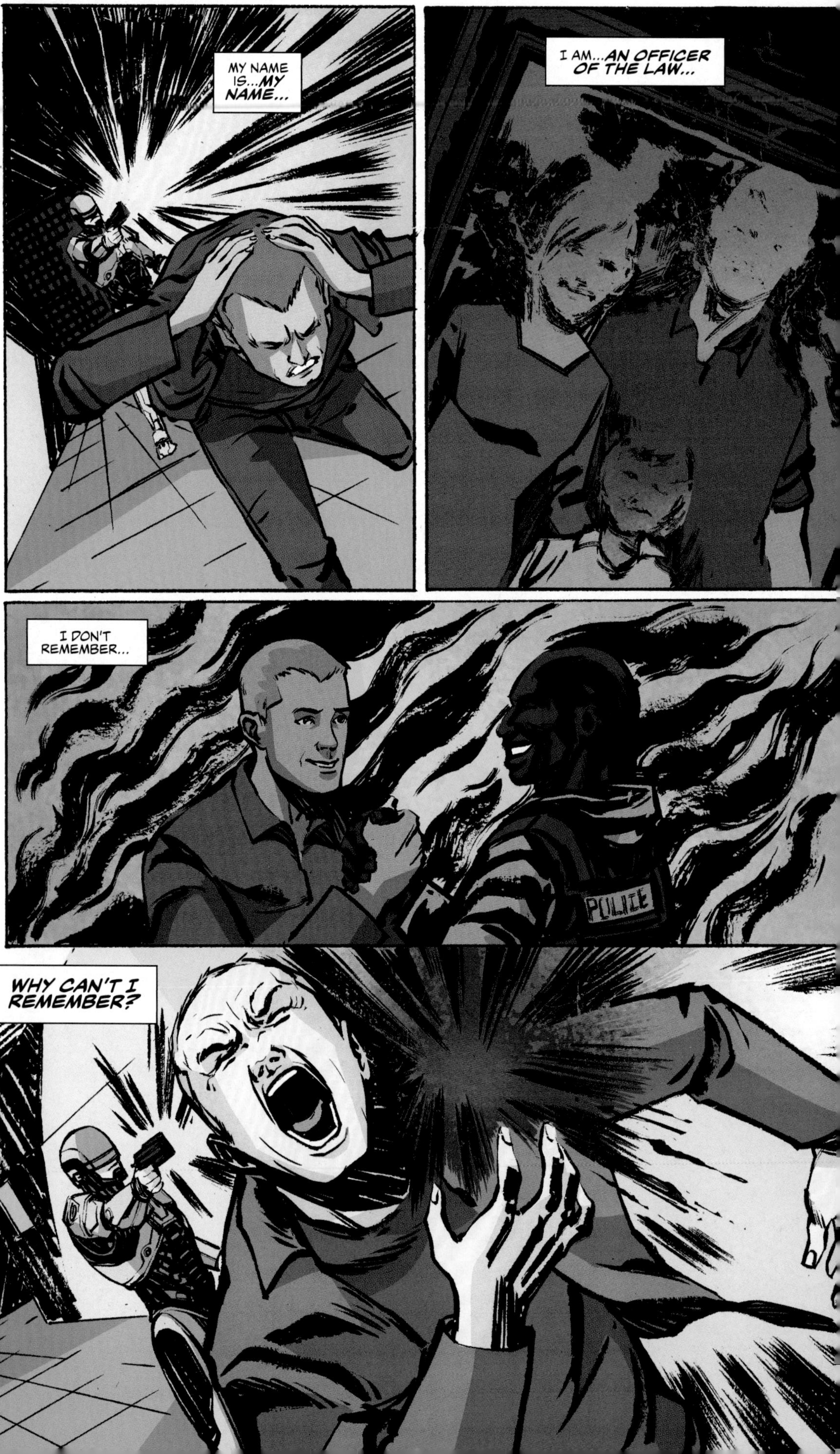
MY NAME IS...MY NAME...
I AM...AN OFFICER OF THE LAW...
I DON'T REMEMBER...
POLICE
WHY CAN'T I REMEMBER?

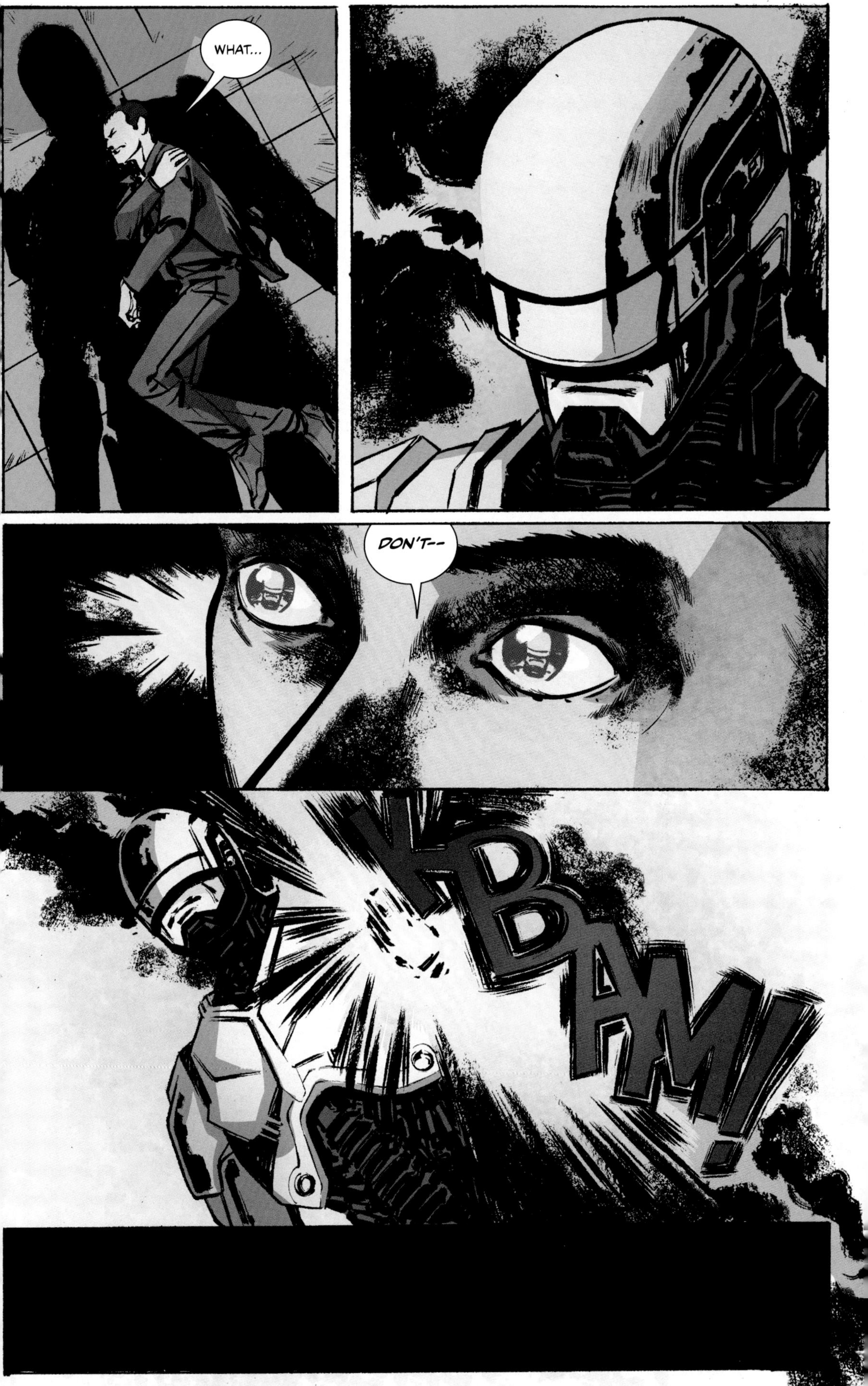
WHAT...
DON'T--
KBAM!

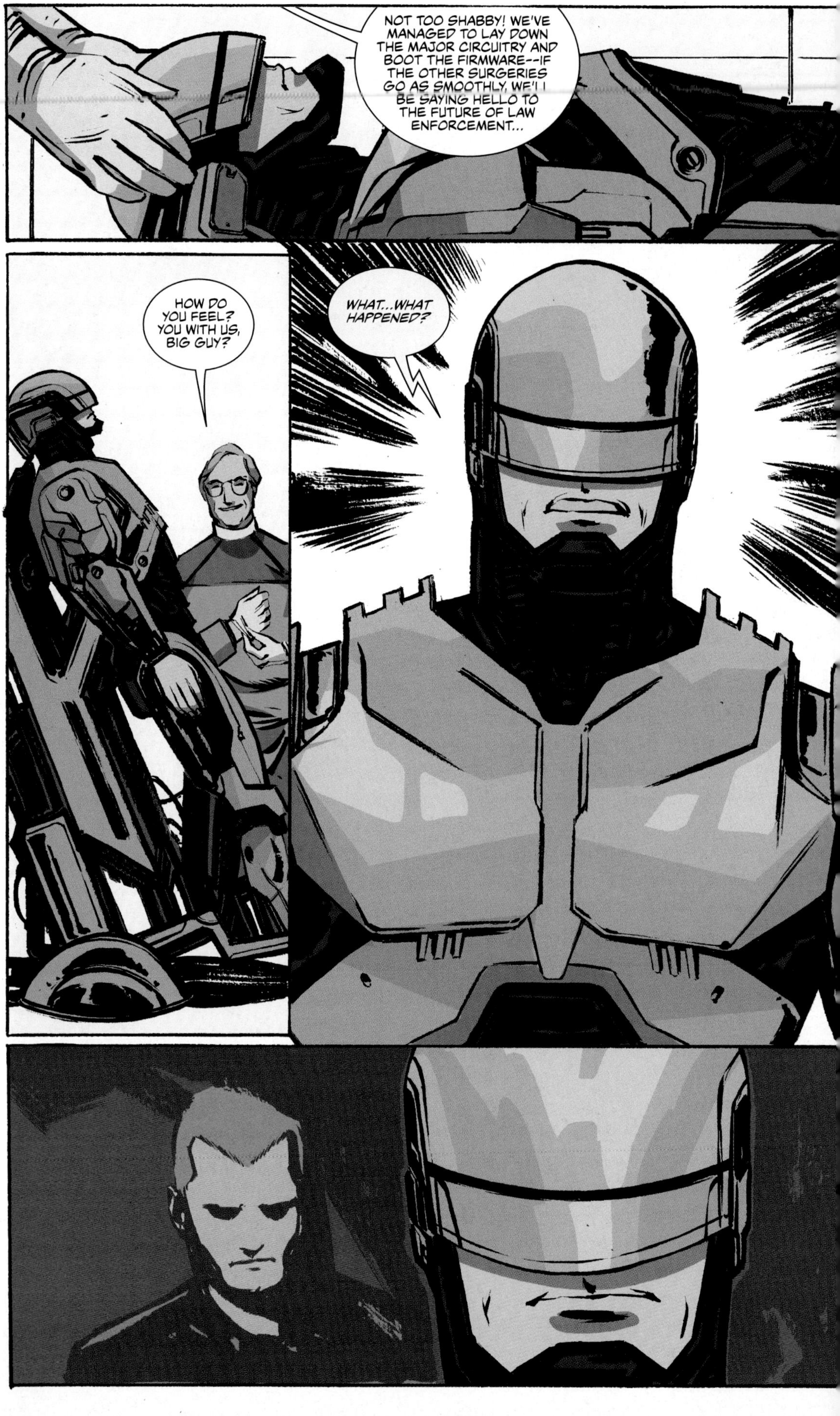
NOT TOO SHABBY! WE'VE MANAGED TO LAY DOWN THE MAJOR CIRCUITRY AND BOOT THE FIRMWARE--IF THE OTHER SURGERIES GO AS SMOOTHLY, WE'LL BE SAYING HELLO TO THE FUTURE OF LAW ENFORCEMENT...
HOW DO YOU FEEL? YOU WITH US, BIG GUY?
WHAT...WHAT HAPPENED?

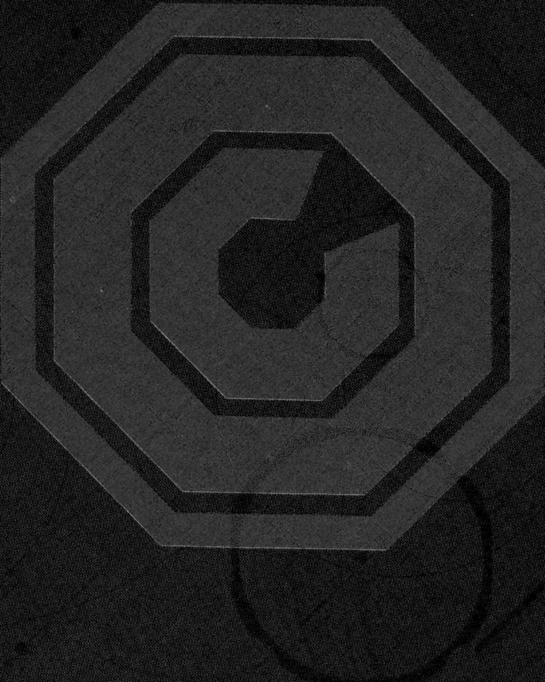

//TO LIVE AND DIE IN DETROIT//

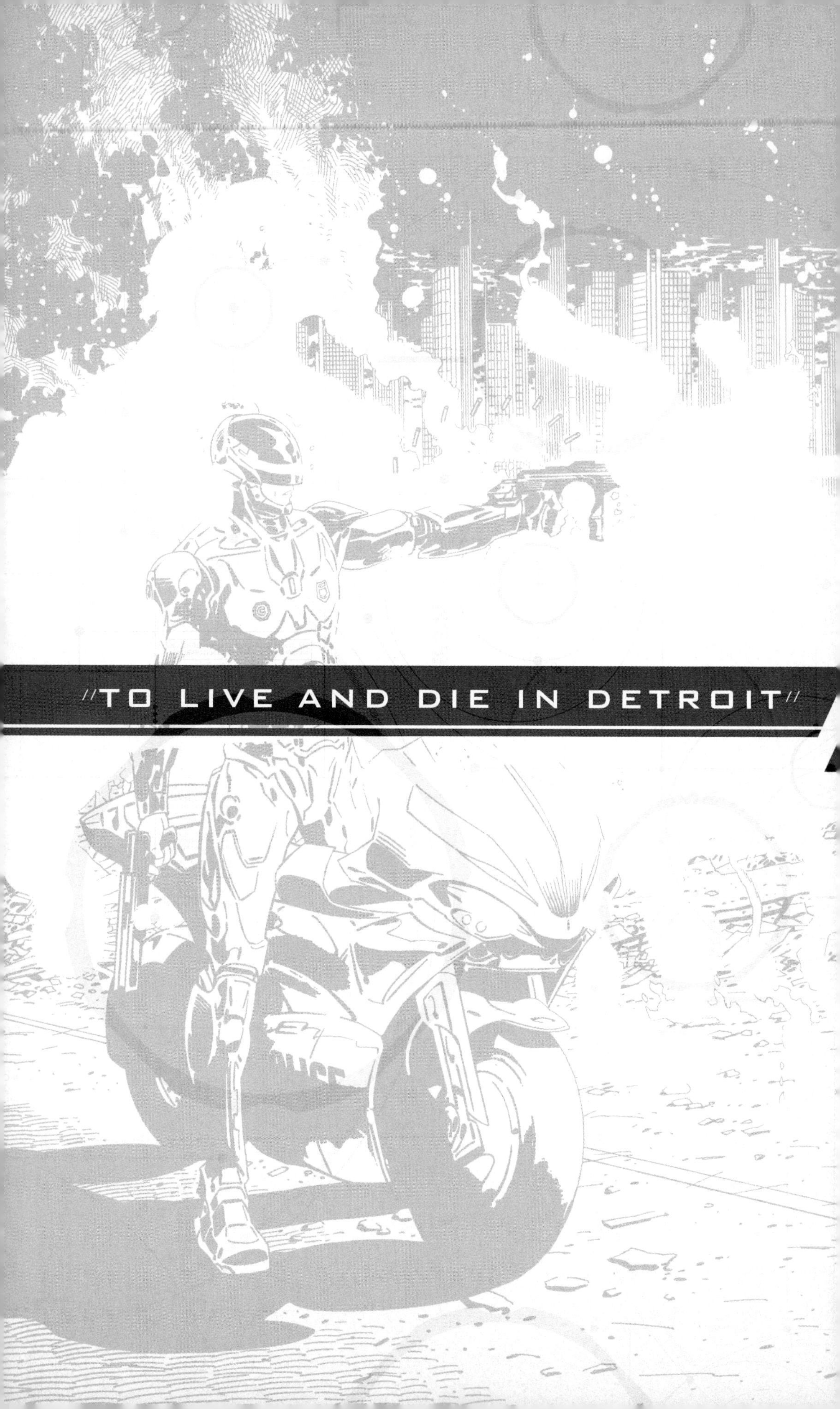

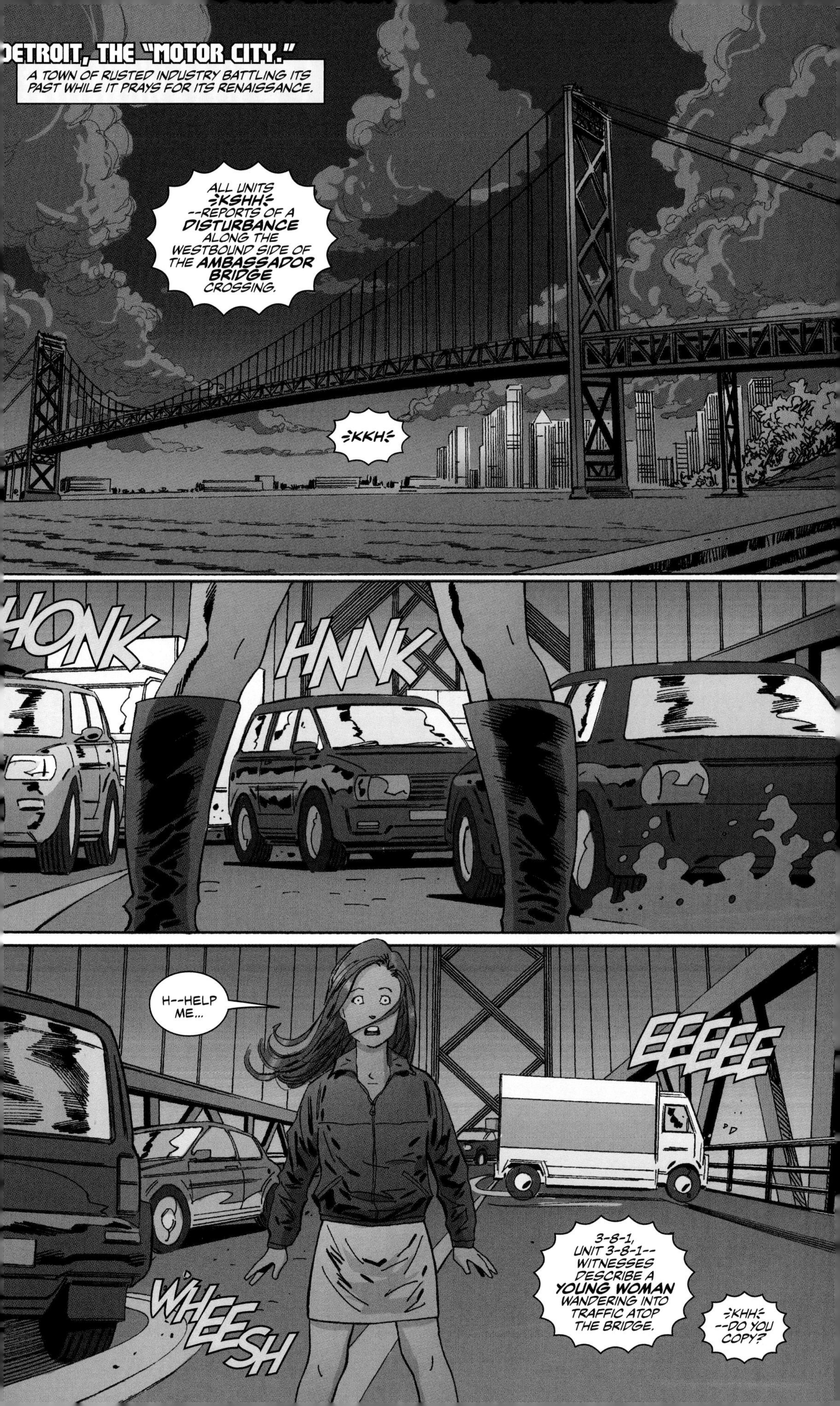
DETROIT, THE "MOTOR CITY."
A TOWN OF RUSTED INDUSTRY BATTLING ITS PAST WHILE IT PRAYS FOR ITS RENAISSANCE.
ALL UNITS -KSHH- --REPORTS OF A DISTURBANCE ALONG THE WESTBOUND SIDE OF THE AMBASSADOR BRIDGE CROSSING.
-KKH-
HONK
HNNK
H--HELP ME...
EEEEE
WHEESH
3-8-1, UNIT 3-8-1-- WITNESSES DESCRIBE A YOUNG WOMAN WANDERING INTO TRAFFIC ATOP THE BRIDGE.
-KHH- --DO YOU COPY?

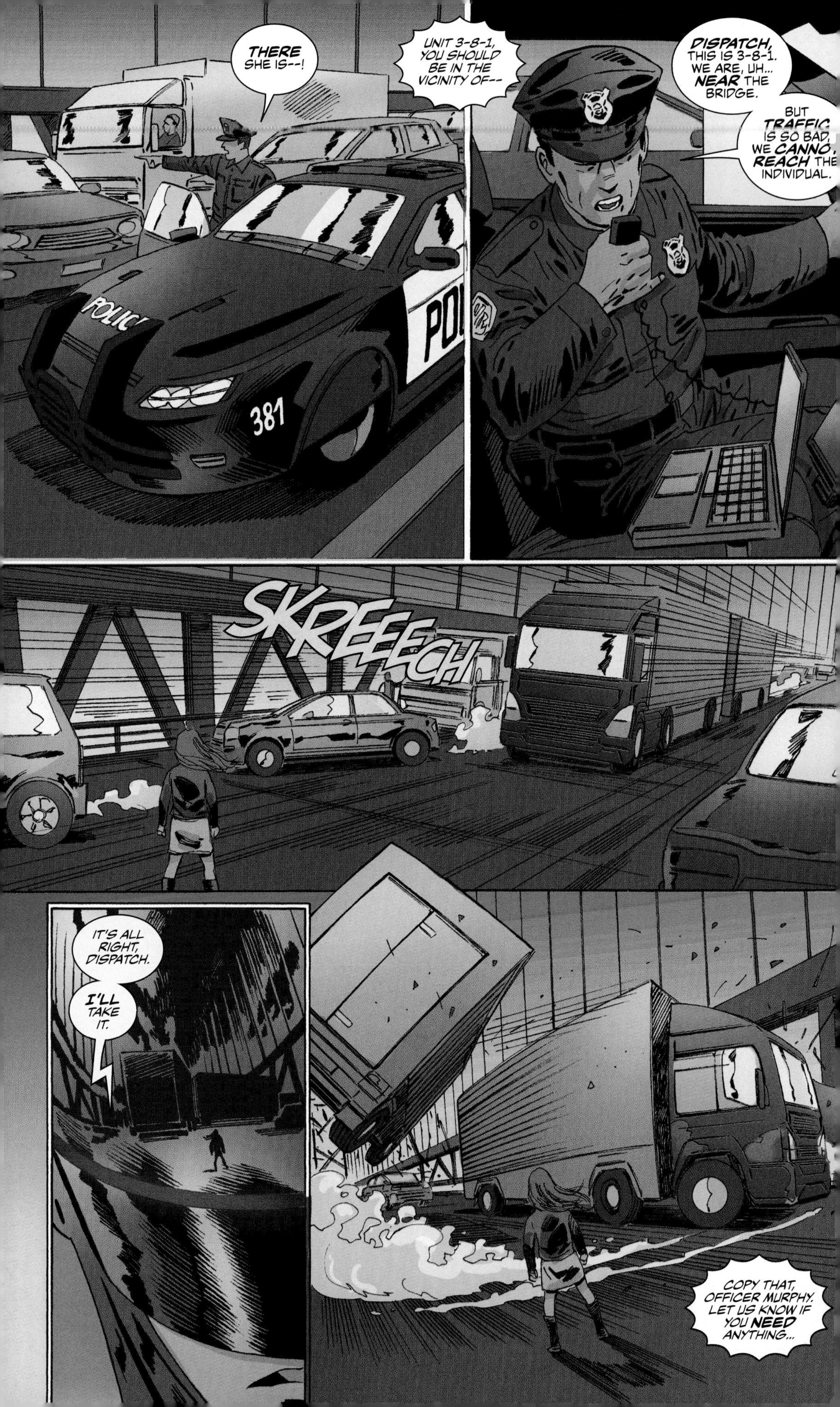

THERE SHE IS--!
UNIT 3-8-1, YOU SHOULD BE IN THE VICINITY OF--
POLICE
381
DISPATCH, THIS IS 3-8-1. WE ARE, UH... NEAR THE BRIDGE.
BUT TRAFFIC IS SO BAD, WE CANNO REACH THE INDIVIDUAL.
SKREEECH
IT'S ALL RIGHT, DISPATCH.
I'LL TAKE IT.
COPY THAT, OFFICER MURPHY. LET US KNOW IF YOU NEED ANYTHING...

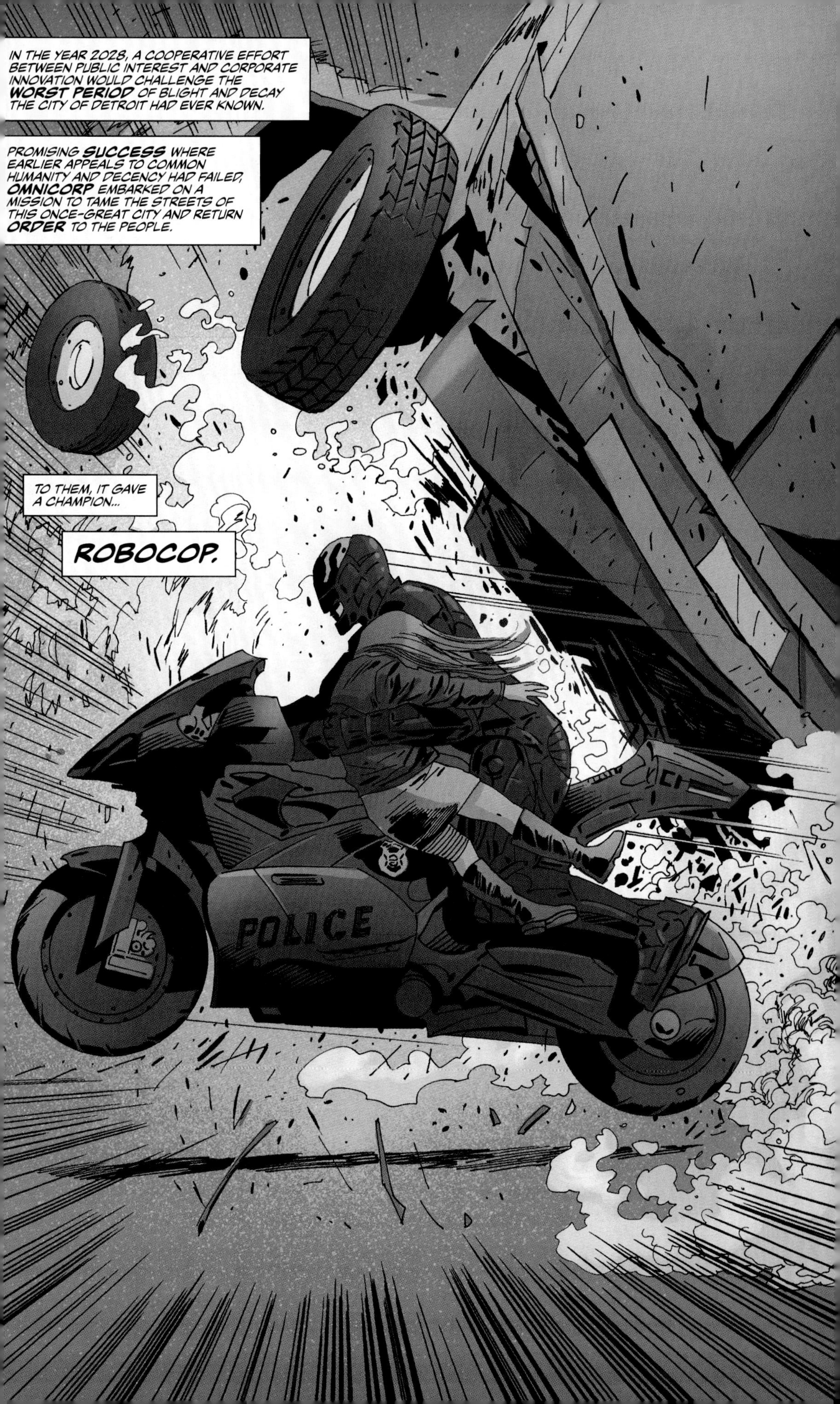
IN THE YEAR 2028, A COOPERATIVE EFFORT BETWEEN PUBLIC INTEREST AND CORPORATE INNOVATION WOULD CHALLENGE THE WORST PERIOD OF BLIGHT AND DECAY THE CITY OF DETROIT HAD EVER KNOWN.
PROMISING SUCCESS WHERE EARLIER APPEALS TO COMMON HUMANITY AND DECENCY HAD FAILED, OMNICORP EMBARKED ON A MISSION TO TAME THE STREETS OF THIS ONCE-GREAT CITY AND RETURN ORDER TO THE PEOPLE.
TO THEM, IT GAVE A CHAMPION...
ROBOCOP.
POLICE

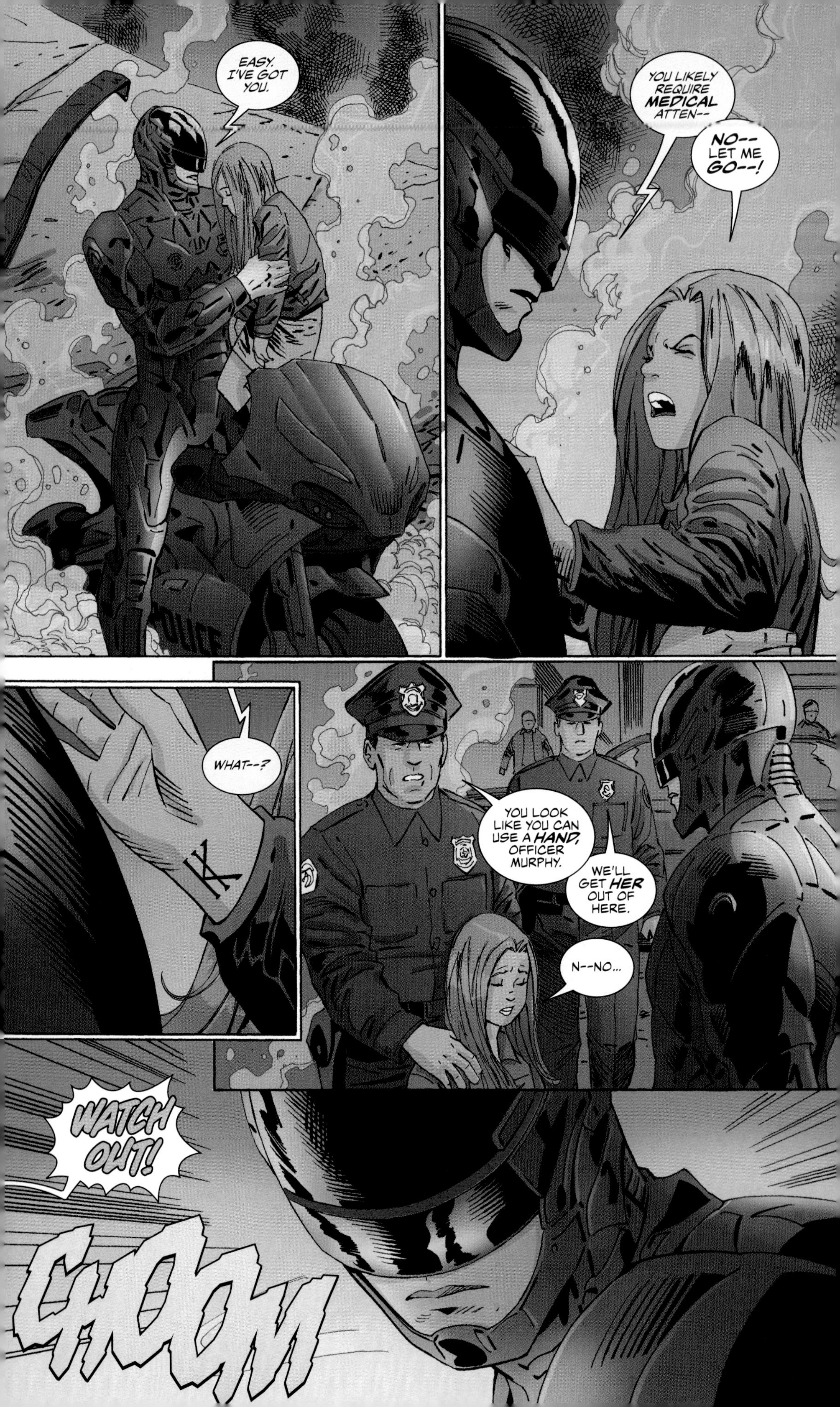
EASY. I'VE GOT YOU.
POLICE
YOU LIKELY REQUIRE MEDICAL ATTEN--
NO-- LET ME GO--!
WHAT--?
YOU LOOK LIKE YOU CAN USE A HAND, OFFICER MURPHY.
WE'LL GET HER OUT OF HERE.
N--NO...
WATCH OUT!
CHOOM

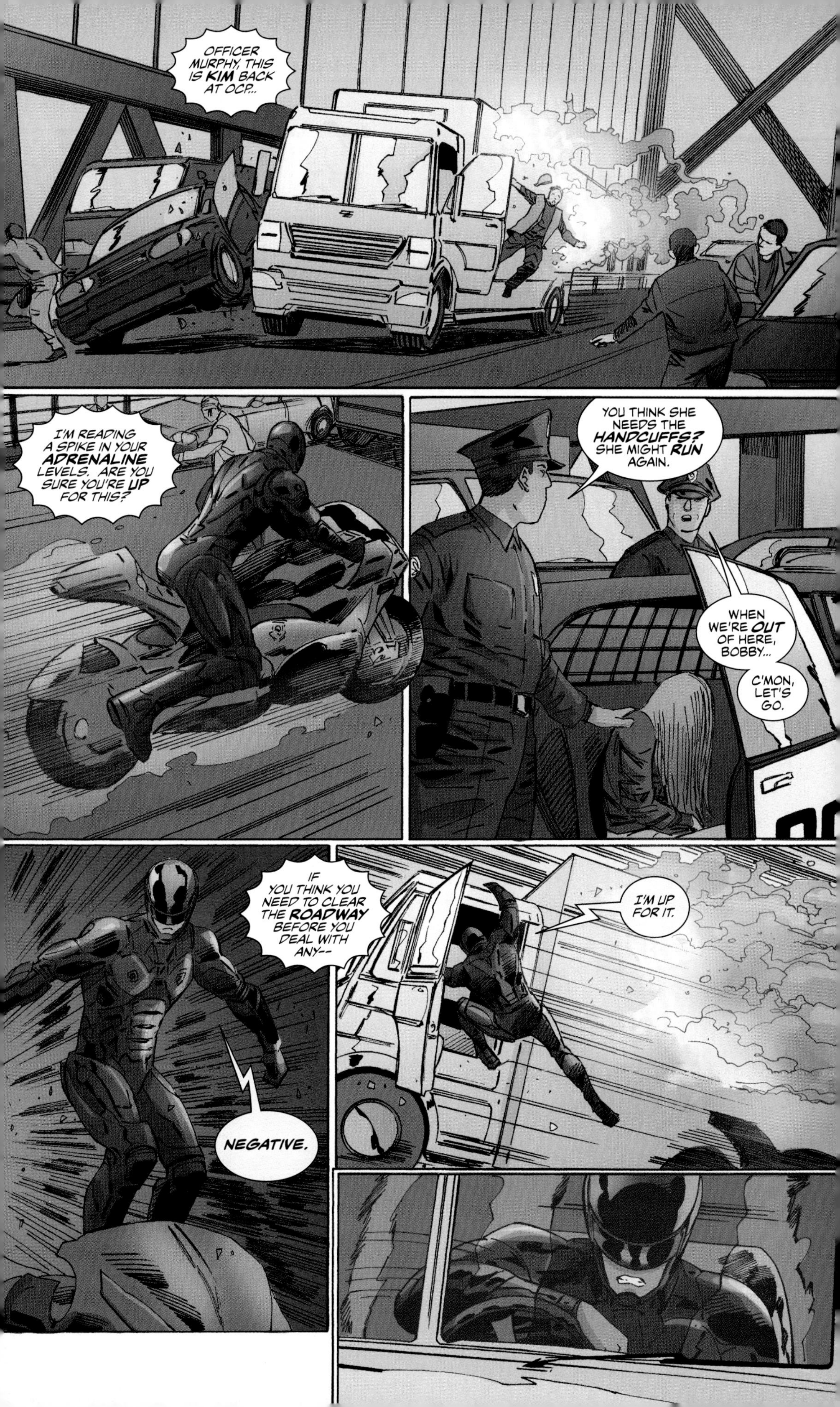
OFFICER MURPHY, THIS IS KIM BACK AT OCP...
I'M READING A SPIKE IN YOUR ADRENALINE LEVELS. ARE YOU SURE YOU'RE UP FOR THIS?
YOU THINK SHE NEEDS THE HANDCUFFS? SHE MIGHT RUN AGAIN.
WHEN WE'RE OUT OF HERE, BOBBY...
C'MON, LET'S GO.
NEGATIVE.
IF YOU THINK YOU NEED TO CLEAR THE ROADWAY BEFORE YOU DEAL WITH ANY--
I'M UP FOR IT.

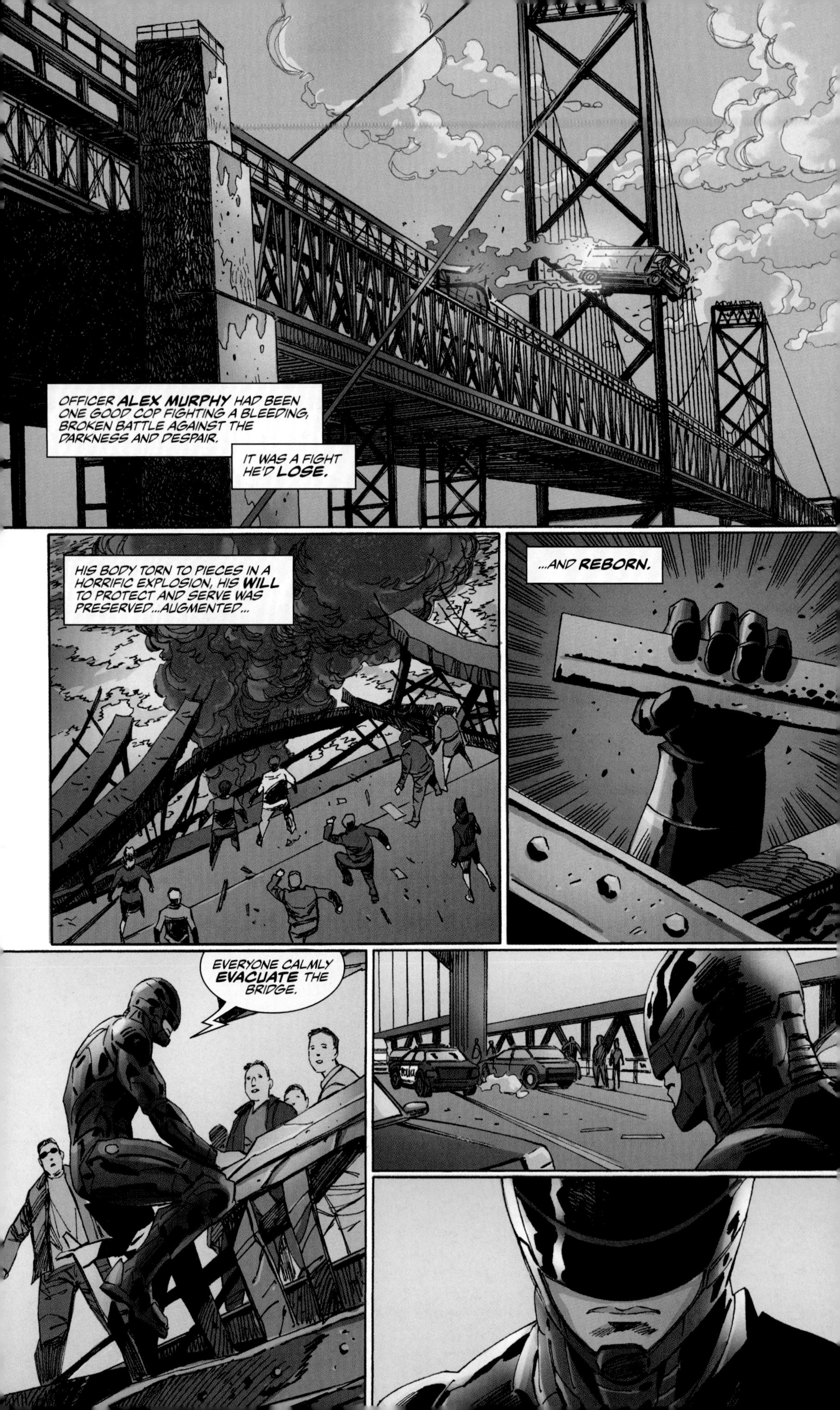
OFFICER ALEX MURPHY HAD BEEN ONE GOOD COP FIGHTING A BLEEDING, BROKEN BATTLE AGAINST THE DARKNESS AND DESPAIR.
IT WAS A FIGHT HE'D LOSE.
HIS BODY TORN TO PIECES IN A HORRIFIC EXPLOSION, HIS WILL TO PROTECT AND SERVE WAS PRESERVED...AUGMENTED...
...AND REBORN.
EVERYONE CALMLY EVACUATE THE BRIDGE.
POLICE

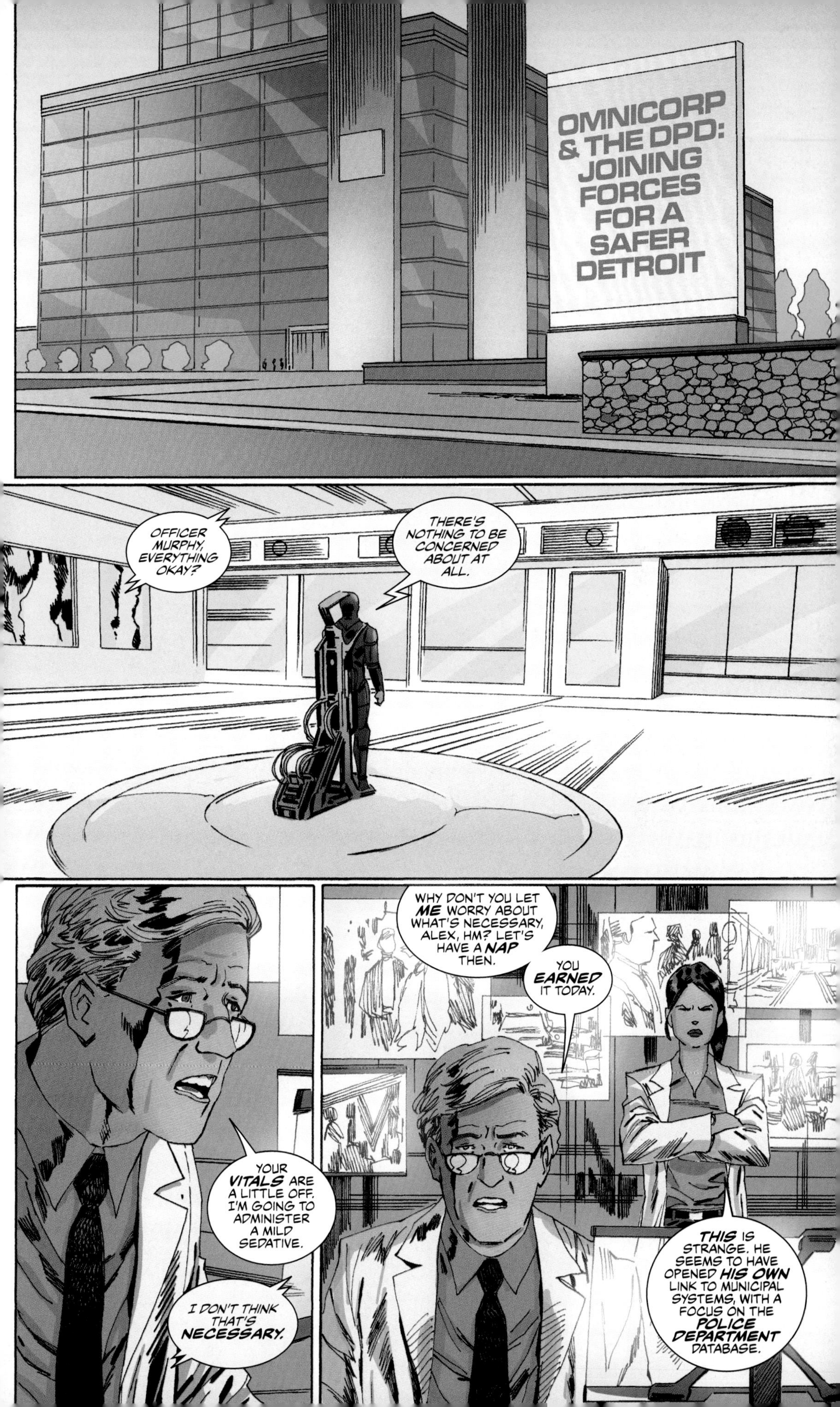
OMNICORP & THE DPD: JOINING FORCES FOR A SAFER DETROIT
OFFICER MURPHY, EVERYTHING OKAY?
THERE'S NOTHING TO BE CONCERNED ABOUT AT ALL.
YOUR VITALS ARE A LITTLE OFF. I'M GOING TO ADMINISTER A MILD SEDATIVE.
I DON'T THINK THAT'S NECESSARY.
WHY DON'T YOU LET ME WORRY ABOUT WHAT'S NECESSARY, ALEX, HM? LET'S HAVE A NAP THEN.
YOU EARNED IT TODAY.
THIS IS STRANGE. HE SEEMS TO HAVE OPENED HIS OWN LINK TO MUNICIPAL SYSTEMS, WITH A FOCUS ON THE POLICE DEPARTMENT DATABASE.

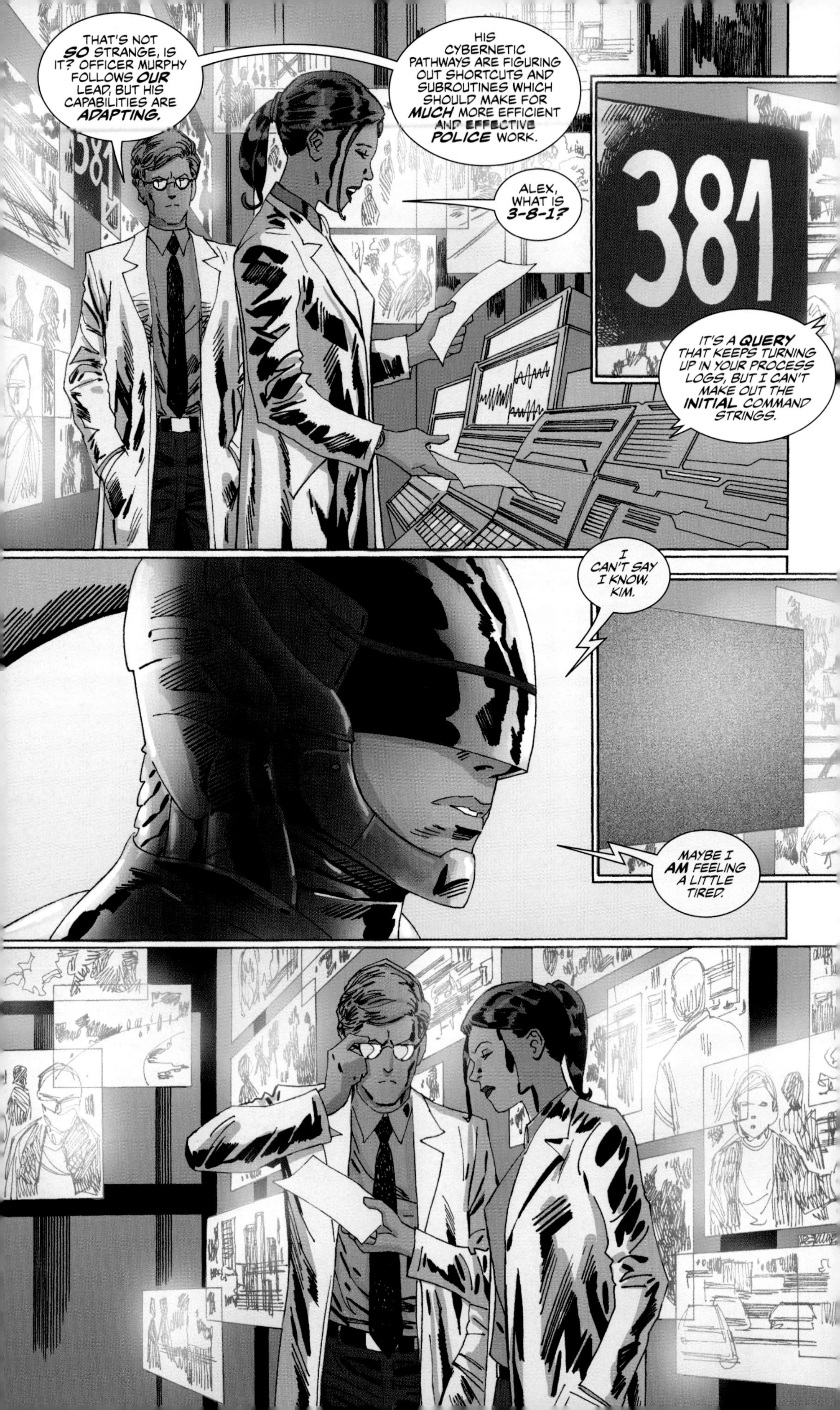

THAT'S NOT SO STRANGE, IS IT? OFFICER MURPHY FOLLOWS OUR LEAD, BUT HIS CAPABILITIES ARE ADAPTING.
HIS CYBERNETIC PATHWAYS ARE FIGURING OUT SHORTCUTS AND SUBROUTINES WHICH SHOULD MAKE FOR MUCH MORE EFFICIENT AND EFFECTIVE POLICE WORK.
381
ALEX, WHAT IS 3-8-1?
IT'S A QUERY THAT KEEPS TURNING UP IN YOUR PROCESS LOGS, BUT I CAN'T MAKE OUT THE INITIAL COMMAND STRINGS.
I CAN'T SAY I KNOW, KIM.
MAYBE I AM FEELING A LITTLE TIRED.

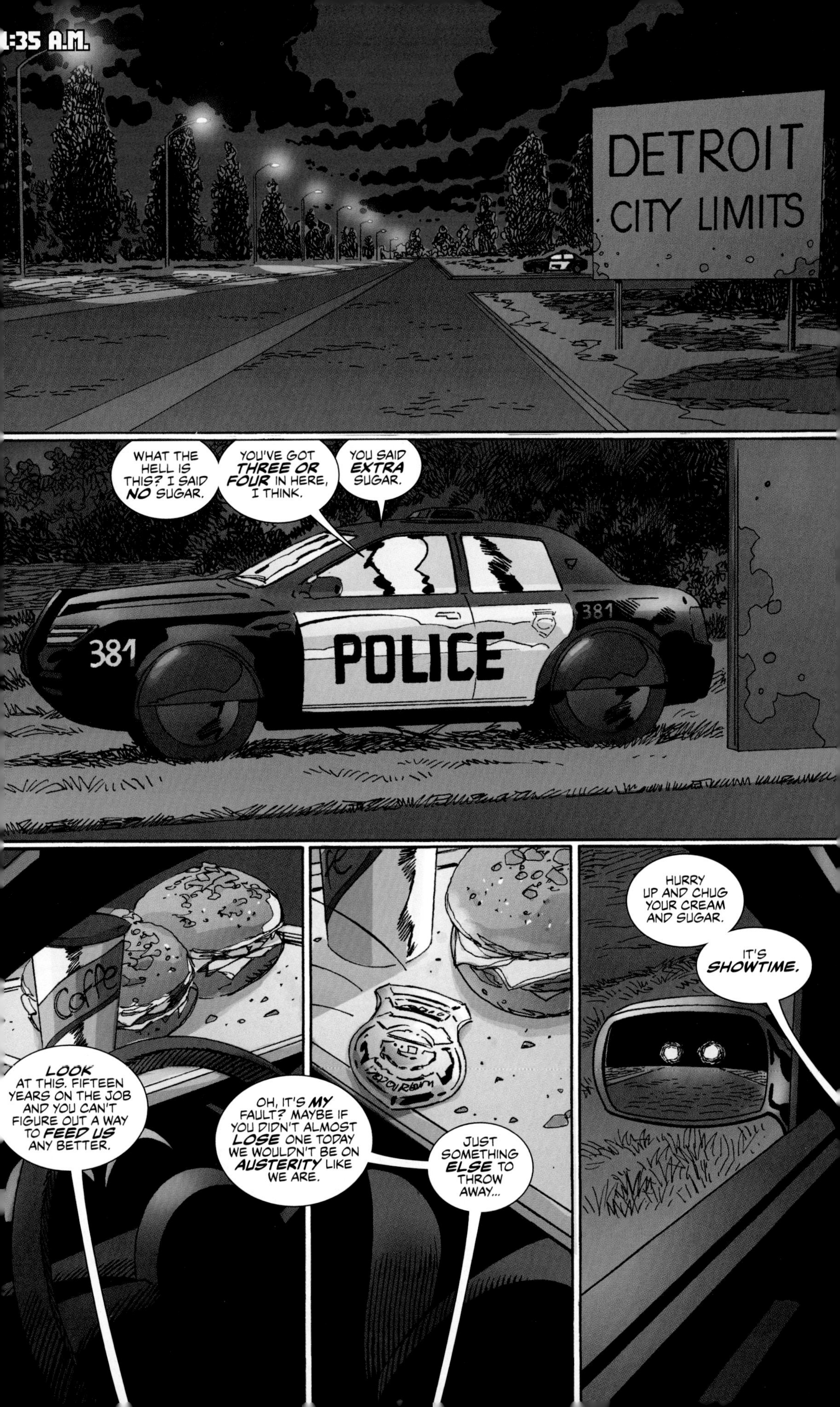
1:35 A.M.
DETROIT CITY LIMITS
WHAT THE HELL IS THIS? I SAID NO SUGAR.
YOU'VE GOT THREE OR FOUR IN HERE, I THINK.
YOU SAID EXTRA SUGAR.
381
POLICE
381
LOOK AT THIS. FIFTEEN YEARS ON THE JOB AND YOU CAN'T FIGURE OUT A WAY TO FEED US ANY BETTER.
OH, IT'S MY FAULT? MAYBE IF YOU DIDN'T ALMOST LOSE ONE TODAY WE WOULDN'T BE ON AUSTERITY LIKE WE ARE.
JUST SOMETHING ELSE TO THROW AWAY...
HURRY UP AND CHUG YOUR CREAM AND SUGAR.
IT'S SHOWTIME.

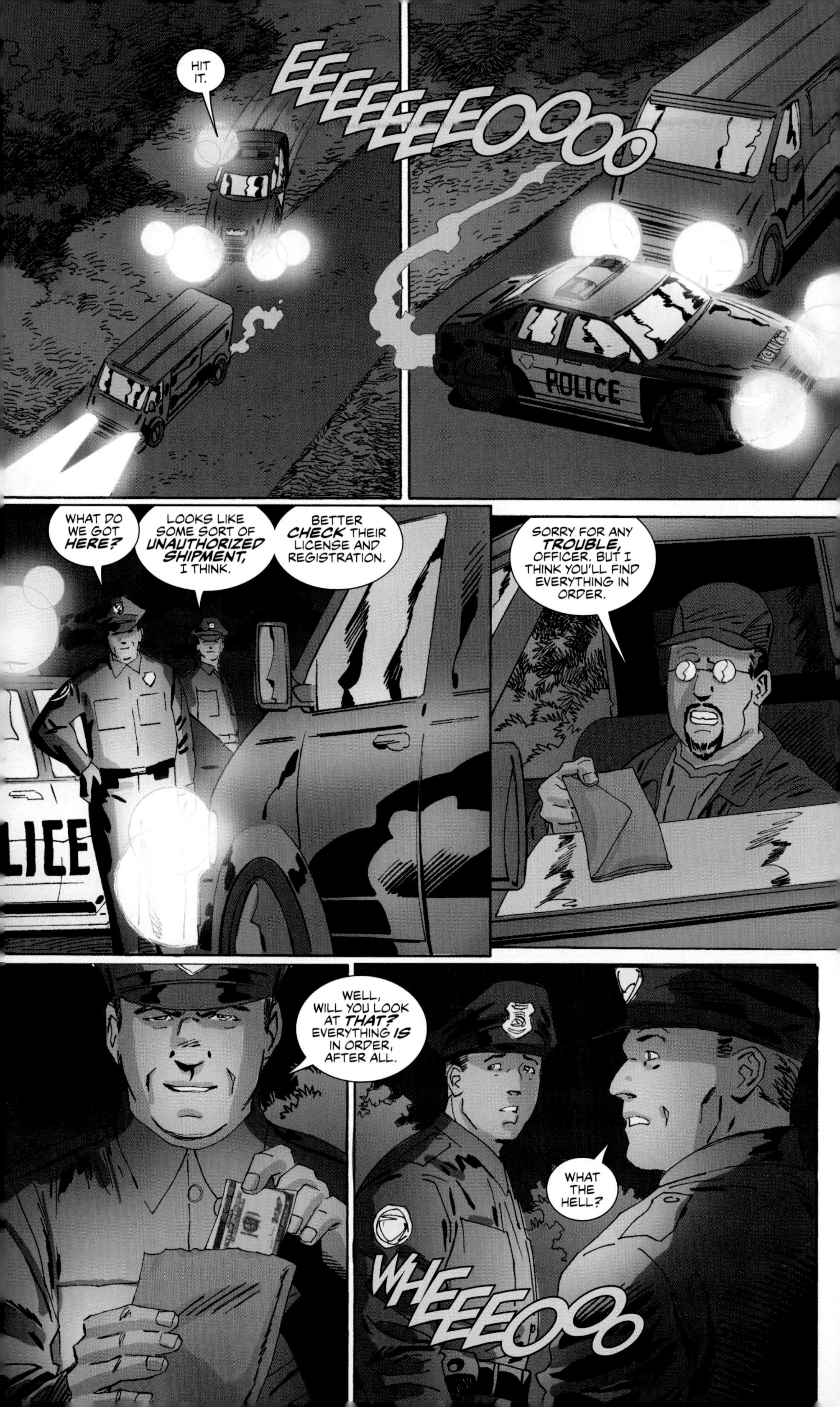
HIT IT.
EEEEEEEOOOO
WHAT DO WE GOT HERE?
LOOKS LIKE SOME SORT OF UNAUTHORIZED SHIPMENT, I THINK.
BETTER CHECK THEIR LICENSE AND REGISTRATION.
SORRY FOR ANY TROUBLE, OFFICER. BUT I THINK YOU'LL FIND EVERYTHING IN ORDER.
WELL, WILL YOU LOOK AT THAT? EVERYTHING IS IN ORDER, AFTER ALL.
WHAT THE HELL?
WHEEEOOO

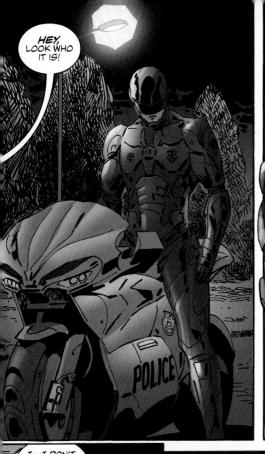

HEY, LOOK WHO IT IS!

WHATSAMATTER, OFFICER MURPHY, YOU DIDN'T GET ENOUGH *GOOD PRESS* OVER ON THE *BRIDGE* THIS MORNING?

I--I DON'T WANT ANY *TROUBLE*, MAN...

FREEZE.

SHRAKT

AGGGH!

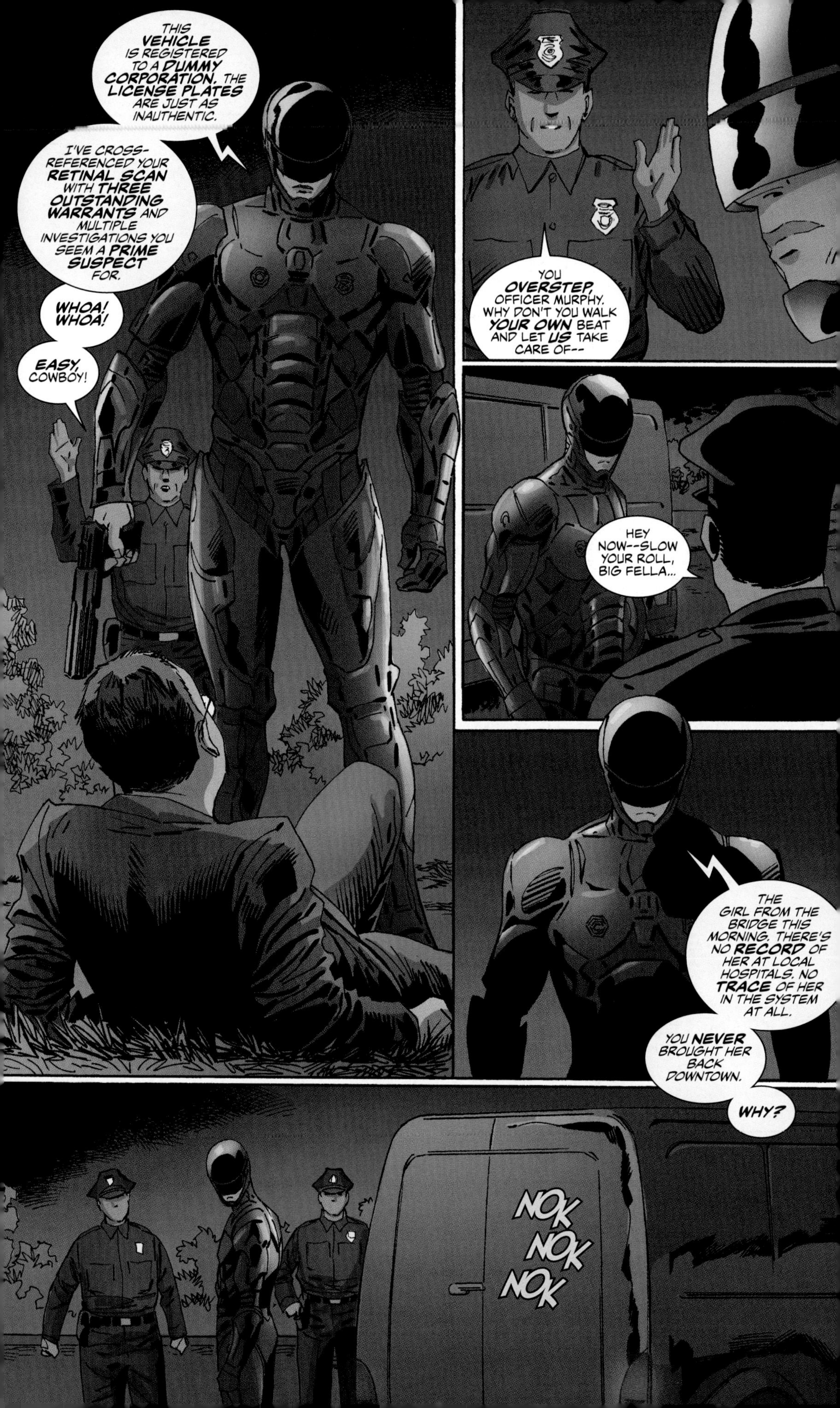

THIS VEHICLE IS REGISTERED TO A DUMMY CORPORATION. THE LICENSE PLATES ARE JUST AS INAUTHENTIC.
I'VE CROSS-REFERENCED YOUR RETINAL SCAN WITH THREE OUTSTANDING WARRANTS AND MULTIPLE INVESTIGATIONS YOU SEEM A PRIME SUSPECT FOR.
WHOA! WHOA!
EASY, COWBOY!
YOU OVERSTEP, OFFICER MURPHY. WHY DON'T YOU WALK YOUR OWN BEAT AND LET US TAKE CARE OF--
HEY NOW--SLOW YOUR ROLL, BIG FELLA...
THE GIRL FROM THE BRIDGE THIS MORNING. THERE'S NO RECORD OF HER AT LOCAL HOSPITALS. NO TRACE OF HER IN THE SYSTEM AT ALL.
YOU NEVER BROUGHT HER BACK DOWNTOWN.
WHY?
NOK NOK NOK

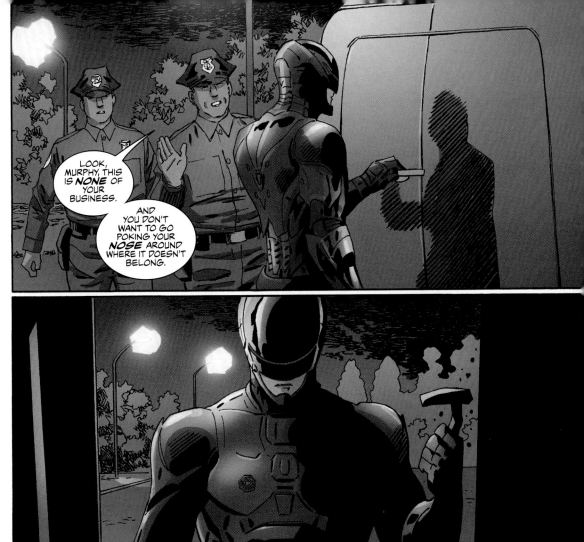

LOOK, MURPHY, THIS IS **NONE** OF YOUR BUSINESS.

AND YOU DON'T WANT TO GO POKING YOUR **NOSE** AROUND WHERE IT DOESN'T BELONG.

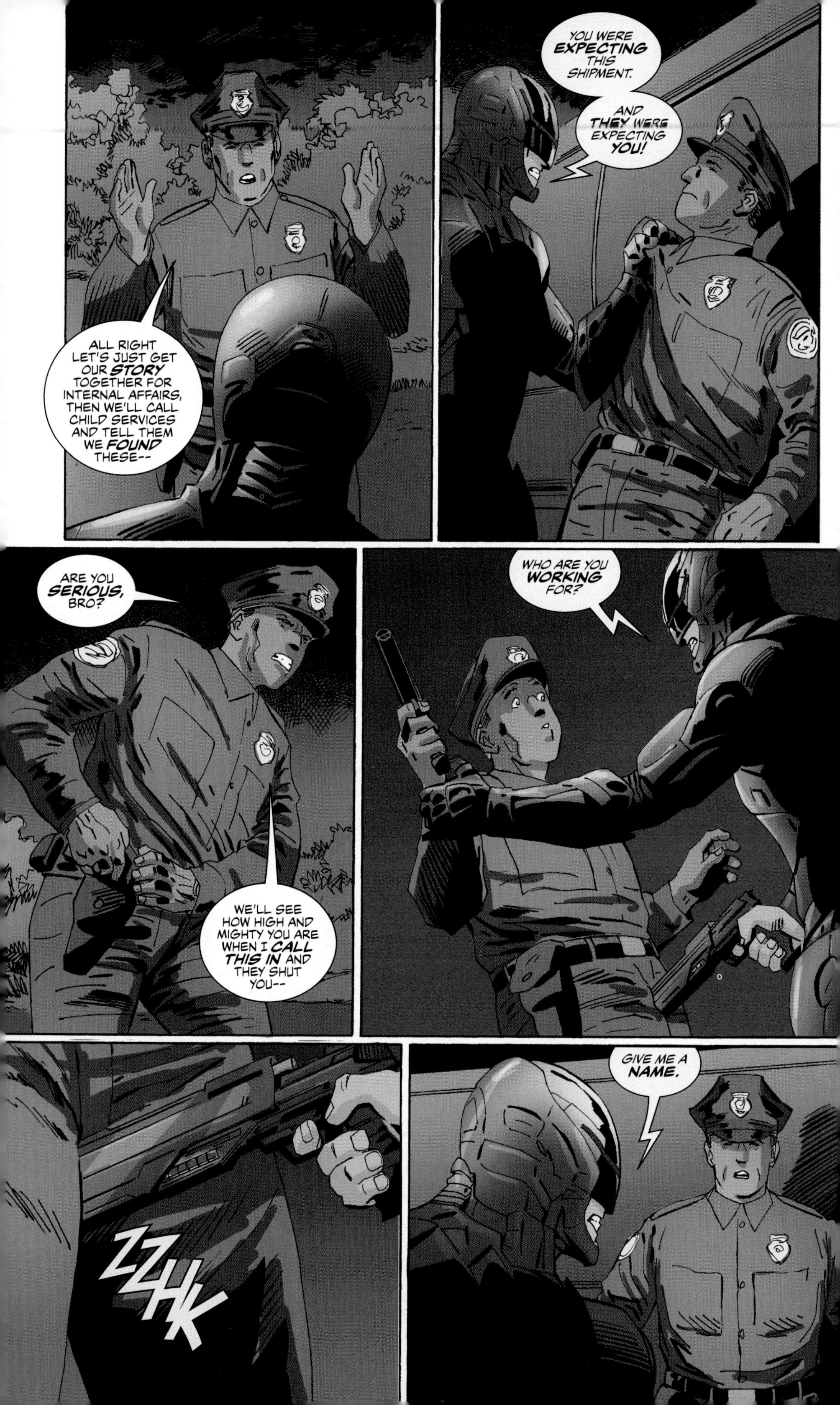
ALL RIGHT LET'S JUST GET OUR STORY TOGETHER FOR INTERNAL AFFAIRS, THEN WE'LL CALL CHILD SERVICES AND TELL THEM WE FOUND THESE--
YOU WERE EXPECTING THIS SHIPMENT.
AND THEY WERE EXPECTING YOU!
ARE YOU SERIOUS, BRO?
WE'LL SEE HOW HIGH AND MIGHTY YOU ARE WHEN I CALL THIS IN AND THEY SHUT YOU--
WHO ARE YOU WORKING FOR?
ZZHK
GIVE ME A NAME.

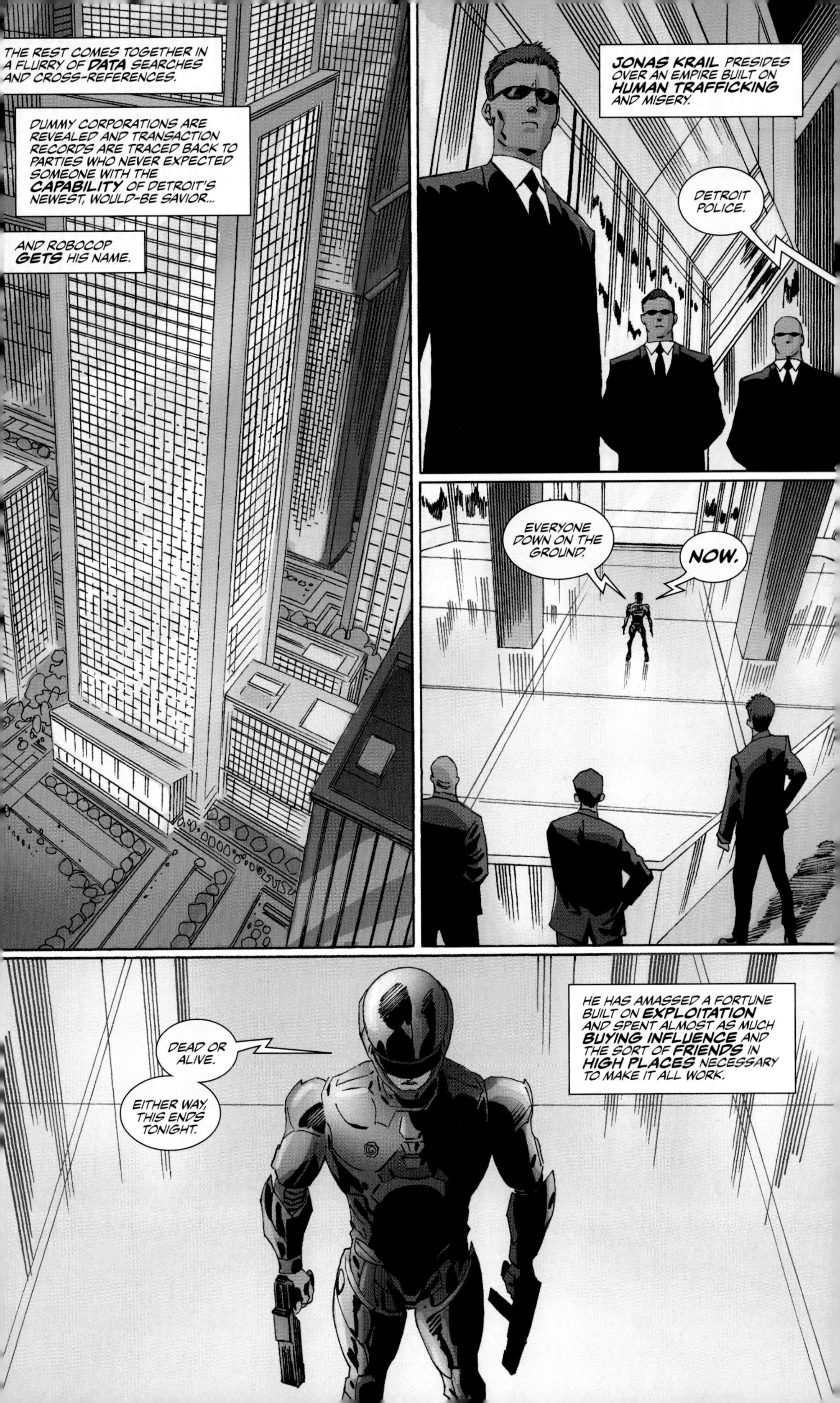
THE REST COMES TOGETHER IN A FLURRY OF DATA SEARCHES AND CROSS-REFERENCES.
DUMMY CORPORATIONS ARE REVEALED AND TRANSACTION RECORDS ARE TRACED BACK TO PARTIES WHO NEVER EXPECTED SOMEONE WITH THE CAPABILITY OF DETROIT'S NEWEST, WOULD-BE SAVIOR...
AND ROBOCOP GETS HIS NAME.
JONAS KRAIL PRESIDES OVER AN EMPIRE BUILT ON HUMAN TRAFFICKING AND MISERY.
DETROIT POLICE.
EVERYONE DOWN ON THE GROUND.
NOW.
HE HAS AMASSED A FORTUNE BUILT ON EXPLOITATION AND SPENT ALMOST AS MUCH BUYING INFLUENCE AND THE SORT OF FRIENDS IN HIGH PLACES NECESSARY TO MAKE IT ALL WORK.
DEAD OR ALIVE.
EITHER WAY, THIS ENDS TONIGHT.

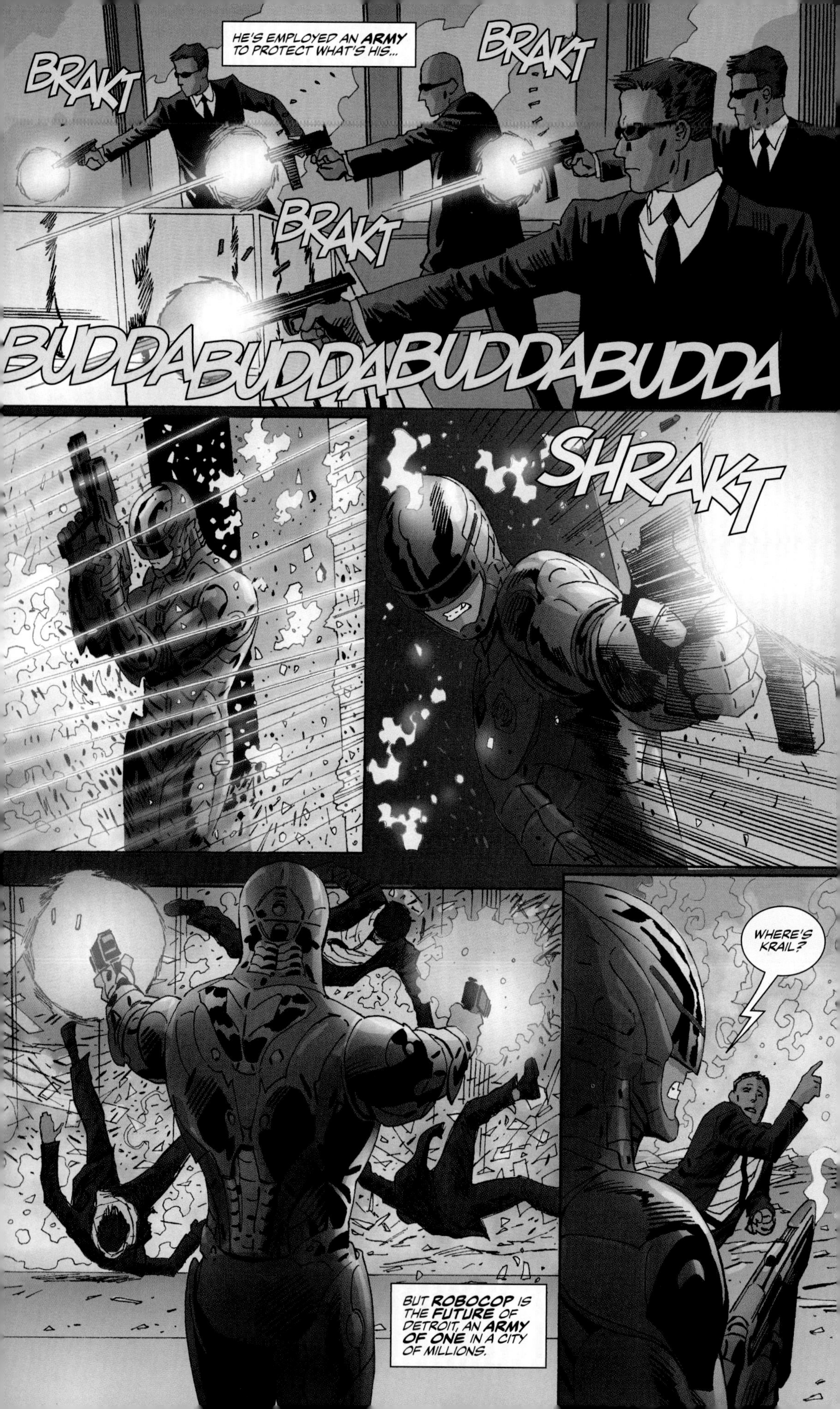
HE'S EMPLOYED AN **ARMY** TO PROTECT WHAT'S HIS...
BRAKT
BRAKT
BRAKT
BUDDABUDDABUDDABUDDA
SHRAKT
WHERE'S KRAIL?
BUT **ROBOCOP** IS THE **FUTURE** OF DETROIT, AN **ARMY OF ONE** IN A CITY OF MILLIONS.

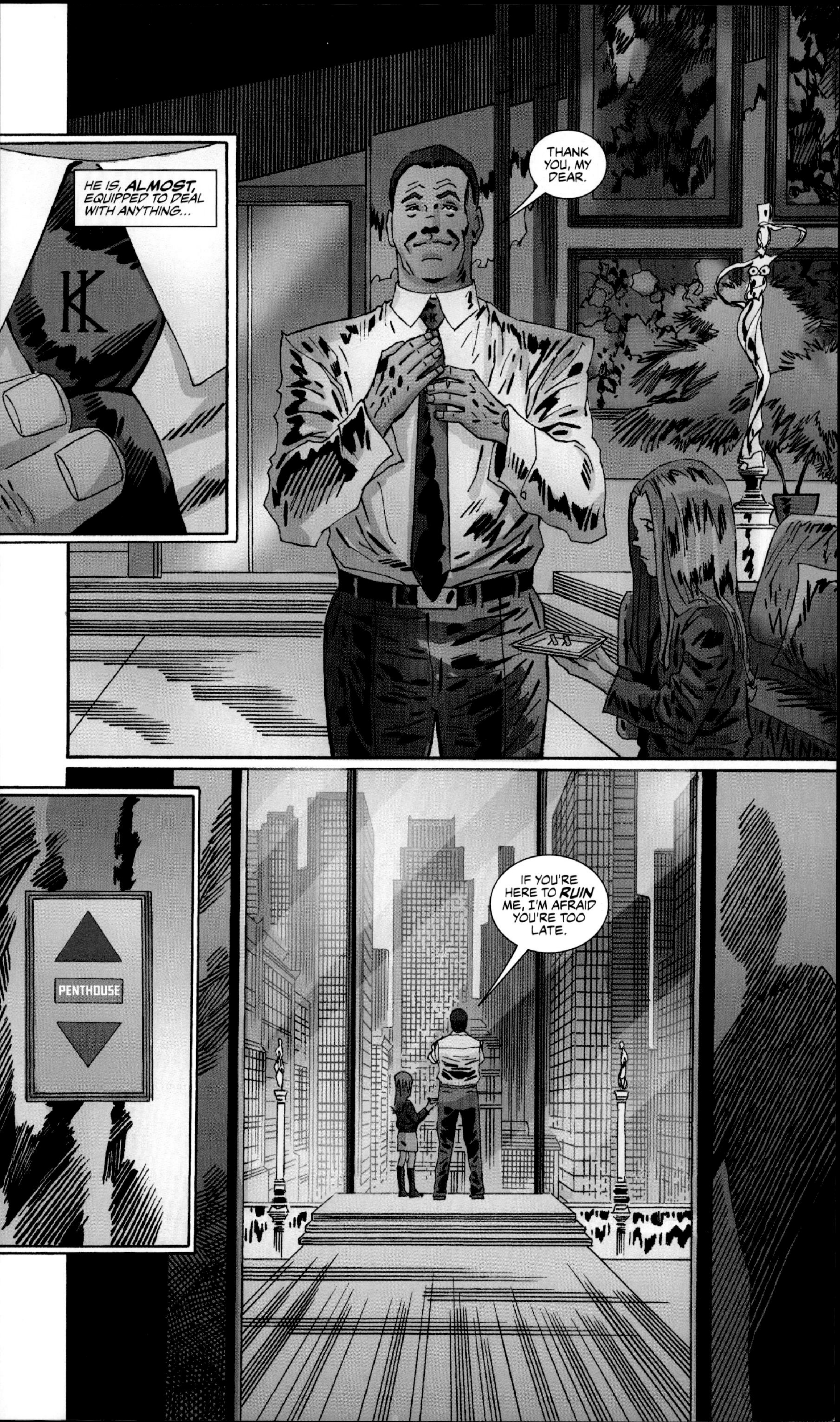
HE IS, ALMOST, EQUIPPED TO DEAL WITH ANYTHING...
THANK YOU, MY DEAR.
PENTHOUSE
IF YOU'RE HERE TO RUIN ME, I'M AFRAID YOU'RE TOO LATE.

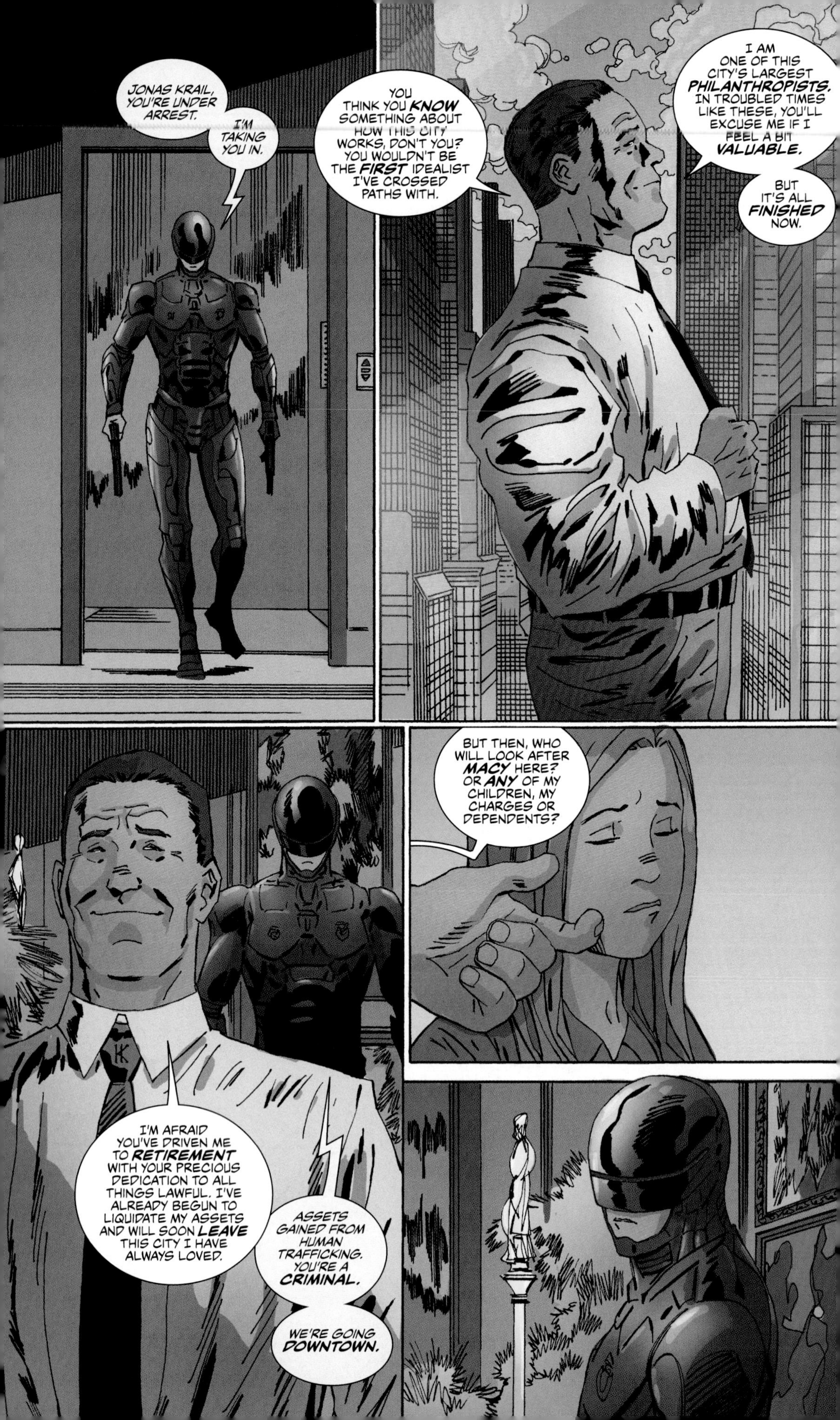
JONAS KRAIL, YOU'RE UNDER ARREST.
I'M TAKING YOU IN.
YOU THINK YOU KNOW SOMETHING ABOUT HOW THIS CITY WORKS, DON'T YOU? YOU WOULDN'T BE THE FIRST IDEALIST I'VE CROSSED PATHS WITH.
I AM ONE OF THIS CITY'S LARGEST PHILANTHROPISTS. IN TROUBLED TIMES LIKE THESE, YOU'LL EXCUSE ME IF I FEEL A BIT VALUABLE.
BUT IT'S ALL FINISHED NOW.
I'M AFRAID YOU'VE DRIVEN ME TO RETIREMENT WITH YOUR PRECIOUS DEDICATION TO ALL THINGS LAWFUL. I'VE ALREADY BEGUN TO LIQUIDATE MY ASSETS AND WILL SOON LEAVE THIS CITY I HAVE ALWAYS LOVED.
ASSETS GAINED FROM HUMAN TRAFFICKING. YOU'RE A CRIMINAL.
WE'RE GOING DOWNTOWN.
BUT THEN, WHO WILL LOOK AFTER MACY HERE? OR ANY OF MY CHILDREN, MY CHARGES OR DEPENDENTS?

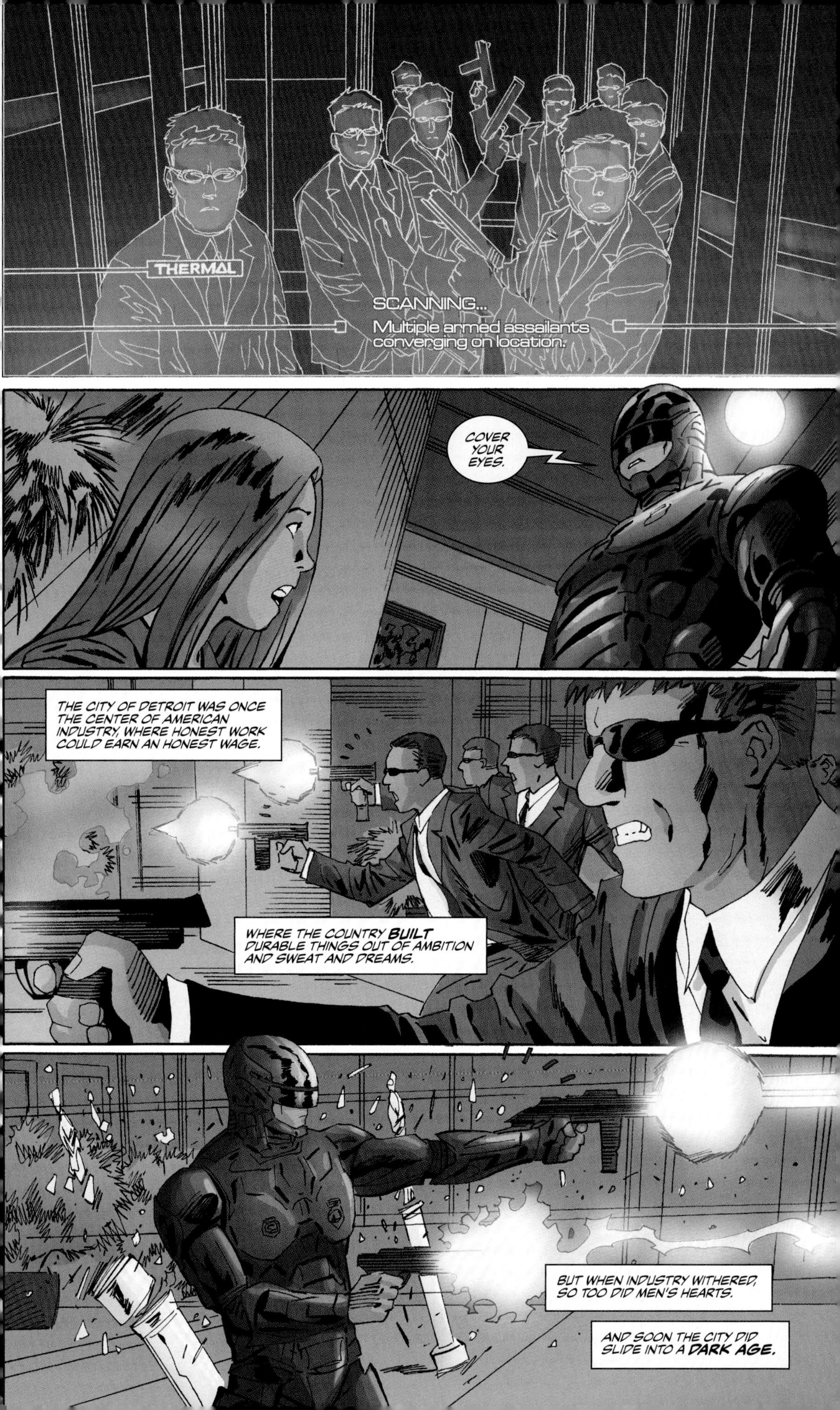
THERMAL
SCANNING...
Multiple armed assailants converging on location.
COVER YOUR EYES.
THE CITY OF DETROIT WAS ONCE THE CENTER OF AMERICAN INDUSTRY, WHERE HONEST WORK COULD EARN AN HONEST WAGE.
WHERE THE COUNTRY BUILT DURABLE THINGS OUT OF AMBITION AND SWEAT AND DREAMS.
BUT WHEN INDUSTRY WITHERED, SO TOO DID MEN'S HEARTS.
AND SOON THE CITY DID SLIDE INTO A DARK AGE.

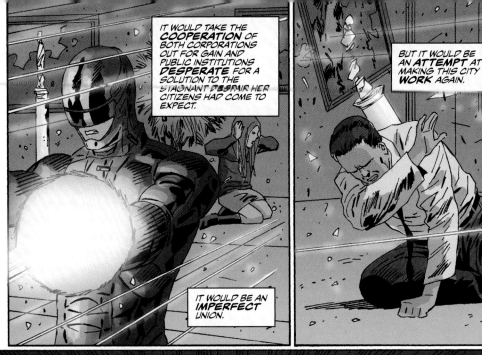

IT WOULD TAKE THE **COOPERATION** OF BOTH CORPORATIONS OUT FOR GAIN AND PUBLIC INSTITUTIONS **DESPERATE** FOR A SOLUTION TO THE STAGNANT DESPAIR HER CITIZENS HAD COME TO EXPECT.

BUT IT WOULD BE AN **ATTEMPT** AT MAKING THIS CITY **WORK** AGAIN.

IT WOULD BE AN **IMPERFECT** UNION.

ONE, LAST CHANCE TO SHOW THE WORLD HOW MUCH **GOOD** COULD BE DONE. AND JUST HOW MUCH DIFFERENCE...

...**ONE** MAN COULD REALLY MAKE.

THIS IS OFFICER ALEX MURPHY REQUESTING SUPPORT.

SYSTEM LOGS WILL INDICATE **MULTIPLE CASUALTIES** LEFT IN SELF-DEFENSE.

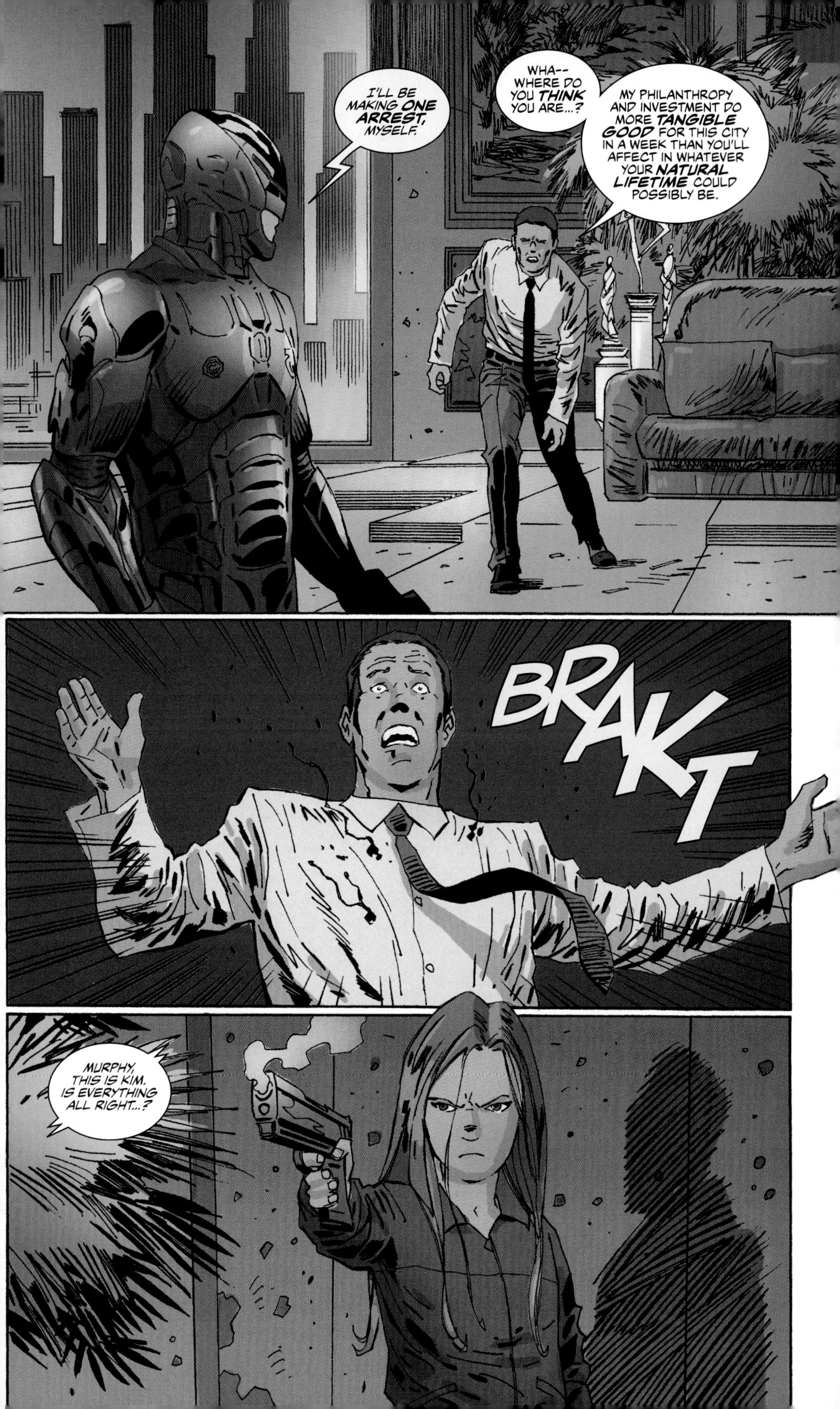
I'LL BE MAKING ONE ARREST, MYSELF.
WHA-- WHERE DO YOU THINK YOU ARE...?
MY PHILANTHROPY AND INVESTMENT DO MORE TANGIBLE GOOD FOR THIS CITY IN A WEEK THAN YOU'LL AFFECT IN WHATEVER YOUR NATURAL LIFETIME COULD POSSIBLY BE.
BRAKT
MURPHY, THIS IS KIM. IS EVERYTHING ALL RIGHT...?

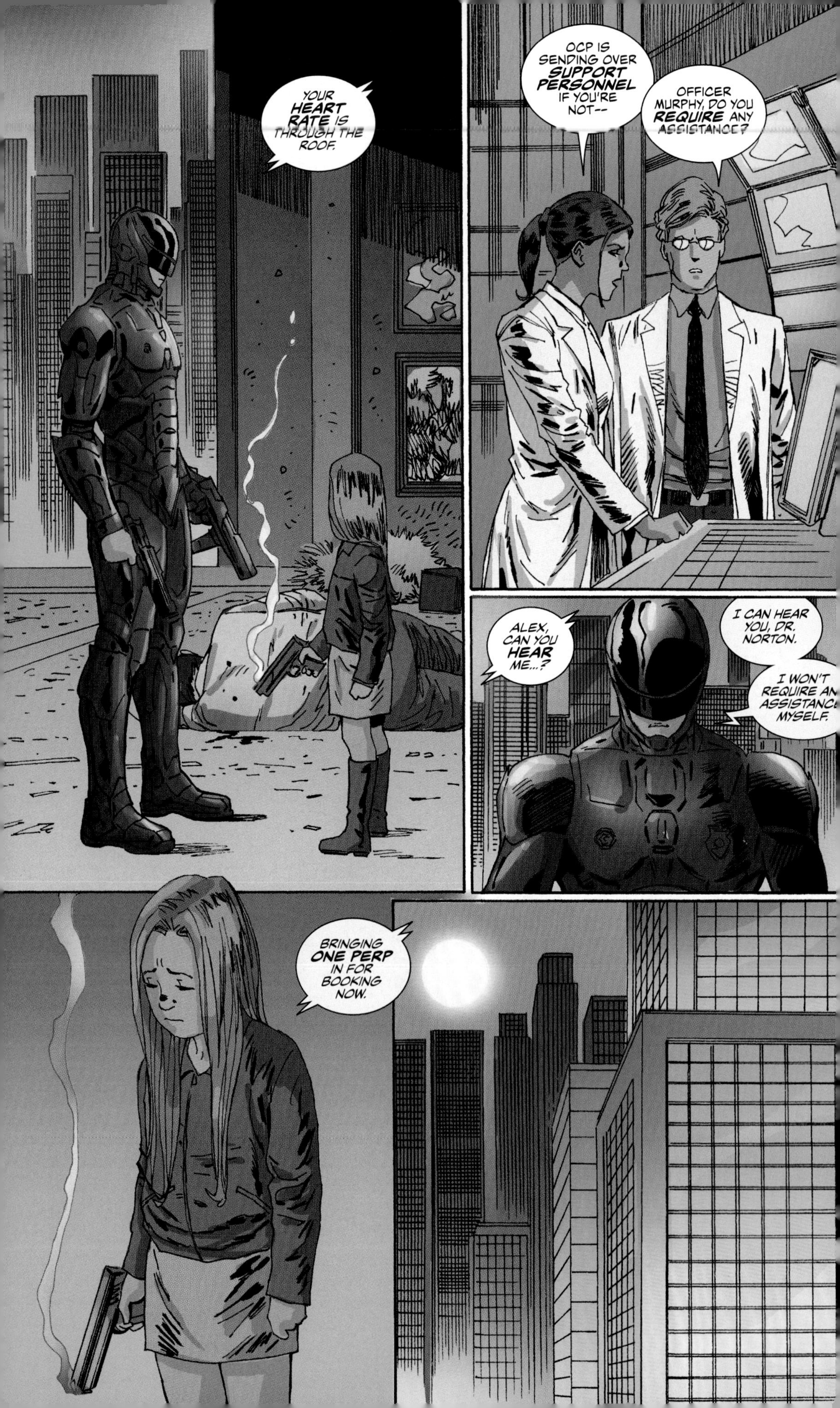

YOUR HEART RATE IS THROUGH THE ROOF.
OCP IS SENDING OVER SUPPORT PERSONNEL IF YOU'RE NOT--
OFFICER MURPHY, DO YOU REQUIRE ANY ASSISTANCE?
ALEX, CAN YOU HEAR ME...?
I CAN HEAR YOU, DR. NORTON.
I WON'T REQUIRE ANY ASSISTANCE MYSELF.
BRINGING ONE PERP IN FOR BOOKING NOW.

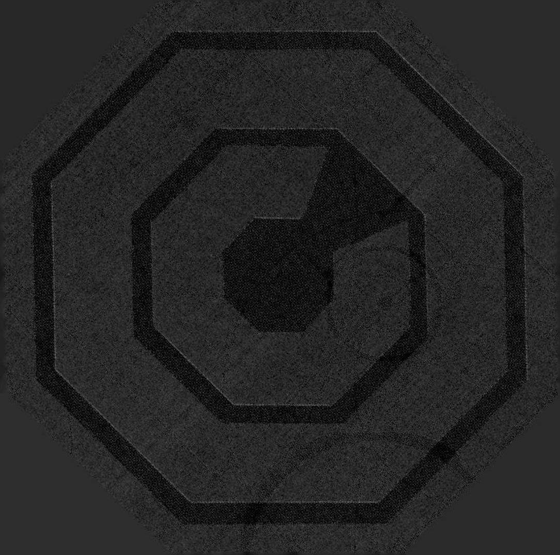

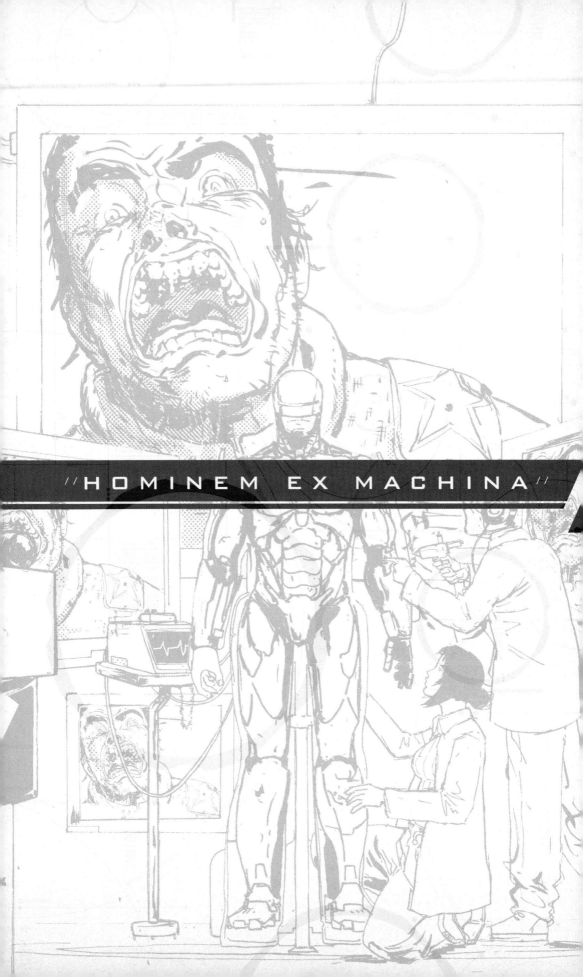

"HOMINEM EX MACHINA"

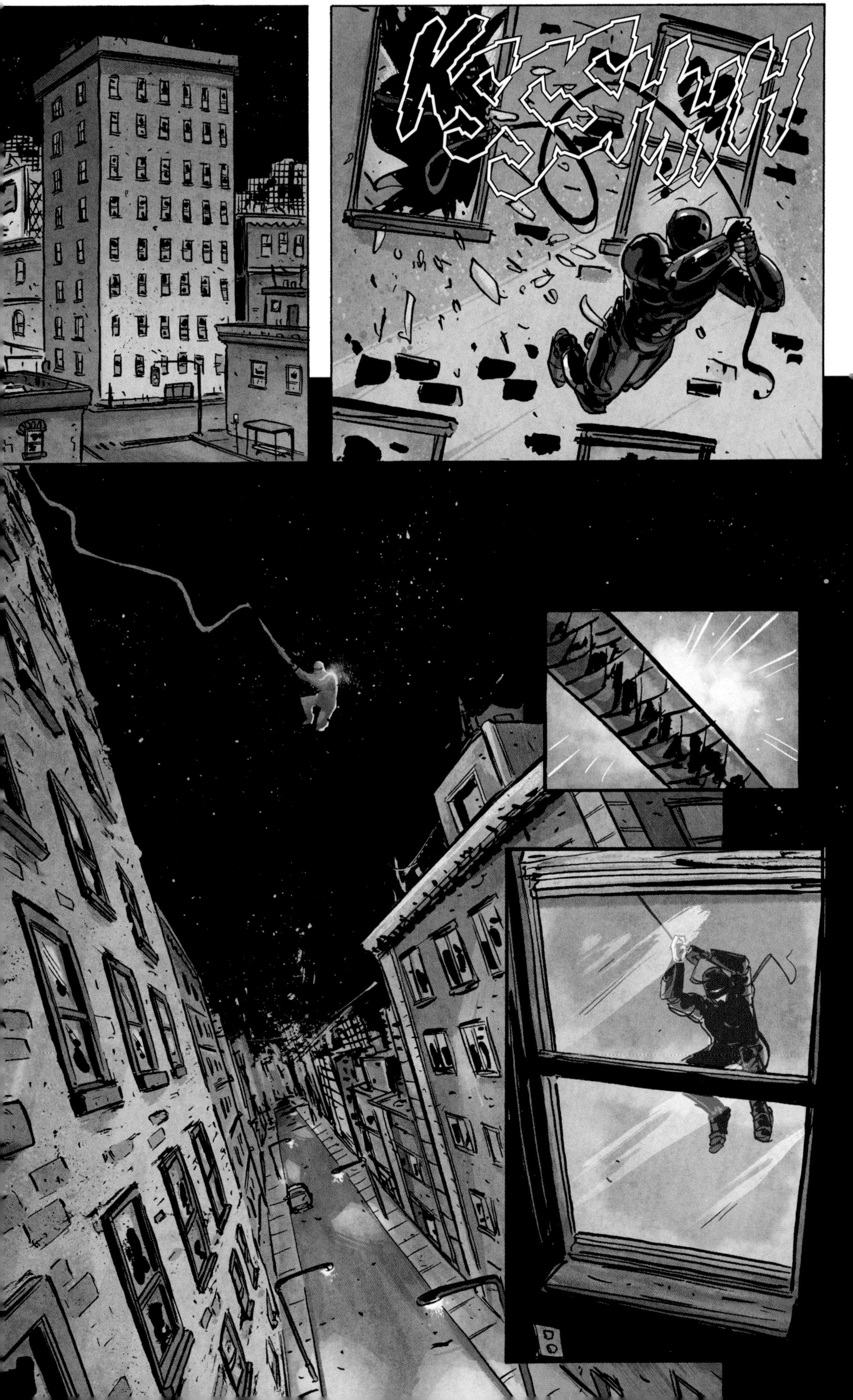

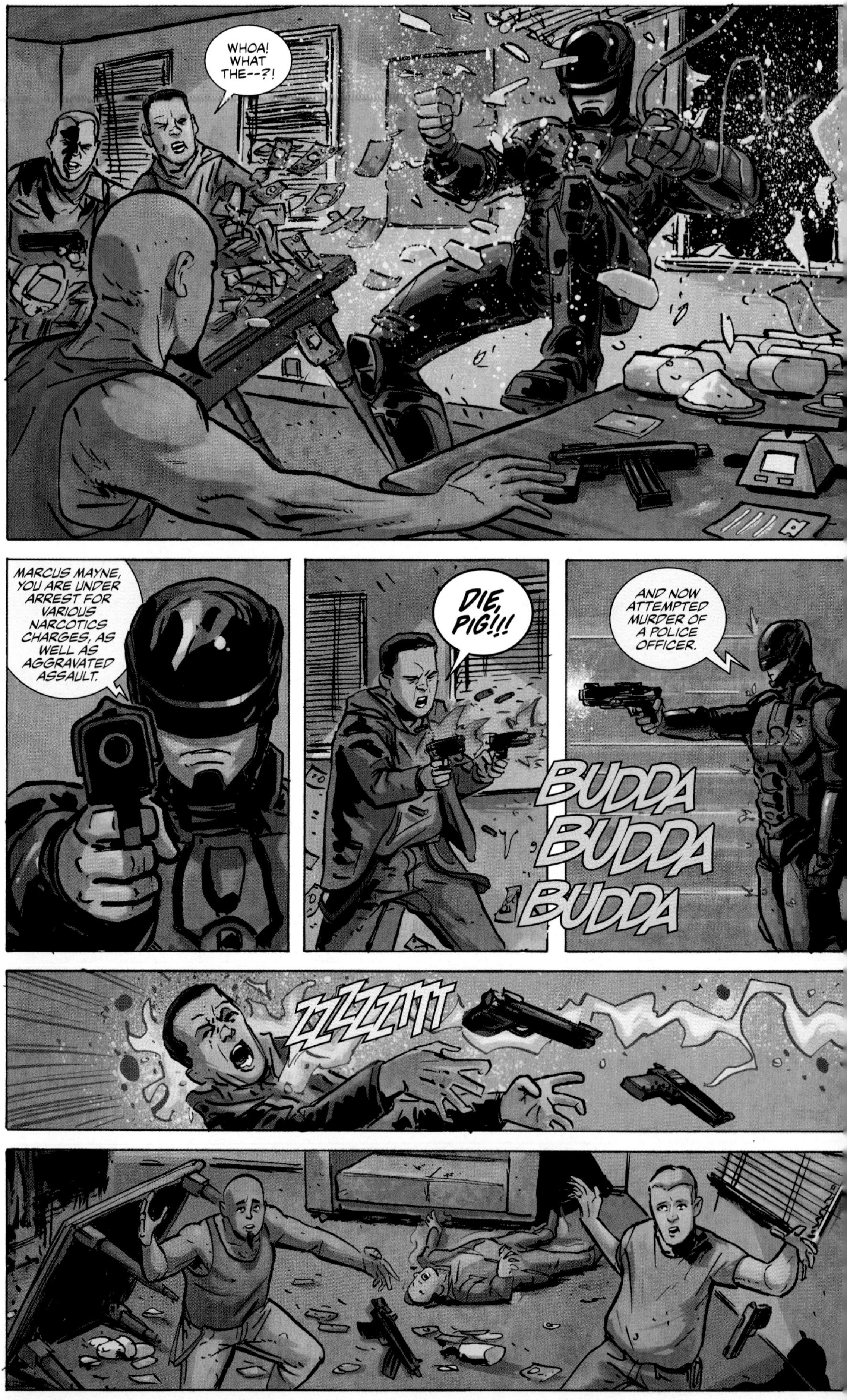
WHOA! WHAT THE--?!
MARCUS MAYNE, YOU ARE UNDER ARREST FOR VARIOUS NARCOTICS CHARGES, AS WELL AS AGGRAVATED ASSAULT.
DIE, PIG!!!
AND NOW ATTEMPTED MURDER OF A POLICE OFFICER.
BUDDA BUDDA BUDDA
ZZZZZTTT

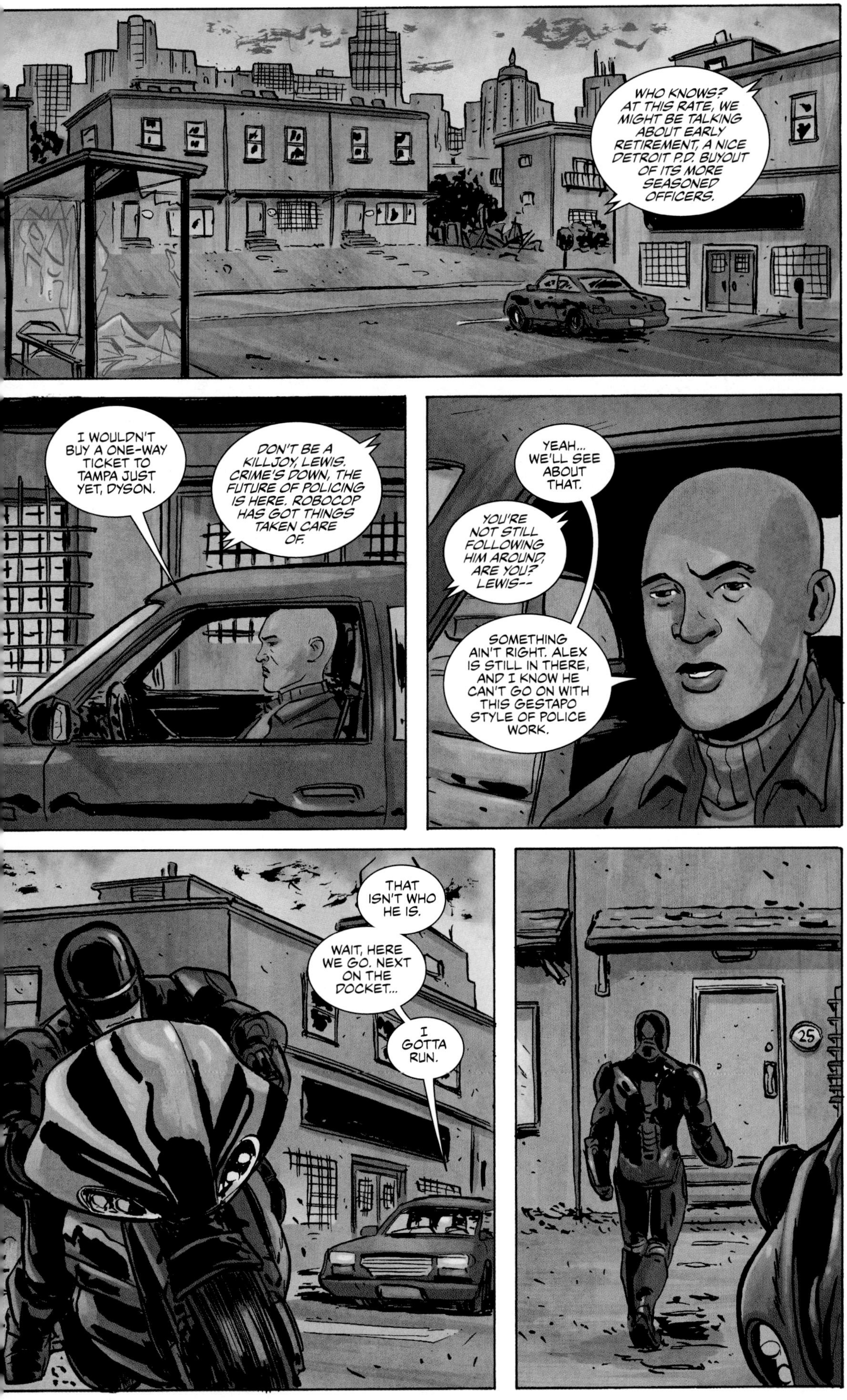
WHO KNOWS? AT THIS RATE, WE MIGHT BE TALKING ABOUT EARLY RETIREMENT, A NICE DETROIT P.D. BUYOUT OF ITS MORE SEASONED OFFICERS.
I WOULDN'T BUY A ONE-WAY TICKET TO TAMPA JUST YET, DYSON.
DON'T BE A KILLJOY, LEWIS. CRIME'S DOWN, THE FUTURE OF POLICING IS HERE. ROBOCOP HAS GOT THINGS TAKEN CARE OF.
YEAH... WE'LL SEE ABOUT THAT.
YOU'RE NOT STILL FOLLOWING HIM AROUND, ARE YOU? LEWIS--
SOMETHING AIN'T RIGHT. ALEX IS STILL IN THERE, AND I KNOW HE CAN'T GO ON WITH THIS GESTAPO STYLE OF POLICE WORK.
THAT ISN'T WHO HE IS.
WAIT, HERE WE GO. NEXT ON THE DOCKET...
I GOTTA RUN.
25

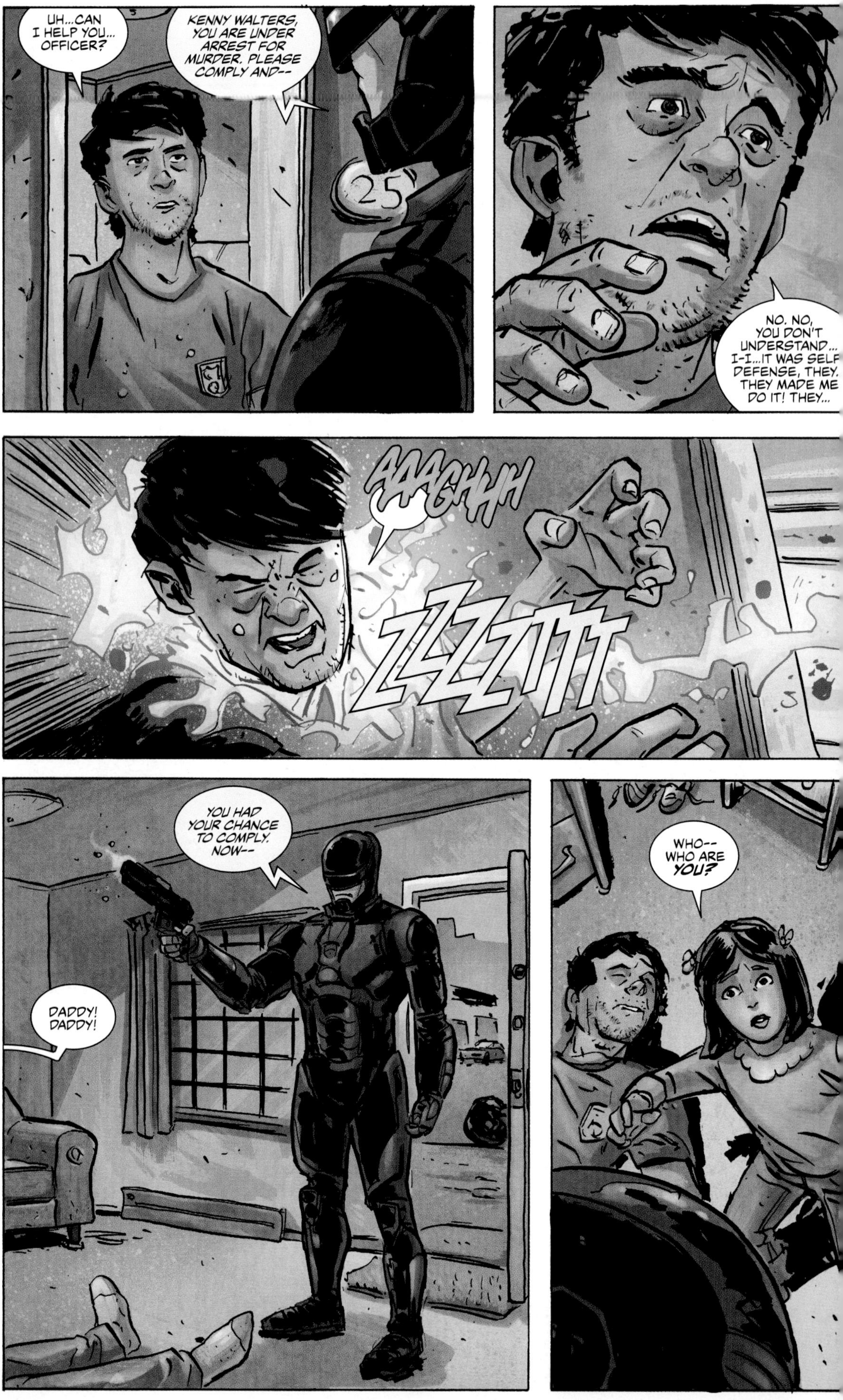
UH...CAN I HELP YOU... OFFICER?
KENNY WALTERS, YOU ARE UNDER ARREST FOR MURDER. PLEASE COMPLY AND--
25
NO. NO, YOU DON'T UNDERSTAND... I-I...IT WAS SELF DEFENSE, THEY. THEY MADE ME DO IT! THEY...
AAAGHHH
ZZZZTTT
YOU HAD YOUR CHANCE TO COMPLY. NOW--
DADDY! DADDY!
WHO-- WHO ARE YOU?

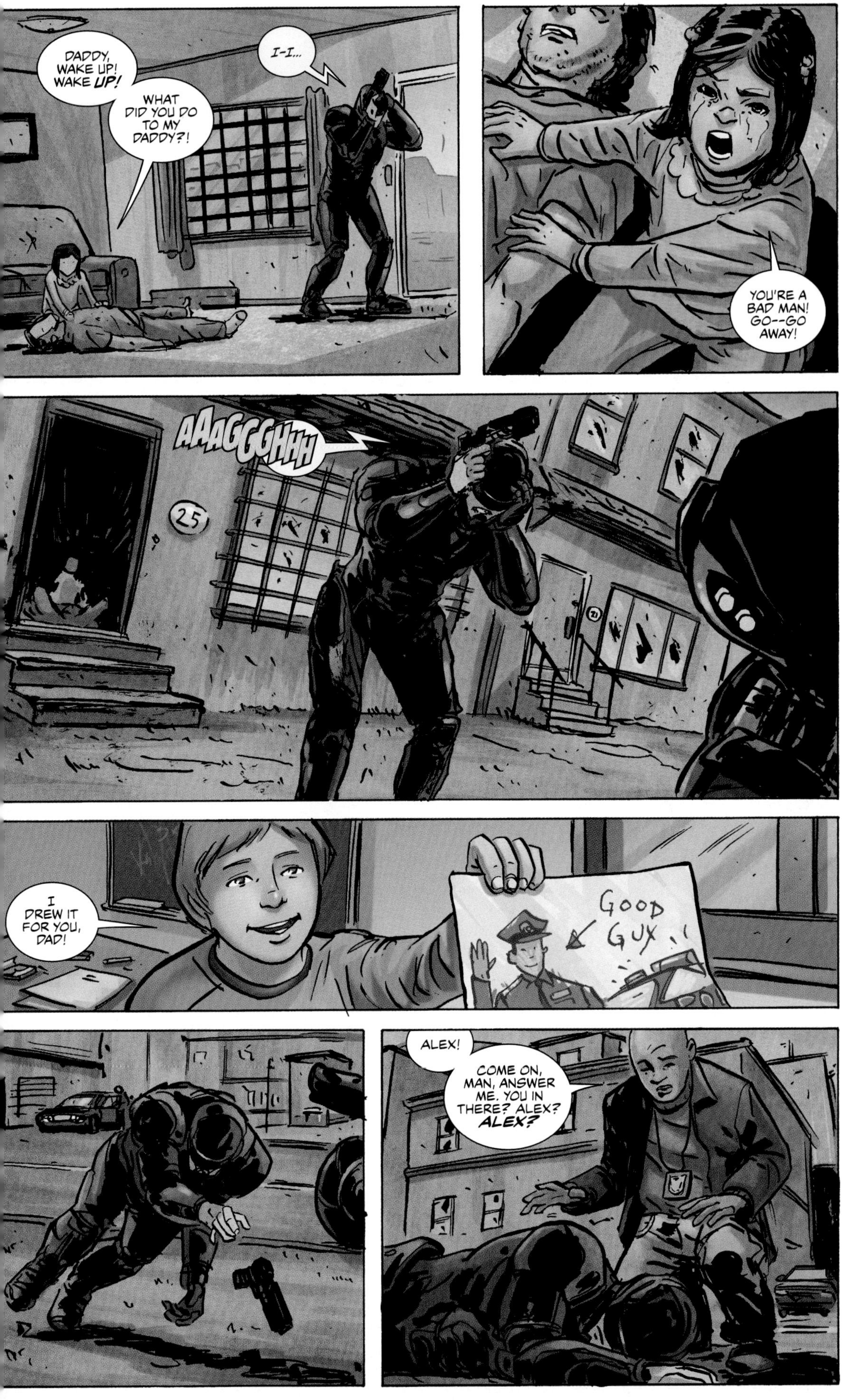

DADDY, WAKE UP! WAKE UP!
WHAT DID YOU DO TO MY DADDY?!
I-I...
YOU'RE A BAD MAN! GO--GO AWAY!
AAAGGGHHH
25
I DREW IT FOR YOU, DAD!
GOOD GUY
ALEX!
COME ON, MAN, ANSWER ME. YOU IN THERE? ALEX? ALEX?

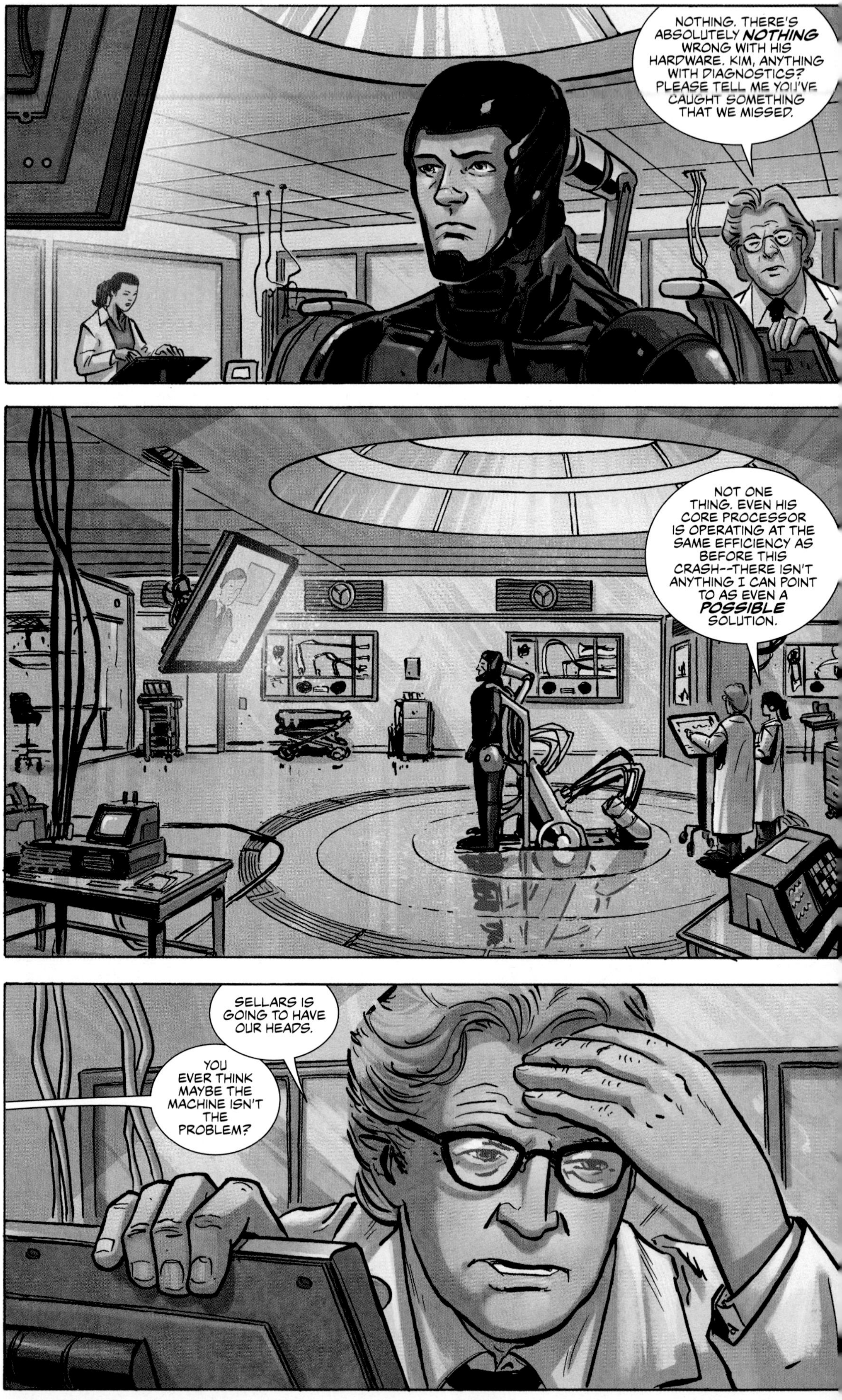
NOTHING. THERE'S ABSOLUTELY NOTHING WRONG WITH HIS HARDWARE. KIM, ANYTHING WITH DIAGNOSTICS? PLEASE TELL ME YOU'VE CAUGHT SOMETHING THAT WE MISSED.
NOT ONE THING. EVEN HIS CORE PROCESSOR IS OPERATING AT THE SAME EFFICIENCY AS BEFORE THIS CRASH--THERE ISN'T ANYTHING I CAN POINT TO AS EVEN A POSSIBLE SOLUTION.
SELLARS IS GOING TO HAVE OUR HEADS.
YOU EVER THINK MAYBE THE MACHINE ISN'T THE PROBLEM?

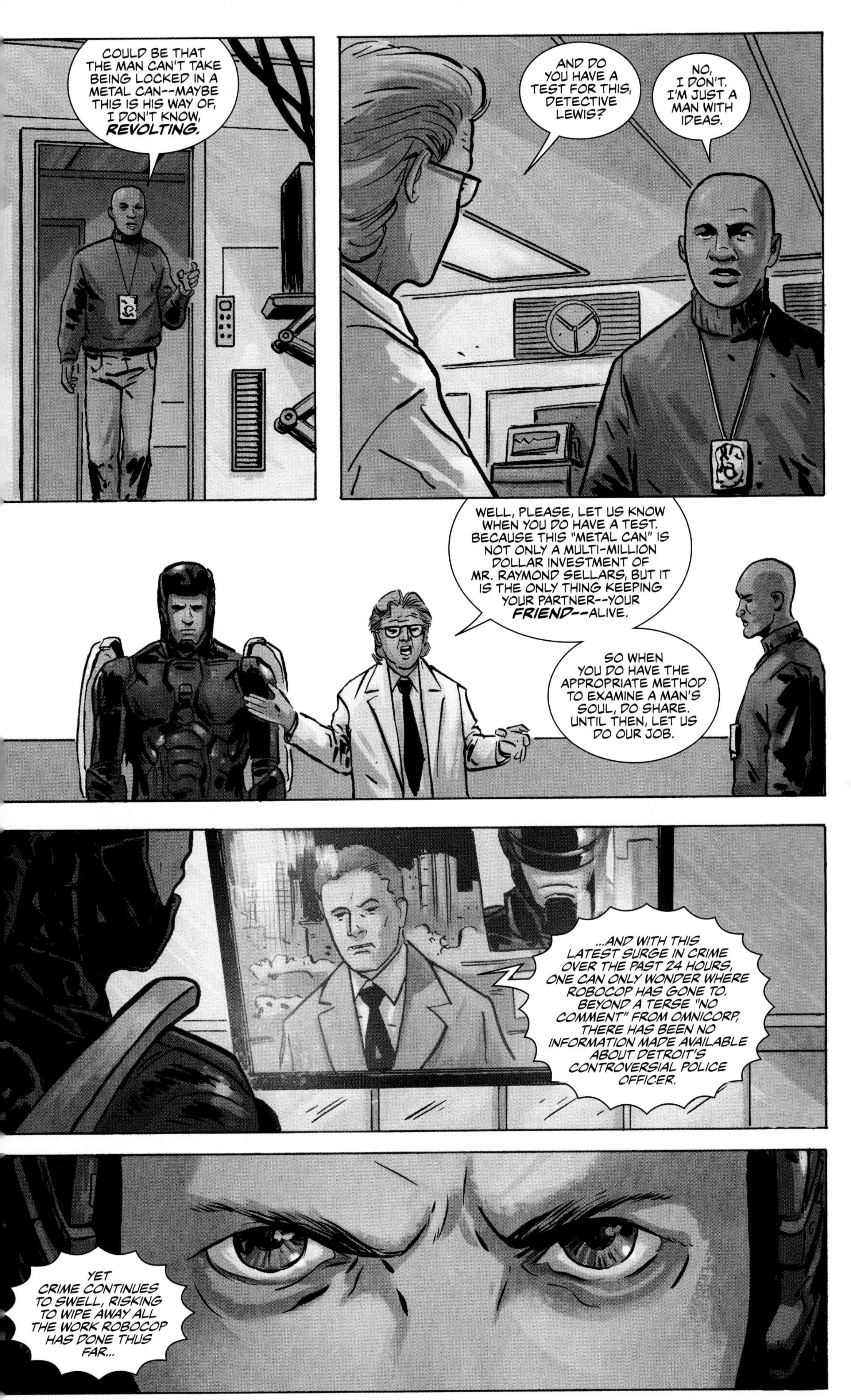
COULD BE THAT THE MAN CAN'T TAKE BEING LOCKED IN A METAL CAN--MAYBE THIS IS HIS WAY OF, I DON'T KNOW, REVOLTING.
AND DO YOU HAVE A TEST FOR THIS, DETECTIVE LEWIS?
NO, I DON'T. I'M JUST A MAN WITH IDEAS.
WELL, PLEASE, LET US KNOW WHEN YOU DO HAVE A TEST. BECAUSE THIS "METAL CAN" IS NOT ONLY A MULTI-MILLION DOLLAR INVESTMENT OF MR. RAYMOND SELLARS, BUT IT IS THE ONLY THING KEEPING YOUR PARTNER--YOUR FRIEND--ALIVE.
SO WHEN YOU DO HAVE THE APPROPRIATE METHOD TO EXAMINE A MAN'S SOUL, DO SHARE. UNTIL THEN, LET US DO OUR JOB.
...AND WITH THIS LATEST SURGE IN CRIME OVER THE PAST 24 HOURS, ONE CAN ONLY WONDER WHERE ROBOCOP HAS GONE TO. BEYOND A TERSE "NO COMMENT" FROM OMNICORP, THERE HAS BEEN NO INFORMATION MADE AVAILABLE ABOUT DETROIT'S CONTROVERSIAL POLICE OFFICER.
YET CRIME CONTINUES TO SWELL, RISKING TO WIPE AWAY ALL THE WORK ROBOCOP HAS DONE THUS FAR...

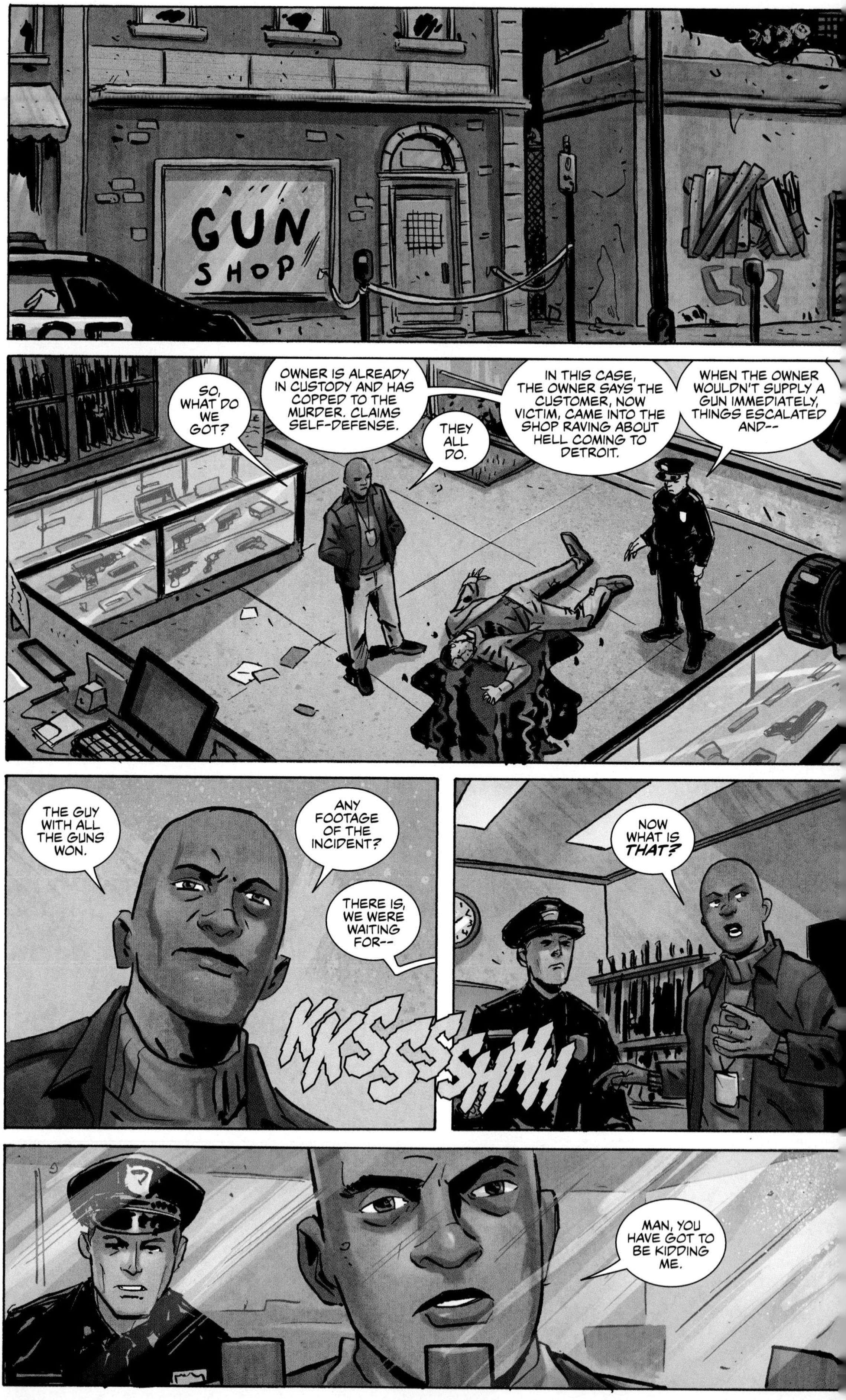
GUN SHOP
SO, WHAT DO WE GOT?
OWNER IS ALREADY IN CUSTODY AND HAS COPPED TO THE MURDER. CLAIMS SELF-DEFENSE.
THEY ALL DO.
IN THIS CASE, THE OWNER SAYS THE CUSTOMER, NOW VICTIM, CAME INTO THE SHOP RAVING ABOUT HELL COMING TO DETROIT.
WHEN THE OWNER WOULDN'T SUPPLY A GUN IMMEDIATELY, THINGS ESCALATED AND--
THE GUY WITH ALL THE GUNS WON.
ANY FOOTAGE OF THE INCIDENT?
THERE IS, WE WERE WAITING FOR--
KKSSSSHHH
NOW WHAT IS *THAT?*
MAN, YOU HAVE GOT TO BE KIDDING ME.

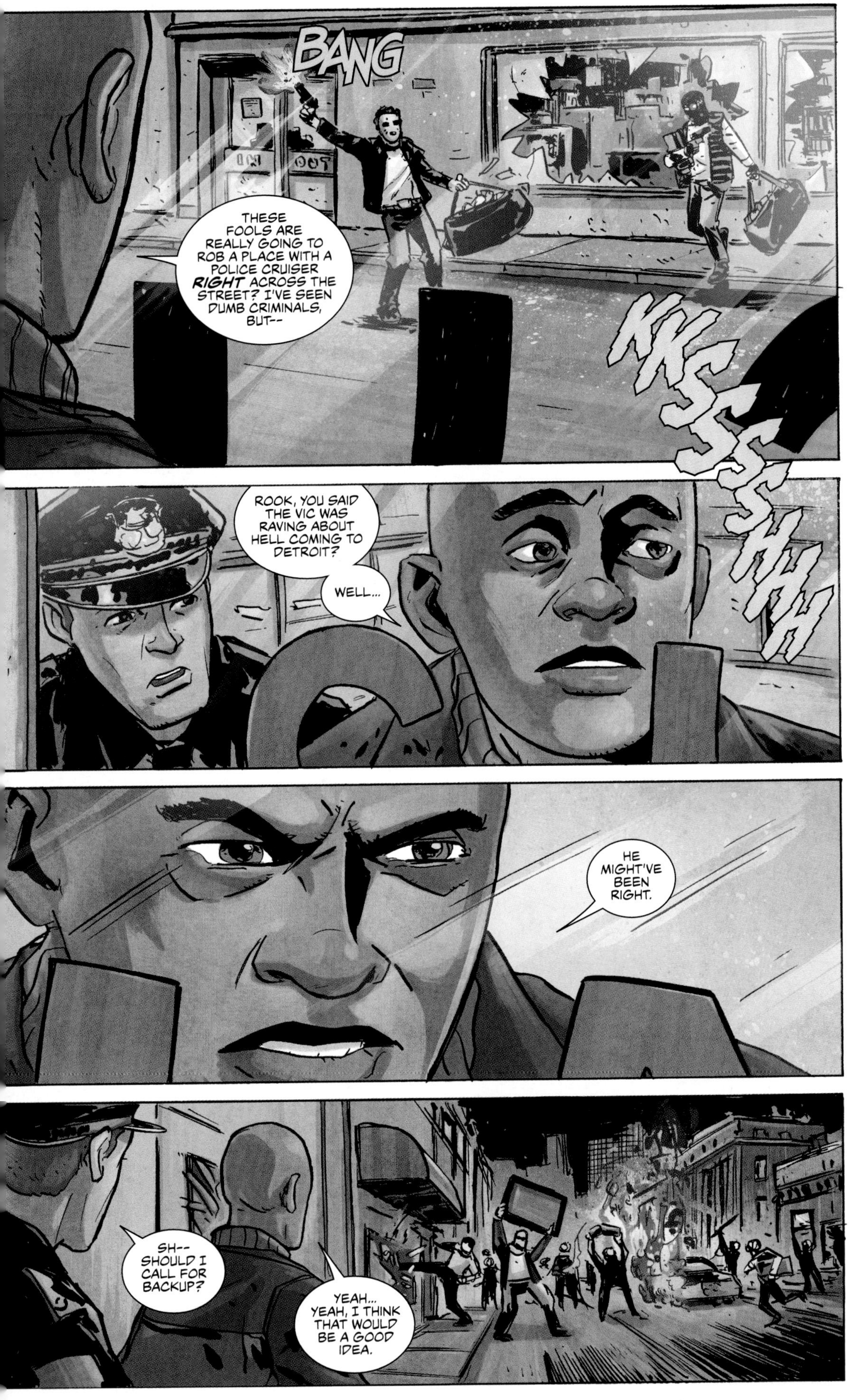
BANG
THESE FOOLS ARE REALLY GOING TO ROB A PLACE WITH A POLICE CRUISER RIGHT ACROSS THE STREET? I'VE SEEN DUMB CRIMINALS, BUT--
KKSSSSHHH
ROOK, YOU SAID THE VIC WAS RAVING ABOUT HELL COMING TO DETROIT?
WELL...
HE MIGHT'VE BEEN RIGHT.
SH-- SHOULD I CALL FOR BACKUP?
YEAH... YEAH, I THINK THAT WOULD BE A GOOD IDEA.

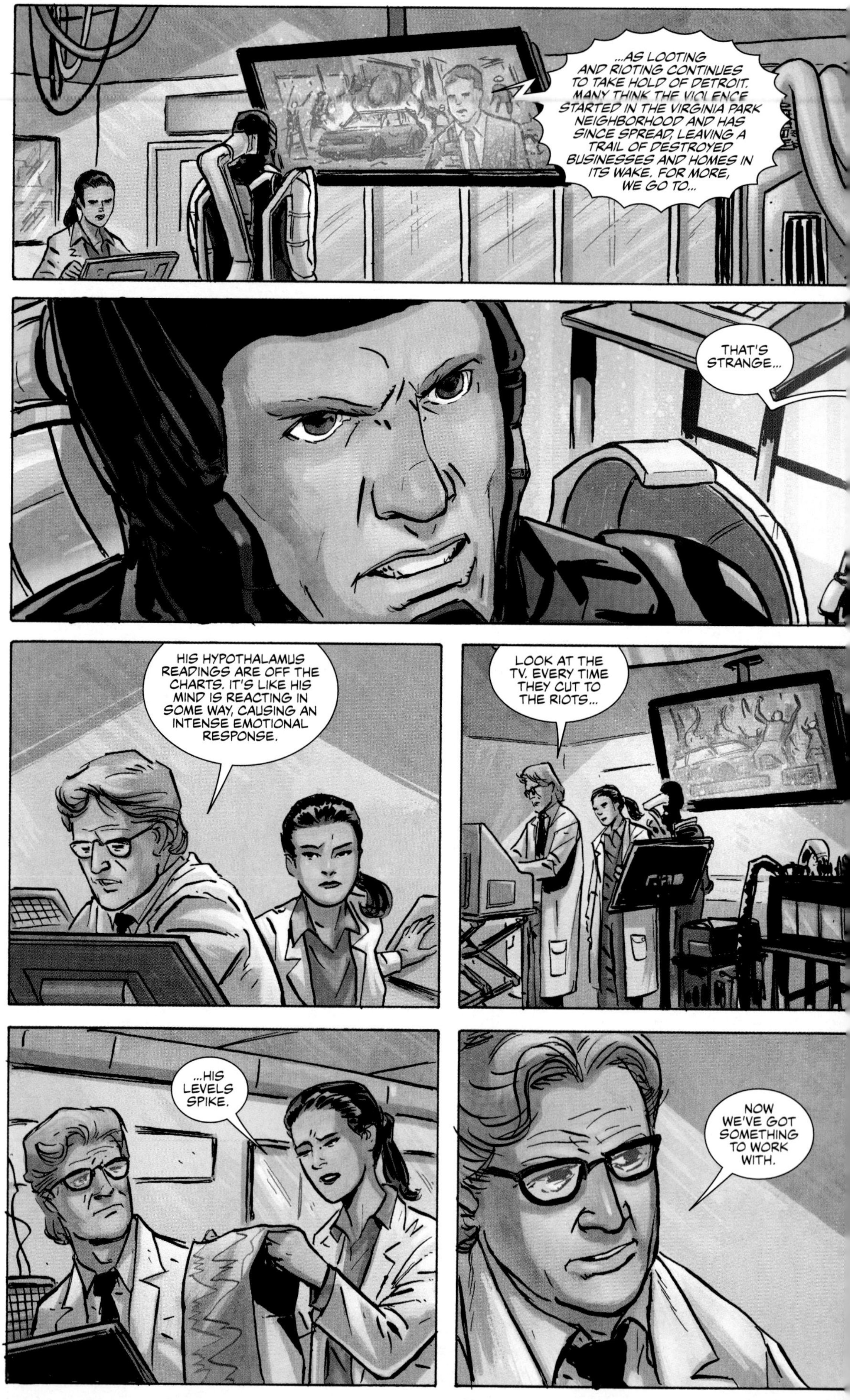
...AS LOOTING AND RIOTING CONTINUES TO TAKE HOLD OF DETROIT, MANY THINK THE VIOLENCE STARTED IN THE VIRGINIA PARK NEIGHBORHOOD AND HAS SINCE SPREAD, LEAVING A TRAIL OF DESTROYED BUSINESSES AND HOMES IN ITS WAKE. FOR MORE, WE GO TO...
THAT'S STRANGE...
HIS HYPOTHALAMUS READINGS ARE OFF THE CHARTS. IT'S LIKE HIS MIND IS REACTING IN SOME WAY, CAUSING AN INTENSE EMOTIONAL RESPONSE.
LOOK AT THE TV. EVERY TIME THEY CUT TO THE RIOTS...
...HIS LEVELS SPIKE.
NOW WE'VE GOT SOMETHING TO WORK WITH.

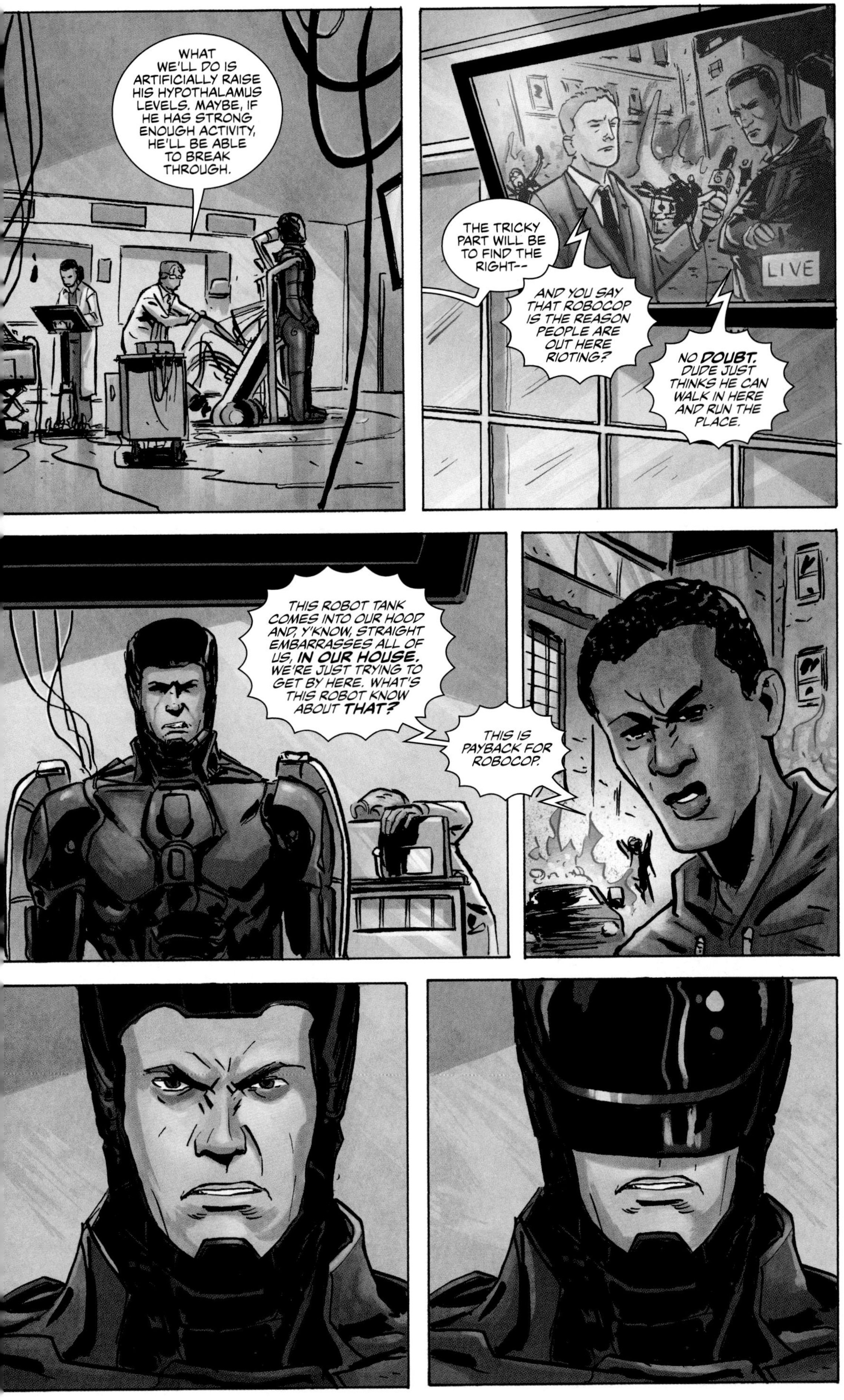
WHAT WE'LL DO IS ARTIFICIALLY RAISE HIS HYPOTHALAMUS LEVELS. MAYBE, IF HE HAS STRONG ENOUGH ACTIVITY, HE'LL BE ABLE TO BREAK THROUGH.
THE TRICKY PART WILL BE TO FIND THE RIGHT--
LIVE
AND YOU SAY THAT ROBOCOP IS THE REASON PEOPLE ARE OUT HERE RIOTING?
NO DOUBT. DUDE JUST THINKS HE CAN WALK IN HERE AND RUN THE PLACE.
THIS ROBOT TANK COMES INTO OUR HOOD AND, Y'KNOW, STRAIGHT EMBARRASSES ALL OF US, IN OUR HOUSE. WE'RE JUST TRYING TO GET BY HERE. WHAT'S THIS ROBOT KNOW ABOUT THAT?
THIS IS PAYBACK FOR ROBOCOP.

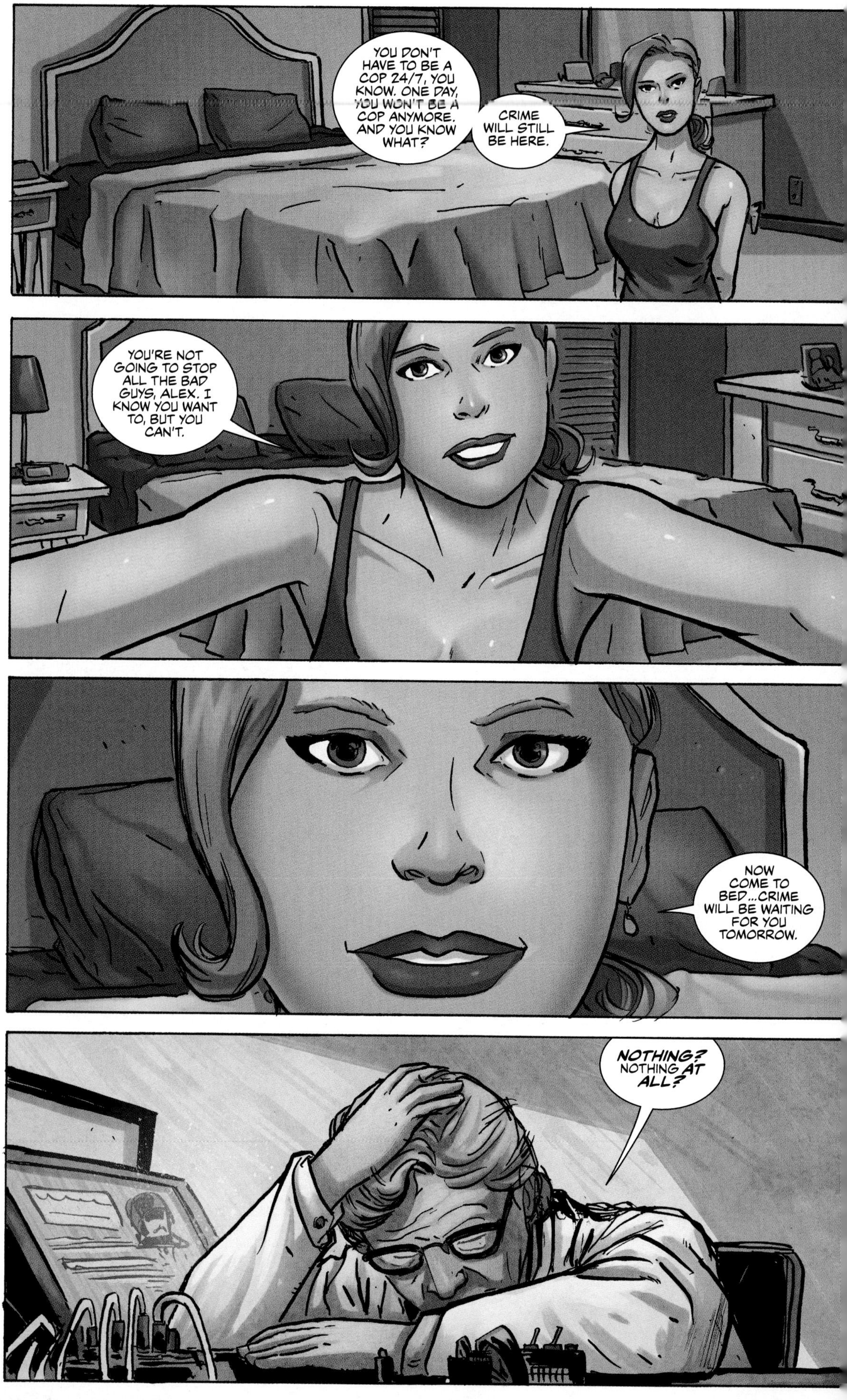
YOU DON'T HAVE TO BE A COP 24/7, YOU KNOW. ONE DAY, YOU WON'T BE A COP ANYMORE. AND YOU KNOW WHAT?
CRIME WILL STILL BE HERE.
YOU'RE NOT GOING TO STOP ALL THE BAD GUYS, ALEX. I KNOW YOU WANT TO, BUT YOU CAN'T.
NOW COME TO BED...CRIME WILL BE WAITING FOR YOU TOMORROW.
NOTHING? NOTHING AT ALL?

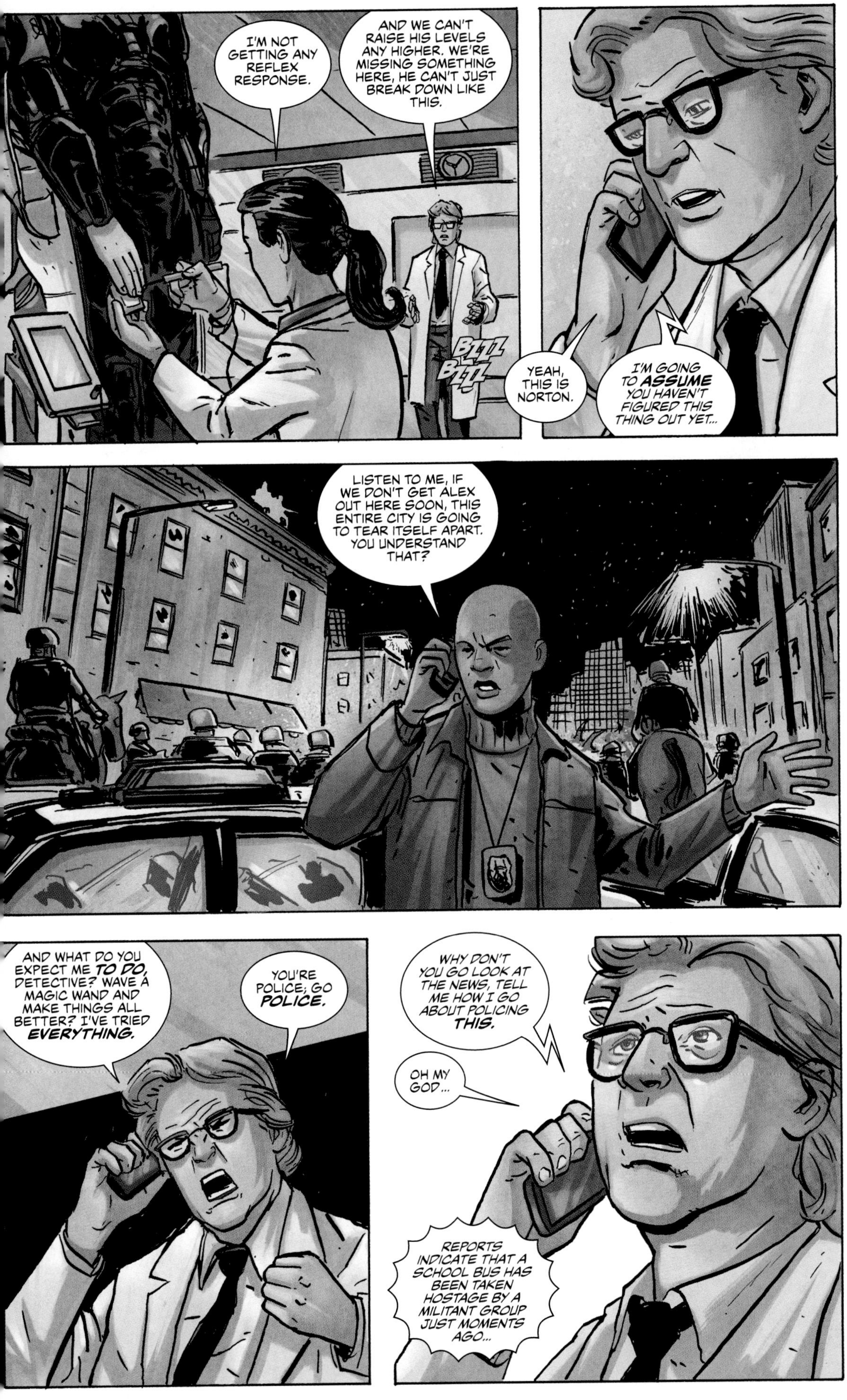
I'M NOT GETTING ANY REFLEX RESPONSE.
AND WE CAN'T RAISE HIS LEVELS ANY HIGHER. WE'RE MISSING SOMETHING HERE, HE CAN'T JUST BREAK DOWN LIKE THIS.
BZZZ BZZZ
YEAH, THIS IS NORTON.
I'M GOING TO ASSUME YOU HAVEN'T FIGURED THIS THING OUT YET...
LISTEN TO ME, IF WE DON'T GET ALEX OUT HERE SOON, THIS ENTIRE CITY IS GOING TO TEAR ITSELF APART. YOU UNDERSTAND THAT?
AND WHAT DO YOU EXPECT ME TO DO, DETECTIVE? WAVE A MAGIC WAND AND MAKE THINGS ALL BETTER? I'VE TRIED EVERYTHING.
YOU'RE POLICE; GO POLICE.
WHY DON'T YOU GO LOOK AT THE NEWS, TELL ME HOW I GO ABOUT POLICING THIS.
OH MY GOD...
REPORTS INDICATE THAT A SCHOOL BUS HAS BEEN TAKEN HOSTAGE BY A MILITANT GROUP JUST MOMENTS AGO...

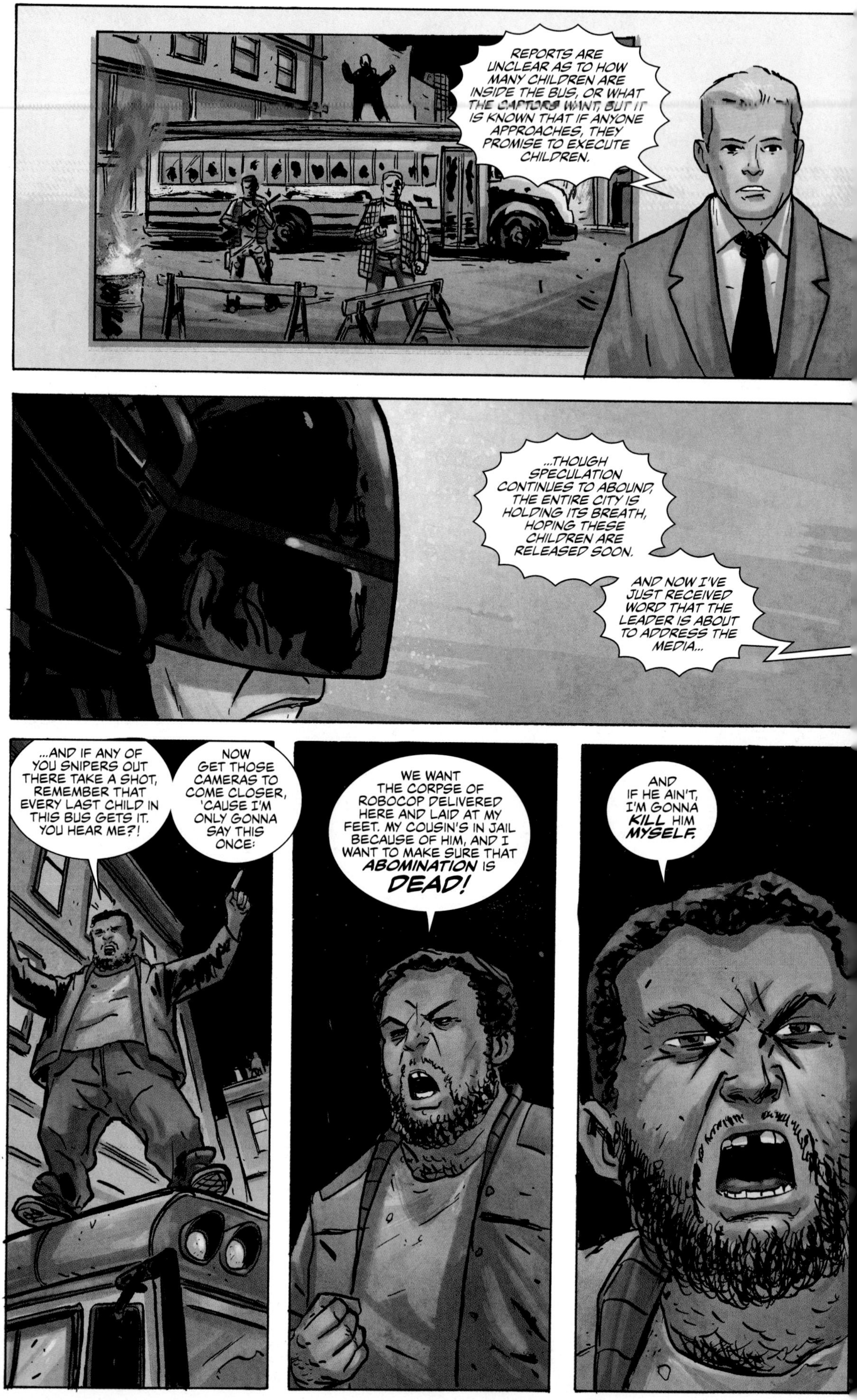
REPORTS ARE UNCLEAR AS TO HOW MANY CHILDREN ARE INSIDE THE BUS, OR WHAT THE CAPTORS WANT, BUT IT IS KNOWN THAT IF ANYONE APPROACHES, THEY PROMISE TO EXECUTE CHILDREN.
...THOUGH SPECULATION CONTINUES TO ABOUND, THE ENTIRE CITY IS HOLDING ITS BREATH, HOPING THESE CHILDREN ARE RELEASED SOON.
AND NOW I'VE JUST RECEIVED WORD THAT THE LEADER IS ABOUT TO ADDRESS THE MEDIA...
...AND IF ANY OF YOU SNIPERS OUT THERE TAKE A SHOT, REMEMBER THAT EVERY LAST CHILD IN THIS BUS GETS IT. YOU HEAR ME?!
NOW GET THOSE CAMERAS TO COME CLOSER, 'CAUSE I'M ONLY GONNA SAY THIS ONCE:
WE WANT THE CORPSE OF ROBOCOP DELIVERED HERE AND LAID AT MY FEET. MY COUSIN'S IN JAIL BECAUSE OF HIM, AND I WANT TO MAKE SURE THAT ABOMINATION IS DEAD!
AND IF HE AIN'T, I'M GONNA KILL HIM MYSELF.

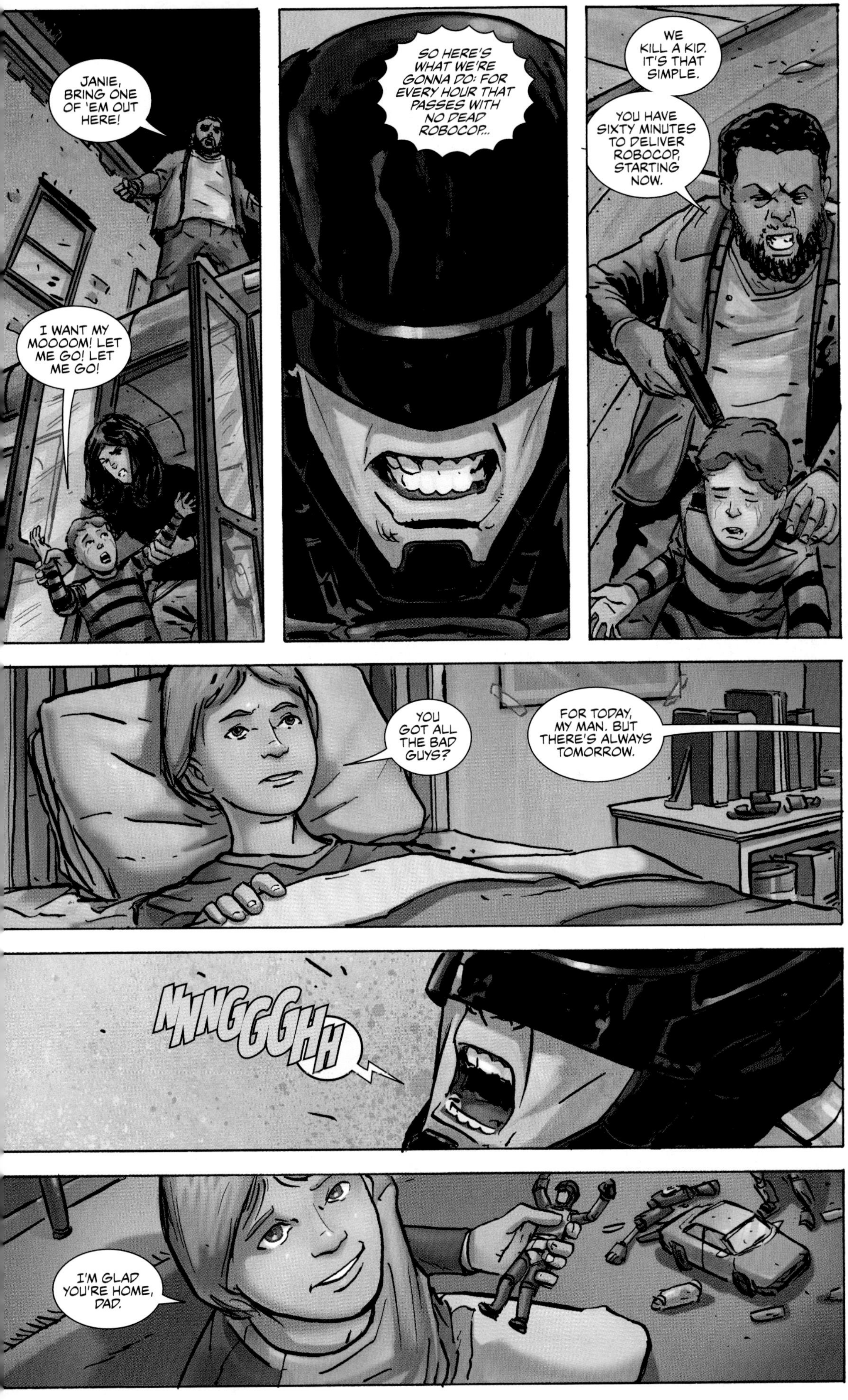

JANIE, BRING ONE OF 'EM OUT HERE!
I WANT MY MOOOOM! LET ME GO! LET ME GO!
SO HERE'S WHAT WE'RE GONNA DO: FOR EVERY HOUR THAT PASSES WITH NO DEAD ROBOCOP...
WE KILL A KID. IT'S THAT SIMPLE.
YOU HAVE SIXTY MINUTES TO DELIVER ROBOCOP, STARTING NOW.
YOU GOT ALL THE BAD GUYS?
FOR TODAY, MY MAN. BUT THERE'S ALWAYS TOMORROW.
NNNGGGHH
I'M GLAD YOU'RE HOME, DAD.

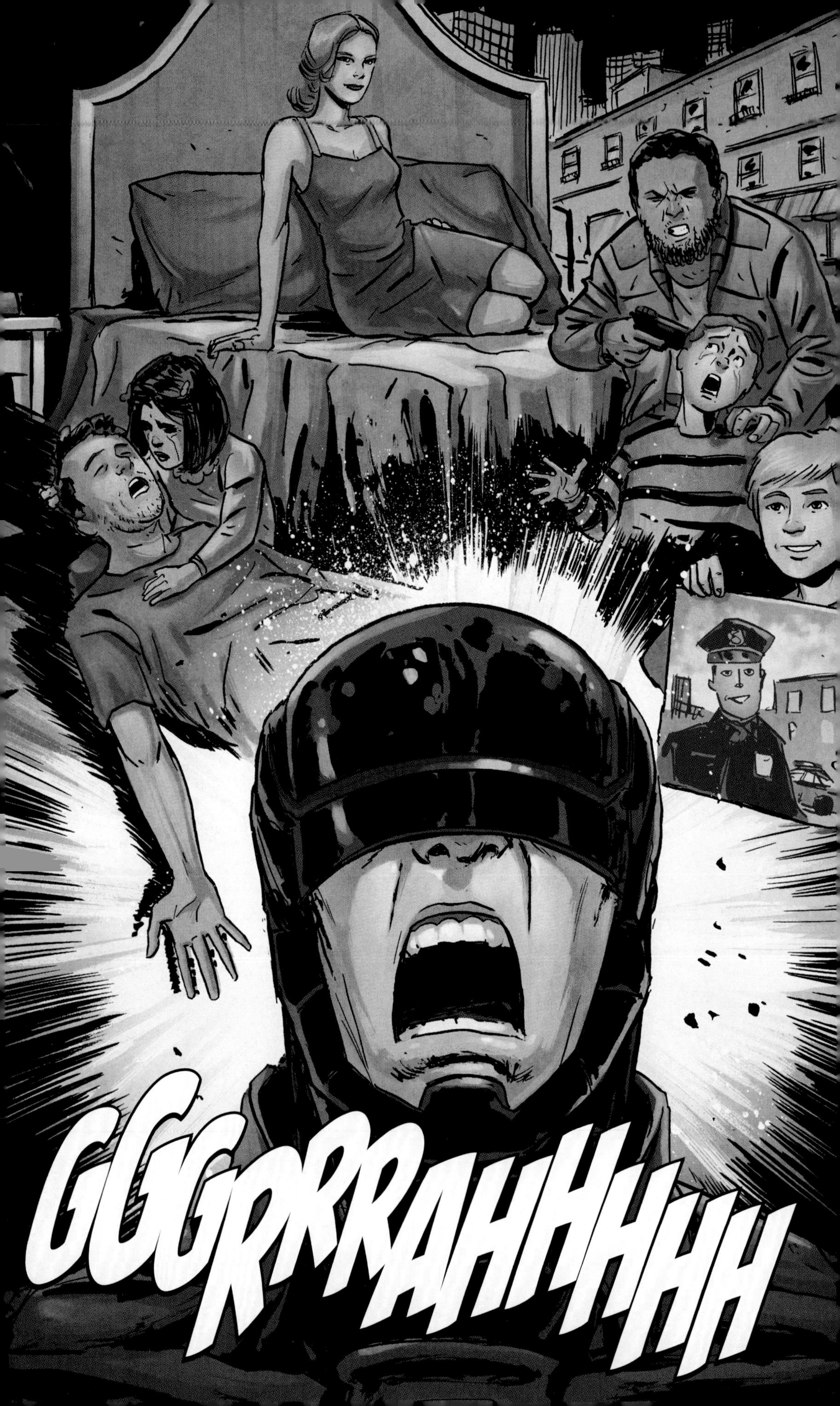
GGGRRRAHHHHHHH

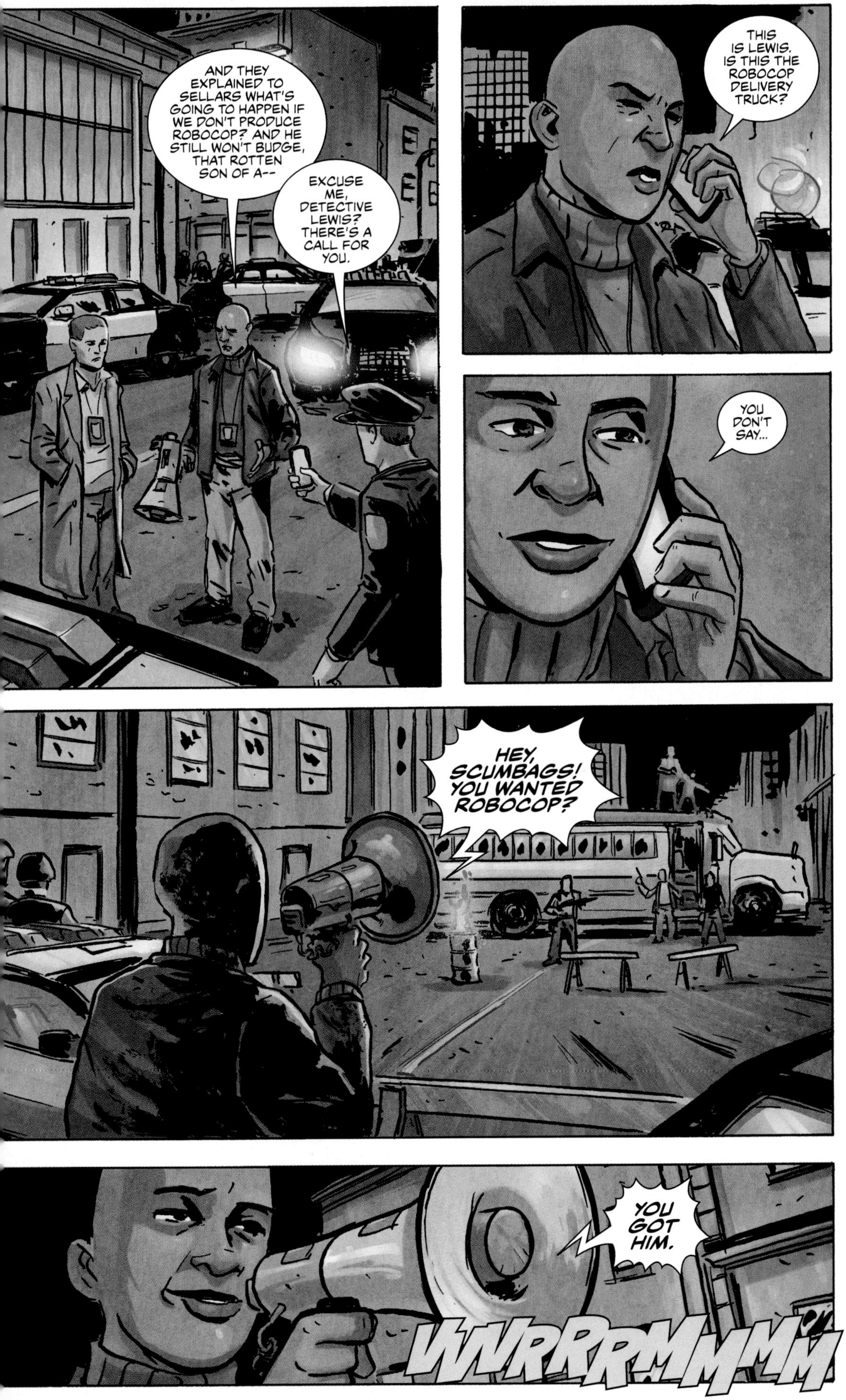
AND THEY EXPLAINED TO SELLARS WHAT'S GOING TO HAPPEN IF WE DON'T PRODUCE ROBOCOP? AND HE STILL WON'T BUDGE, THAT ROTTEN SON OF A--
EXCUSE ME, DETECTIVE LEWIS? THERE'S A CALL FOR YOU.
THIS IS LEWIS. IS THIS THE ROBOCOP DELIVERY TRUCK?
YOU DON'T SAY...
HEY, SCUMBAGS! YOU WANTED ROBOCOP?
YOU GOT HIM.
WWRRRMMMMM

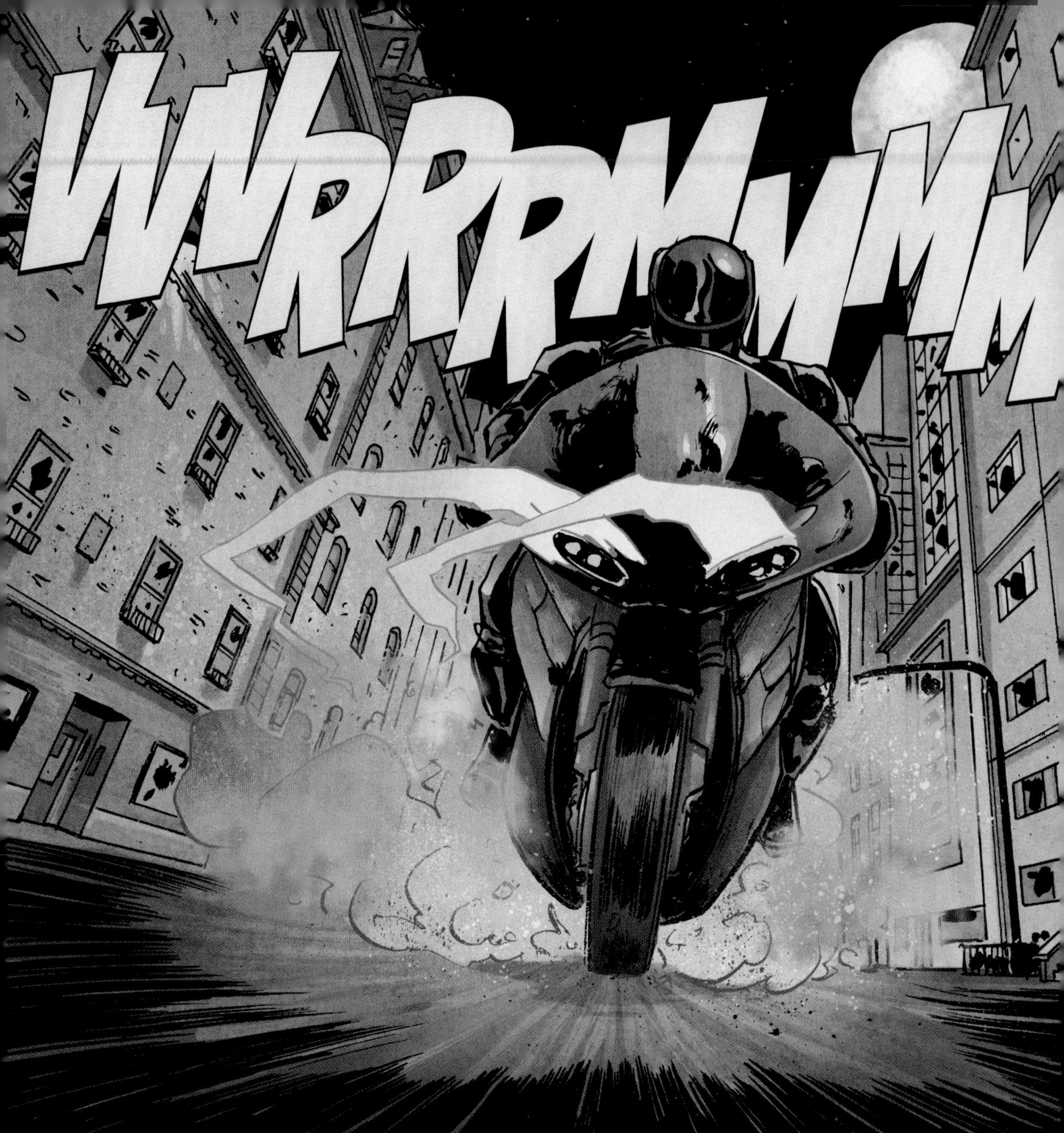
VVVRRRMMMMM

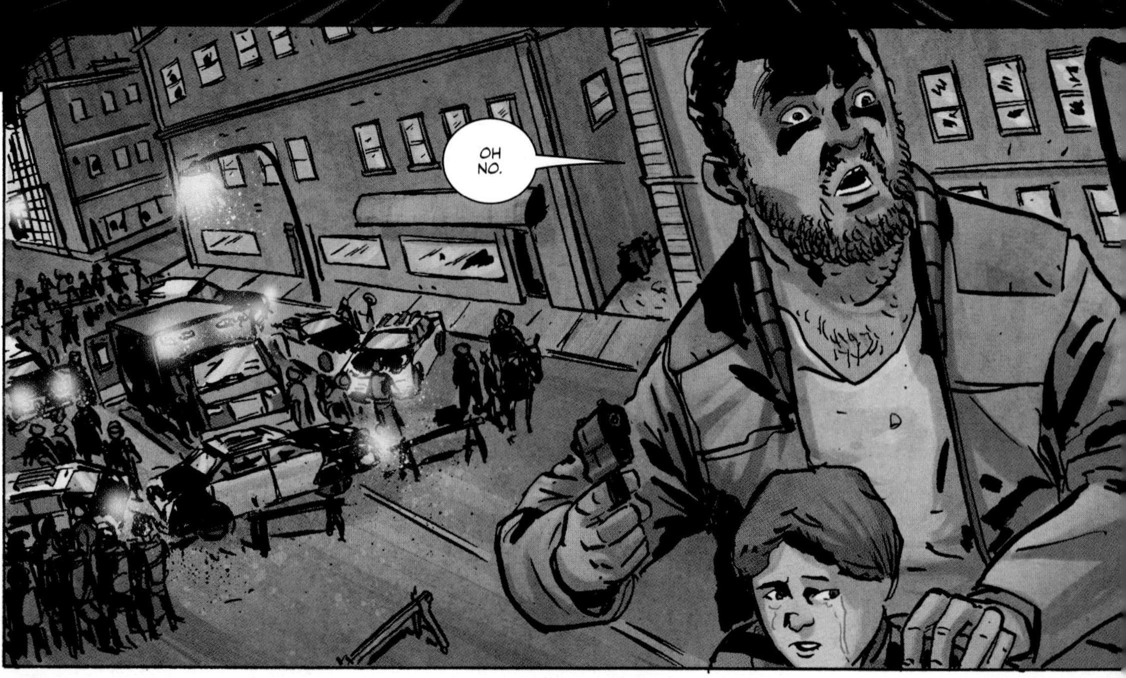
OH NO.

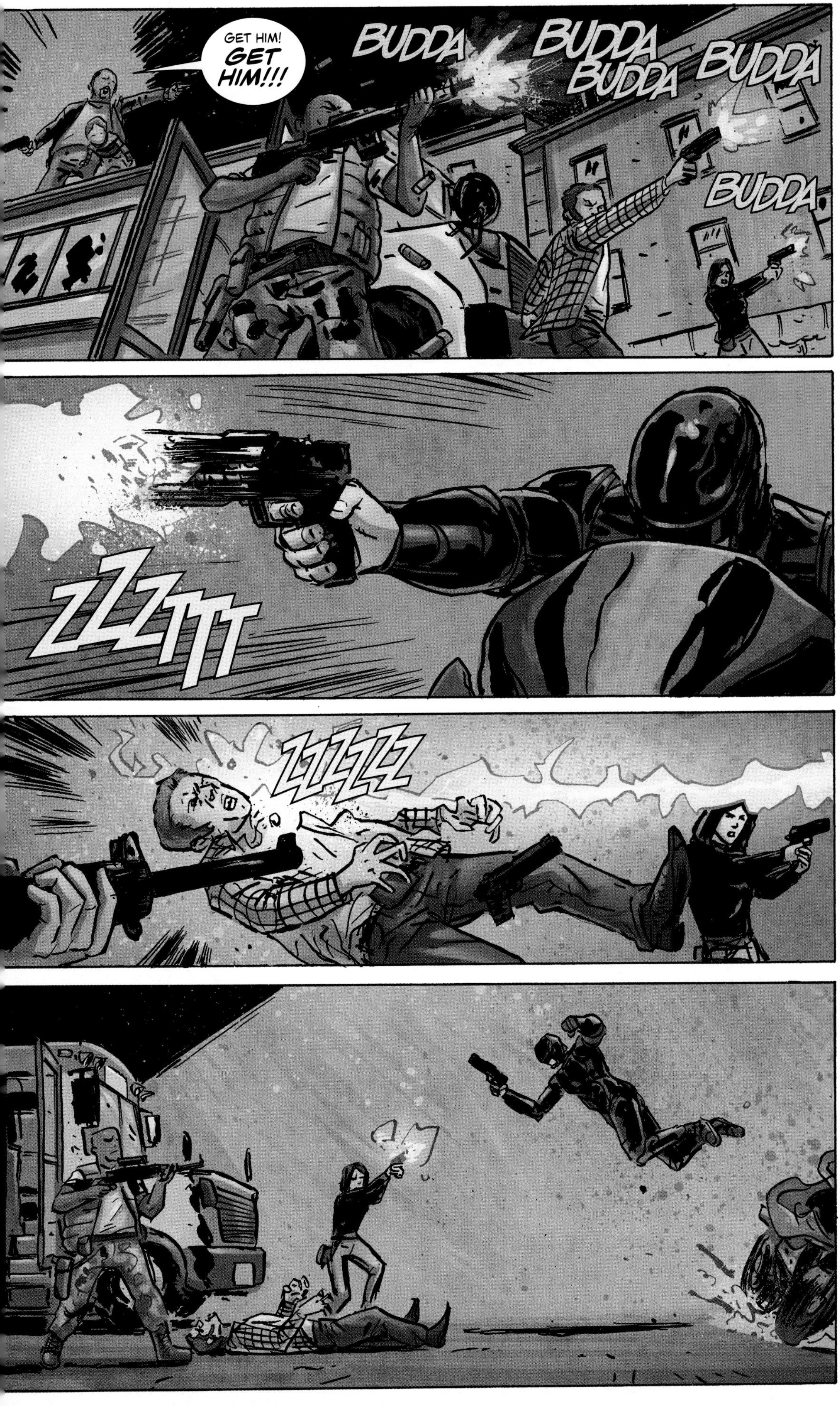

GET HIM! GET HIM!!!
BUDDA
BUDDA
BUDDA
BUDDA
BUDDA
ZZZTTT
ZZZZZ

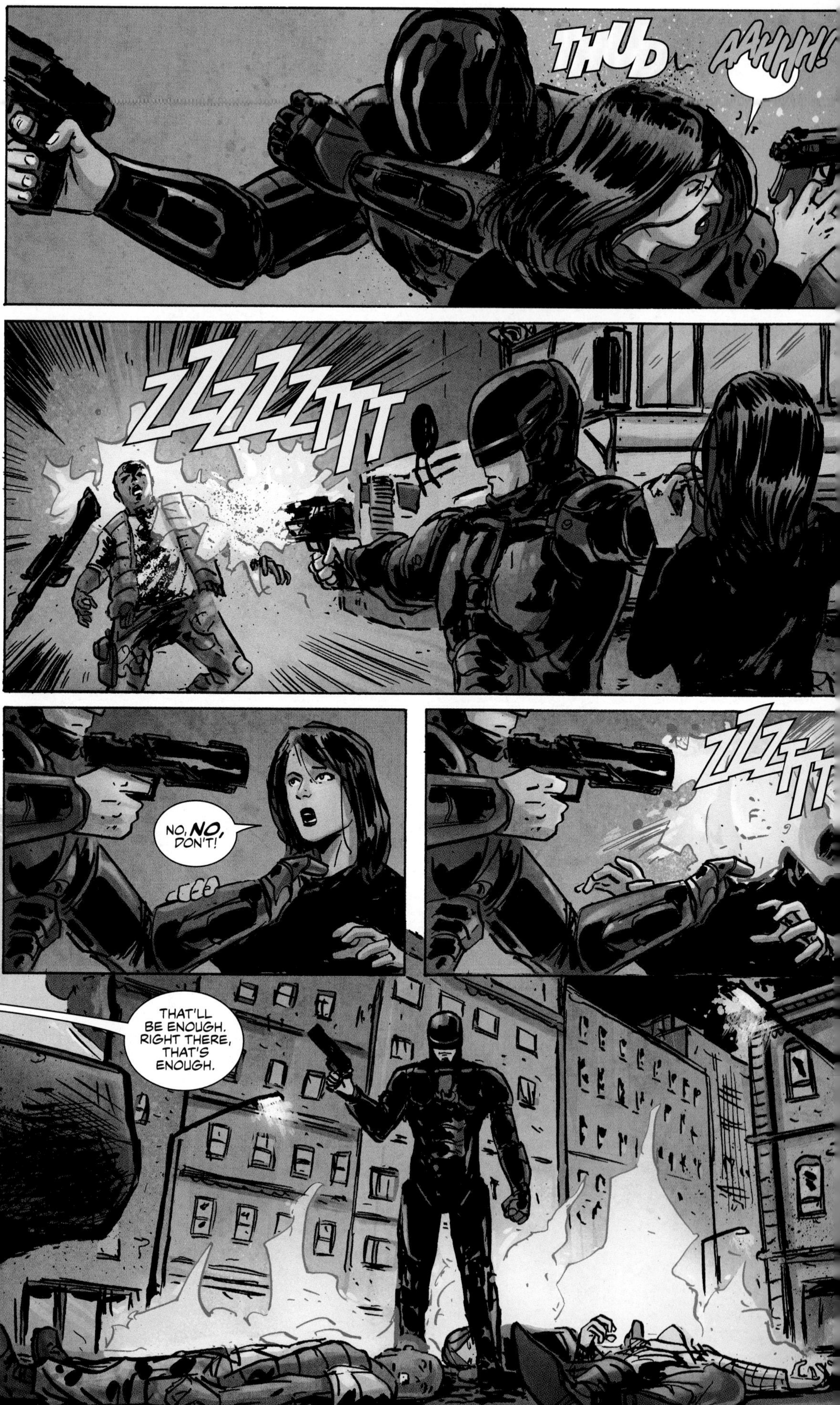
THUD
AAHHH!
ZZZZZTTT
NO, NO, DON'T!
ZZZTTT
THAT'LL BE ENOUGH. RIGHT THERE, THAT'S ENOUGH.

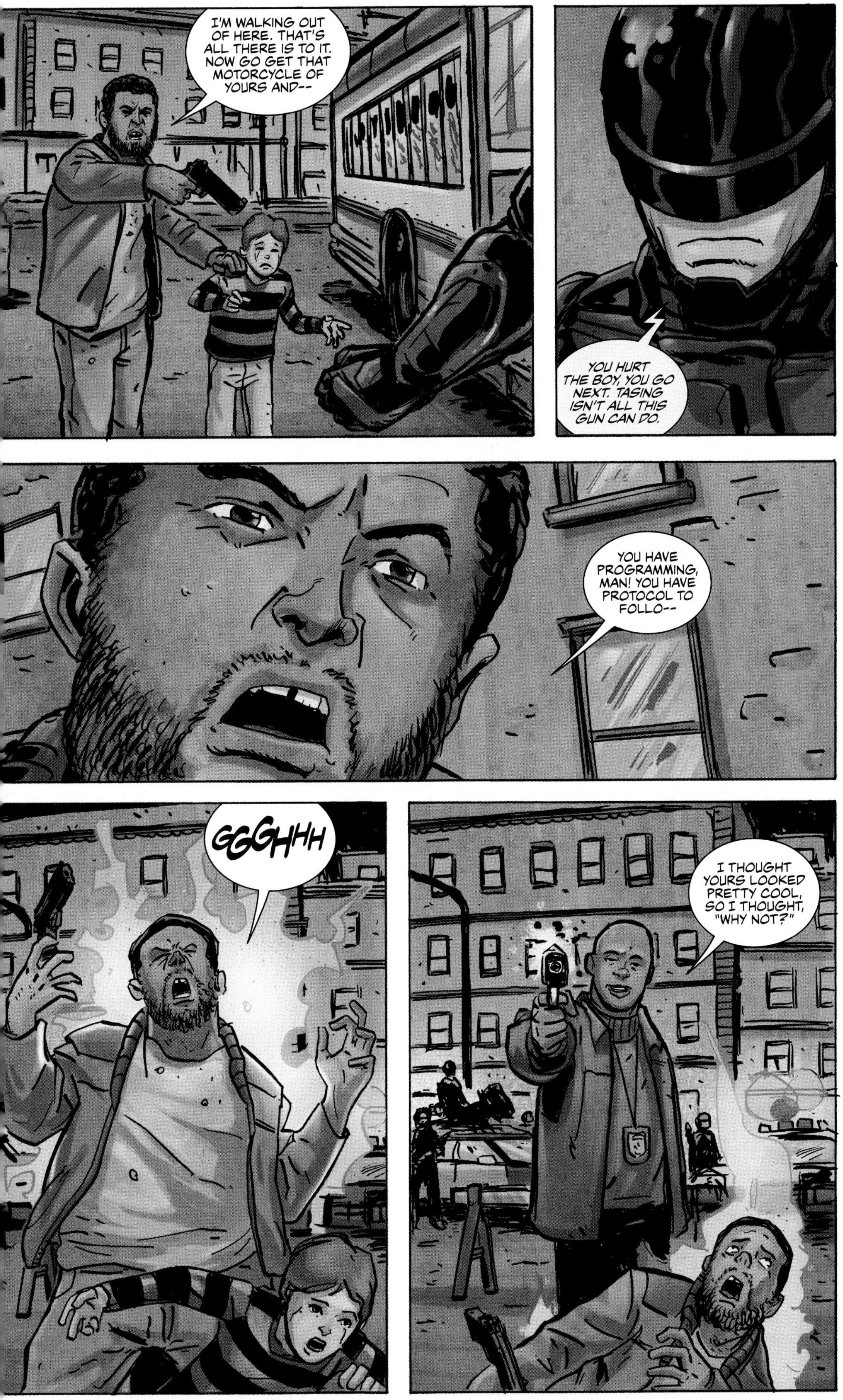

I'M WALKING OUT OF HERE. THAT'S ALL THERE IS TO IT. NOW GO GET THAT MOTORCYCLE OF YOURS AND--
YOU HURT THE BOY, YOU GO NEXT. TASING ISN'T ALL THIS GUN CAN DO.
YOU HAVE PROGRAMMING, MAN! YOU HAVE PROTOCOL TO FOLLO--
GGGHHH
I THOUGHT YOURS LOOKED PRETTY COOL, SO I THOUGHT, "WHY NOT?"

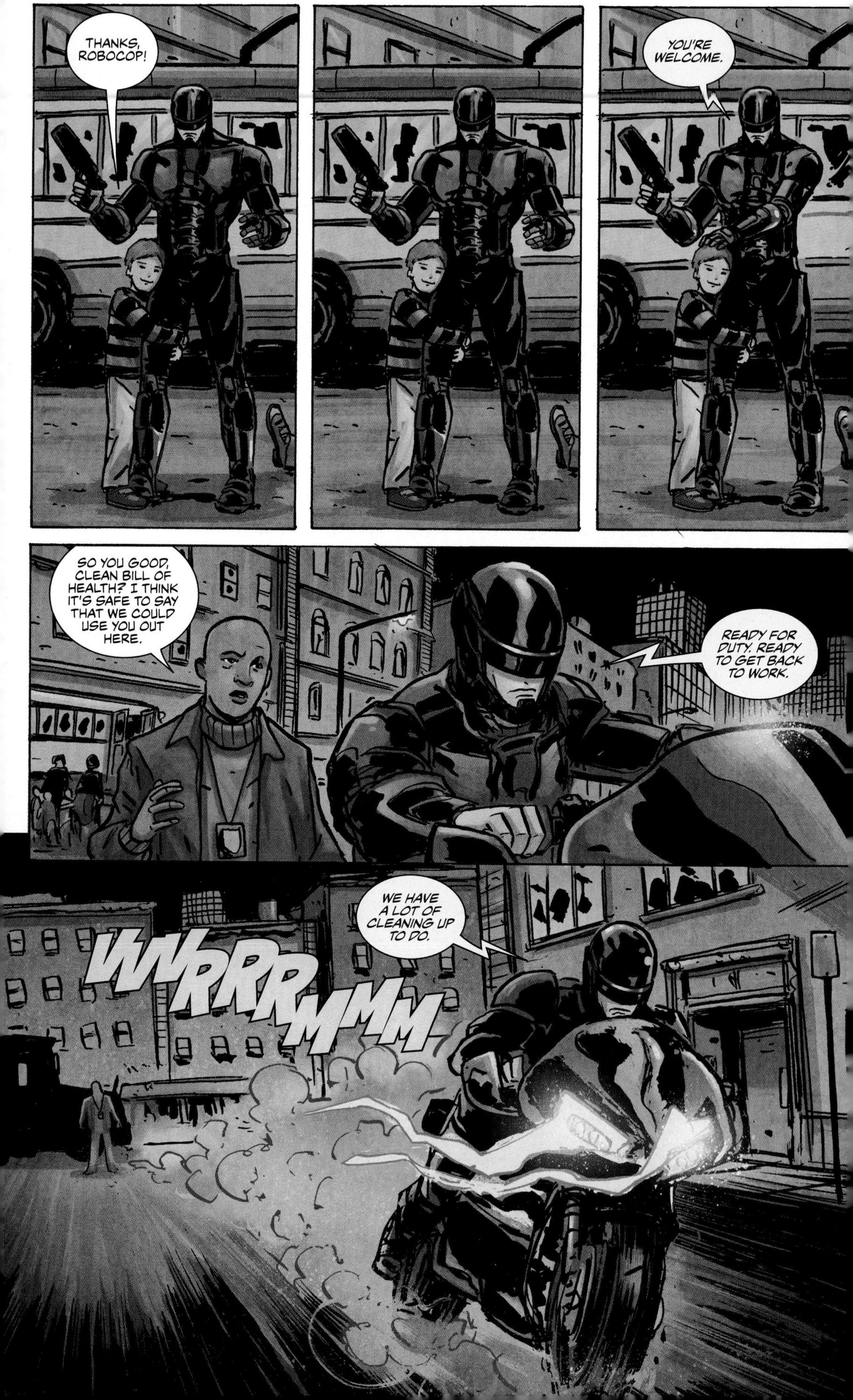
THANKS, ROBOCOP!
YOU'RE WELCOME.
SO YOU GOOD, CLEAN BILL OF HEALTH? I THINK IT'S SAFE TO SAY THAT WE COULD USE YOU OUT HERE.
READY FOR DUTY. READY TO GET BACK TO WORK.
WE HAVE A LOT OF CLEANING UP TO DO.
VVVRRRRMMMM

//COVER GALLERY//

ROBOCOP "BETA"
ART BY GREG SMALLWOOD

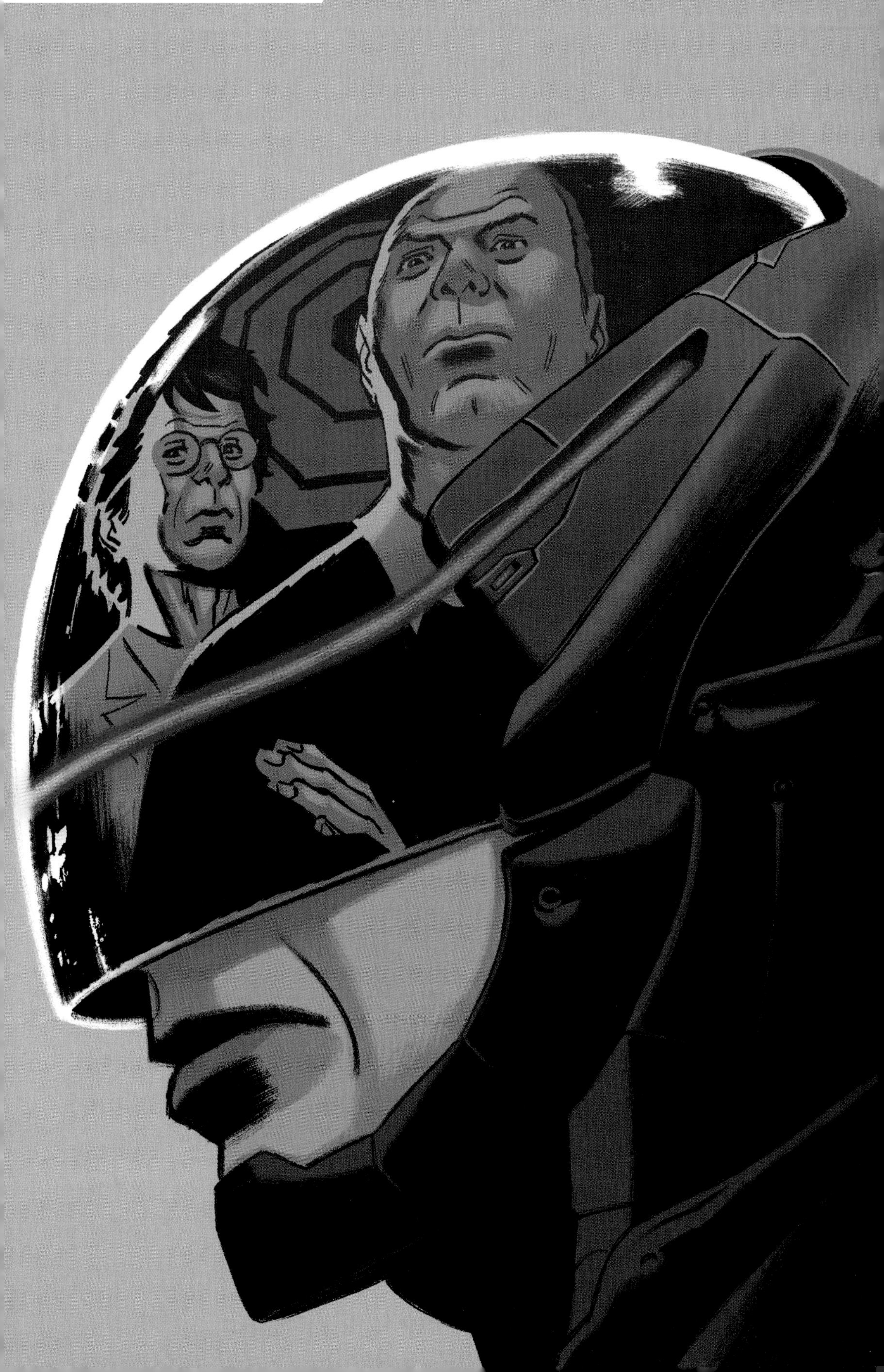

ROBOCOP "BETA" EMERALD CITY COMICON EXCLUSIVE

ART BY JOHNNIE CHRISTMAS COLORS BY SHARI CHANKHAMMA

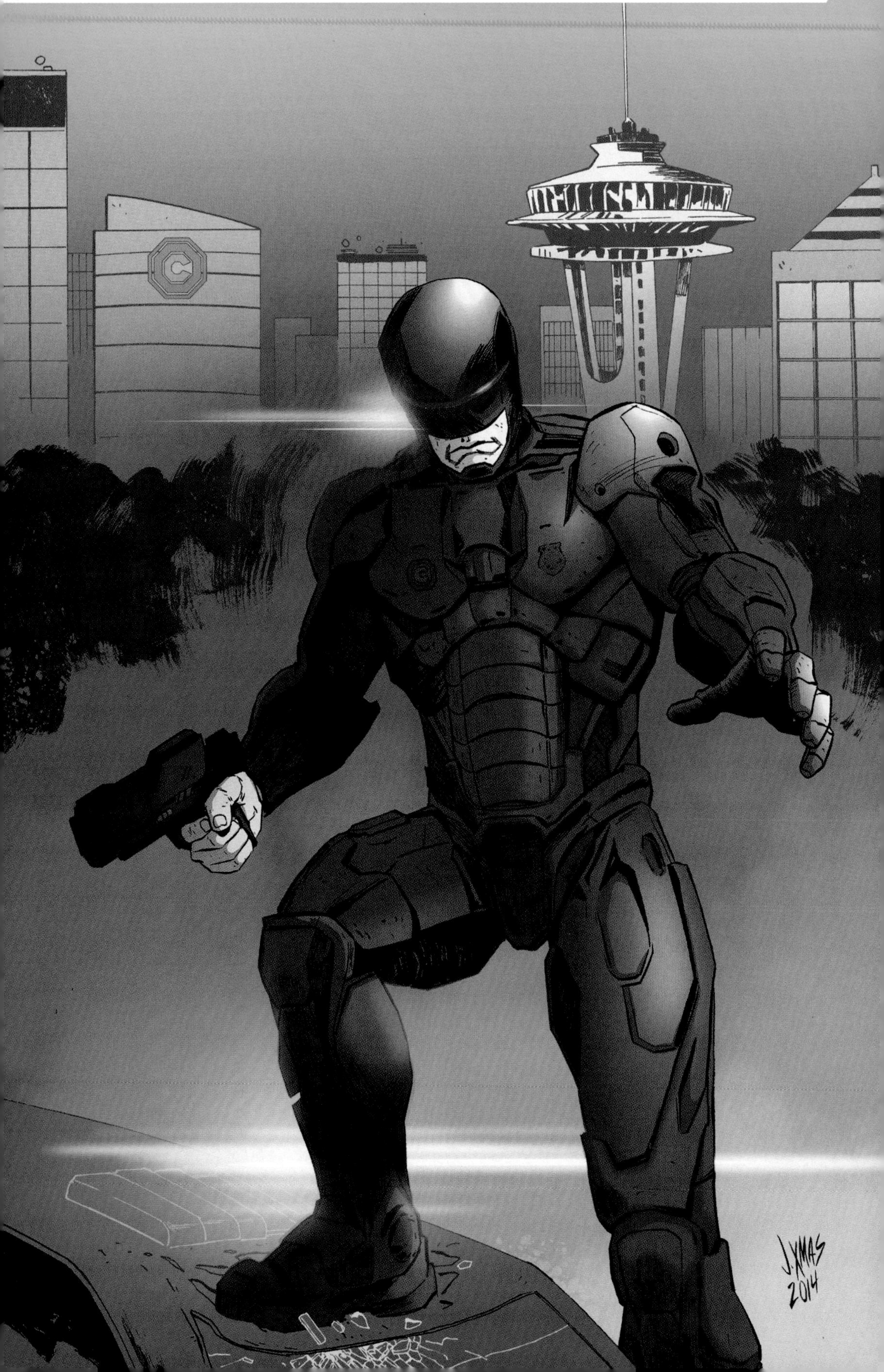
J.XMAS
2014

ROBOCOP "MEMENTO MORI"
ART BY CHRIS MOONEYHAM

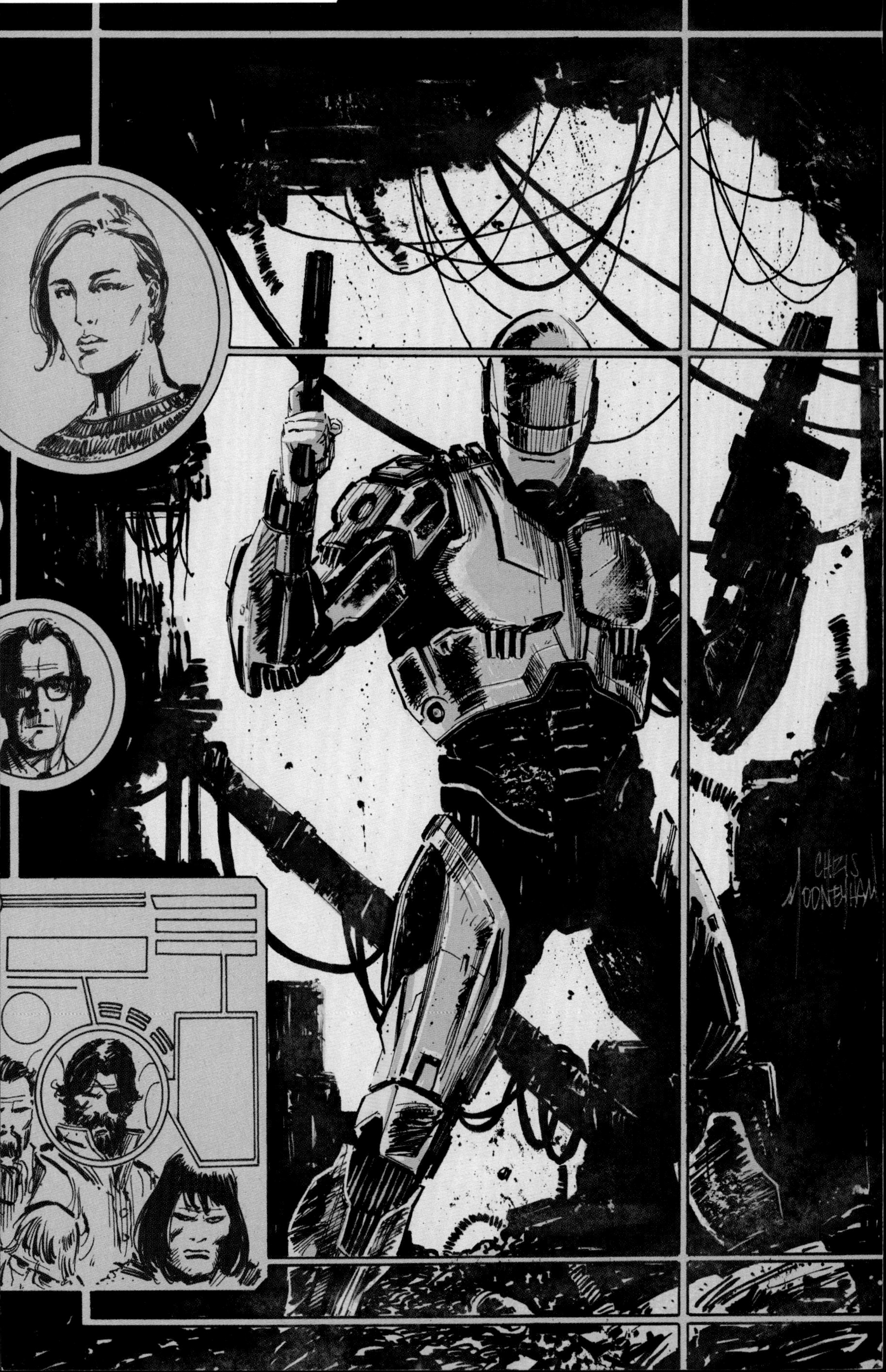
CHRIS MOONEYHAM

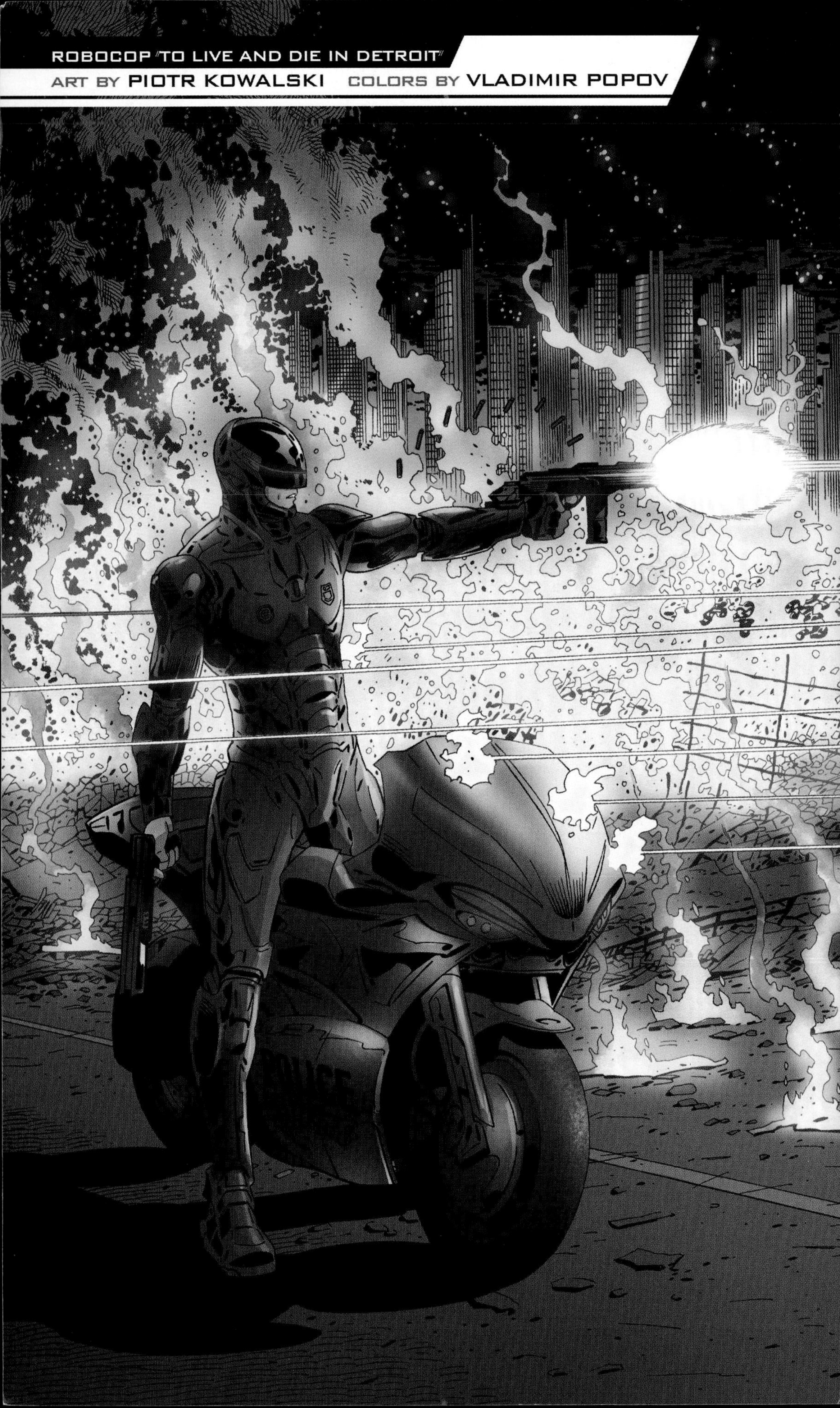
ROBOCOP "TO LIVE AND DIE IN DETROIT"
ART BY PIOTR KOWALSKI COLORS BY VLADIMIR POPOV

ROBOCOP "HOMINEM EX MACHINA"
ART BY RILEY ROSSMO

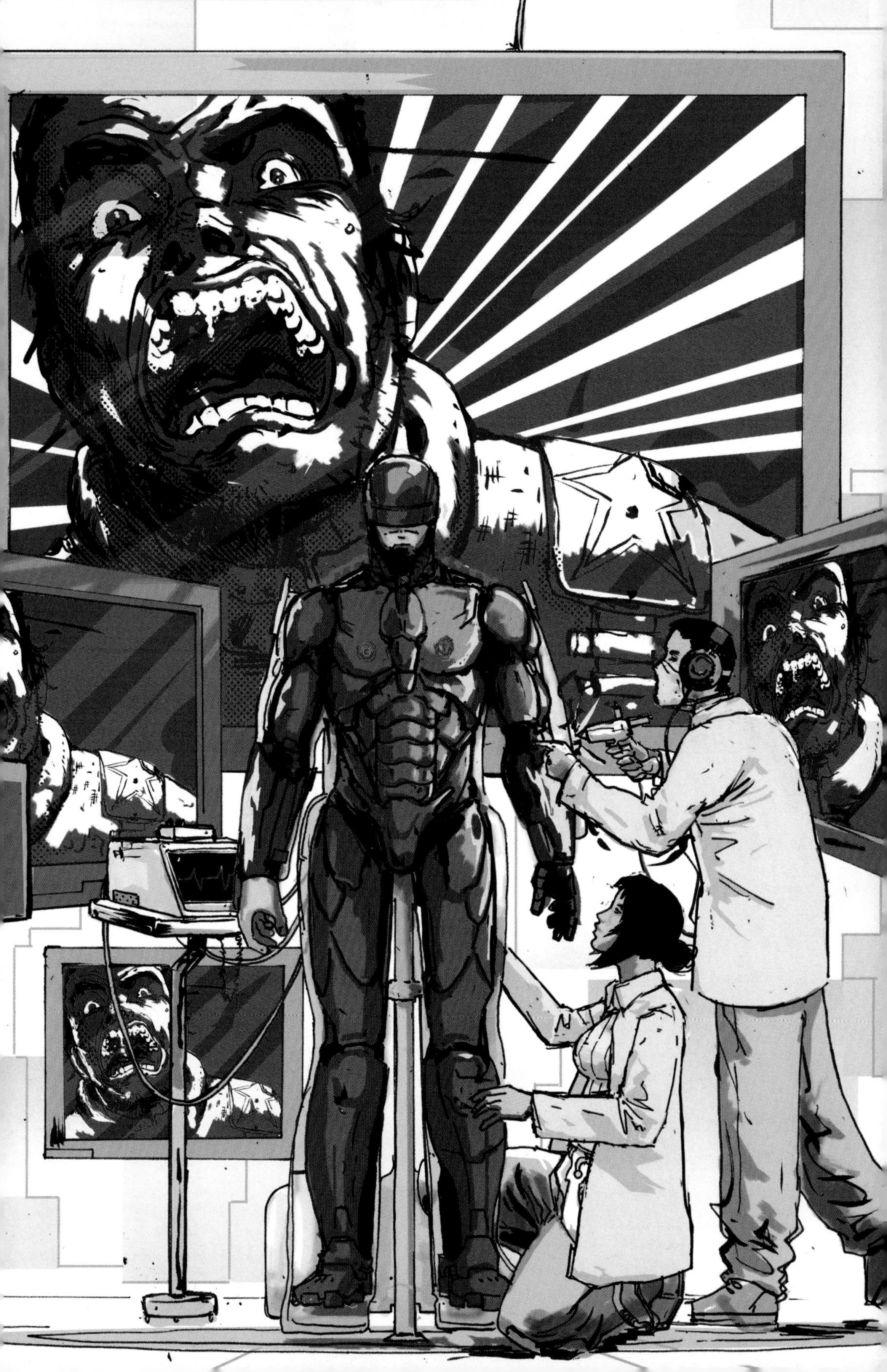

COVER PROCESS GALLERY

ROBOCOP
MURDER 187
CHRIS MOONEYHAM

ART BY CHRIS MOONEYHAM

POLICE
B
C

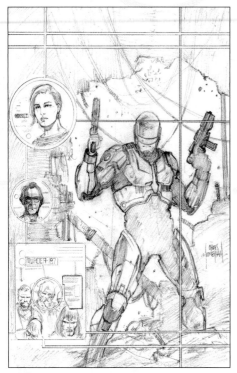

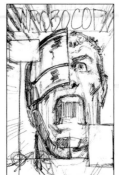

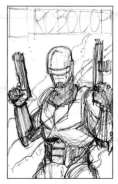

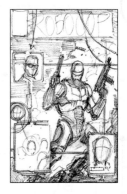

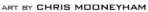

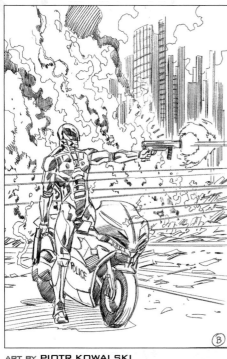

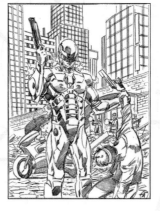

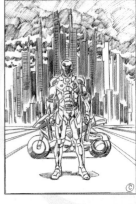

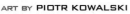

ART BY PIOTR KOWALSKI

THANK YOU
FOR YOUR
COOPERATION

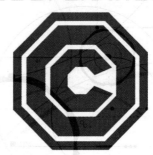